La Chicana

La Chicana

The Mexican-American Woman

Alfredo Mirandé
Evangelina Enríquez

The University of Chicago Press
Chicago and London

ALFREDO MIRANDÉ is associate professor of sociology and Chicano studies at the University of California at Riverside.

EVANGELINA ENRÍQUEZ is a doctoral candidate in comparative literature at the University of California at Riverside.

The University of Chicago Press, Chicago 60637
The University of Chicago Press, Ltd., London

© 1979 by the University of Chicago
All rights reserved. Published 1979
Printed in the United State of America
83 82 81 80 79 5 4 3 2 1

Library of Congress Cataloging in Publication Data

Mirandé, Alfredo.
  La Chicana.

  Bibliography: p.
  Includes index.
  1. Mexican American women.   I. Enríquez, Evangelina
joint author.   II. Title.
E184.M5M55   301.41′2′0973   79–13536
ISBN 0–226–53159–7

para Lucía
para la Lucy de Riverside

Contents

Preface

This book was inspired both by a real need for a definitive, comprehensive study of the Chicana and by our intense personal interest in the Mexican-American woman. What began as osmotic, random discussions and eventually developed into several proposed research studies finally evolved into a full-fledged effort to document the contributions of Chicanas to their history and culture in Mexico and the United States.

Despite our initial enthusiasm, we quickly discovered that there existed little if any field research, theoretical work, or compiled information on the subject. However, although our task at first seemed enormous, our labors in time proved fruitful and rewarding. Interestingly, although we were up to the challenge of undertaking to write a book on Chicanas, we were psychologically unprepared for what was to ensue in its formulation and actual writing.

The Aztec codices detail a neat, sane division of labor in their social order, and the same neat division in the roles of men and women in their society. But while they spell out a hierarchy on one hand and ostensible equality on the other, they fail to issue a prescription for harmony among their members and between the sexes.

There was never any question at the outset of this endeavor that we had an inherent respect for our undertaking and for each other; but, alas, we had failed to anticipate the tension and lack of harmony that could arise when two modern-day members of opposite sexes decide to undertake together a book about one sex.

La Chicana examines a number of dualities in the Mexican and Chicano experience that impinge on the Mexican-American woman. These dualities are often at odds, as in the "good-bad woman" syndrome and in traditional expectations of the Chicana as opposed to contemporary reality. But as often as these dualities are at odds, they are complements to one another. We believe that the inspiration, the formulation, and the execution of this book are a microcosm of these processes of tension.

While these tensions have led to many pitfalls along the way, we are confident that harmony and balance have prevailed. *La Chicana* is thus the product of a successful mingling of brawn and brains, analysis and passion, trial and victory. Ultimately, we claim victory, individually and collectively. We hope that the culmination of our efforts can begin to pay sufficient tribute to the *mexicanas* of the past and the Chicanas of today and the future, who have inspired this work.

One

La Chicana
An
Introduction

Public awareness of the status of social minorities in American society has grown rapidly in recent years. The civil rights movement of the 1950s and 1960s and the urban unrest which characterized this period served not only to dramatize the subordination and exploitation of black Americans but also to increase awareness of the exploitation of other groups. In the aftermath of this turbulent period in American history, it became clear that racial oppression was not limited to blacks but extended to native Americans, Asian Americans, Chicanos, and other groups with racial and cultural characteristics that differed from the white Anglo-Saxon Protestant ideal. The women's liberation movement shifted attention to the subordination and exploitation of women. It attempted to show that women were subjected to differential and unequal treatment and that their subjugation cut across racial, ethnic, and social class groupings.

While the women's movement ostensibly sought to liberate all women, it was to focus more on the needs of middle-class Anglo women. Founded and led by middle-class women, ultimately the movement reflected their needs, concerns, and biases. In the process of establishing goals and priorities, the unique needs and concerns of minority women were not taken into account.

As racial-ethnic movements developed and their goals and tactics solidified, it became clear

1

that minority women would be neglected by their men as they had been by their Anglo sisters. A major goal of the Chicano movement was to end the colonial oppression of Chicanos. It was said to concentrate on concerns common to all Chicanos but in fact focused on male issues and for the most part ignored the problems of women. Not wishing to divide or split the movement, Chicanas subordinated their needs to the good of the entire group. Many came to believe that some semblance of equality had to be achieved for their people as a whole before feminine concerns could be voiced. Internal division would be taken by the larger society as a sign of weakness or a lack of solidarity.

The net result has been that Chicanas and other minority women have suffered benign neglect at the hands of Anglo women and their oppressed brothers. Of late, interest in the status of black women has intensified, as witnessed by the publication of articles that deal with their unique problems and concerns.[1] The Chicana, however, remains an enigma. Little is known about her needs, goals, problems, or history.

While some knowledge of the history and contemporary status of Chicanos is critical to an understanding of the Chicana and there are many parallels between the status of Chicanas and other minority women, especially black women, there is a need to focus on her unique problems. We hope that parallels between the condition of Chicanas and other minority women became apparent as the text unfolds, but we feel that Chicanas have been neglected for too long for a study of them to be diluted by extensive discussion of other women. The Chicana is unique and has a rich cultural heritage that deserves more extensive treatment than is possible even in this book.

We have sought to gather diverse materials on the Chicana analyzing and evaluating her position in society. Though our focus is sociological and contemporary, we believe that a sociohistorical perspective is essential to an understanding of the Chicana today. The importance of history becomes apparent when one considers the colonial legacy of the Chicana. Our analysis proceeds on the assumption that Chicanos are colonized and that their colonial heritage has had a profound impact not only on Chicanos as a people but specifically on their women. Chicanas are colonized women and must be understood within this context.

The Legacy of Conquest

The colonial roots of the Chicana, in Mexico and in the United States, date back to the conquest of Mexico in 1519. The conquest was facilitated by two powerful forces: the missionary zeal of the Spaniards, which led them to see native culture and institutions as inferior and their destruction ordained by God, and elements in Aztec religion and mythology which saw the arrival of the Spaniard as an ominous sign which foretold their demise. The ironic coupling of these diverse forces, plus the military advantage of the Spaniard, spelled the inevitable destruction of an ancient civilization which by the conquerors' own accounts was equal, if not superior, to its European counterpart. The conquest was so pervasive that it has been depicted as not only a physical but a moral and spiritual conquest as well (Paz 1961; Ramos 1962; Ricard 1966; and Fuentes 1970).

Since the conquest was divinely willed and sanctioned, the conversion of the *indio* to Christianity and to European conceptions of morality was an integral part of pacification.[2] Codices, temples, and religious relics and idols were destroyed and replaced with Christian symbols (Ricard 1966, p. 287; Moreno, 1971, p. 14; and Valdez, 1972, p. xx). The Spanish mission was not only commissioned by His Majesty Carlos V but mandated by God. Before entering battle, their practice was to read a *requerimiento*. This document, usually written in Latin and read aloud, served notice to the heathens that "there was one God, that His vicar on earth was the Pope, and that the Pope had granted power to the Spanish ruler, who was now obliged to use this power for the salvation of the Indians" (Blacker and Rosen 1962, p. xvi). The king would grant many favors to those who accepted his legitimacy, but he would wage war against, subjugate, and enslave those who questioned his authority. The declaration that "the deaths and disasters which may come about because of this action will be the fault of yourselves and not of his majesty, nor of me" (quoted ibid., p. xvi) absolved them of any wrongdoing. As emissary of the king, Cortés took great pains to insure that the "rights" of the Indians were protected. Efforts were made to instruct them in the faith, baptize them, and urge them to embrace Christianity, before war was waged. The Indians were to be subjugated only if they resisted conversion and refused to abandon their worship of pagan deities. In his dispatches to Carlos V, Cortés reported,

> I overturned the idols in which these people believe the most and rolled them down the stairs. Then I had those chapels cleansed, for they were full of blood from the sacrifices; and I set up images of Our Lady and other Saints in them. . . . I made them understand by the interpreters how deceived they were in putting their hope in idols made of unclean things by their own hands. I told them that they should know there was but one God, the Universal Lord of all, Who

had created the heavens and earth and all things, and them, and us. . . . [Ibid., p. 57]

Cortés was painfully aware that the destruction of the Aztec empire could only be justified by the fact that Motecuhzoma was not a Christian and his authority was not ordained by God (ibid., p. xvi). When the Aztec emperor was taken prisoner, Cortés therefore took great care to explain the reasons for his imprisonment and to insure that he was well cared for (ibid., p. 47).

The Spaniard can thus be seen as motivated by a divine imperative. Even Fray Bernardino de Sahagún, who is considered to have written one of the most objective and authoritative accounts of the Indians, espoused this view:

> Nuestro Señor Dios (a propósito) ha tenido ocultada esta media parte del mundo hasta nuestros tiempos, que por su divina ordenación ha tenido por bien de manifestarla a la Iglesia Romana Católica, no con propósito que fuesen destruidos y tiranizados sus naturales, sino con propósito que sean alumbrados de las tinieblas de la idolatría en que han vivido, y sean introducidos en la Iglesia Católica, e informados en la religión cristiana, y para que alcancen el reino de los cielos, muriendo en la fe de verdaderos cristianos.[3]

He saw Cortés as God's valiant soldier. "A este negocio muy grande y muy importante, tuvo nuestro Señor Dios por bien de que hiciese camino y derrocase el muro conque esta infidelidad estaba cercada y murada, el valentísimo capitán D. Hernando Cortés, en cuya presencia y por cuyos medios, hizo Dios nuestro Señor muchos milagros en la conquista."[4]

The Spaniard's religious fervor was aided by elements in Aztec religion and mythology. Ten years before the arrival of the Spaniards, Aztec mythology asserts that there were eight signs or omens which foretold their downfall. One was a gigantic, resplendent flame—so bright that it made the night like day. The flame appeared nightly for approximately one year. People feared that it signaled a bad end (ibid., p. 15). A second sign was a large water fowl containing a round mirror in the middle of its head that reflected an image of the sky and stars. Motecuhzoma was frightened when he saw this bird, for the second time that he looked into the mirror he saw many people armed and clustered together, and riding on horses (ibid., pp. 16–17).

Thus, prior to the arrival of the conquistadores the doom of the Aztec empire had been foretold. Motecuhzoma himself initially took Cortés to be Quetzalcóatl, a returning deposed god. Quetzalcóatl was the self-sacrificing, penitent god of life, love, peace, and wisdom, who represented all that is good in man; he was the benevolent father and creator of man who symbolized the cosmic struggle between good and evil (Caso 1958, pp. 24–26). Forced to leave Tula by necromancers and other evil forces (Sahagún 1946, 1:297), he departed to the mythical Tlillan Tlapallan, "the land of the black and the red," and promised to return from the east in the year "One Reed" (1519) (Caso 1958, p. 25). Fortuitously for the Spaniards, this date coincided with Cortés's arrival, and his physical characteristics resembled those of the departed god, who was also fair haired, fair skinned, and bearded. Motecuhzoma sent representatives to the coast to greet the returning god with obeisances and to present him with the treasure of Quetzalcóatl (Leon-Portilla 1962, pp. 22–26). He cautioned his messengers to treat Cortés with the deference and reverence normally accorded a deity: "Mirad que han dicho que ha llegado nuestro señor Quetzalcóatl, id y recibirle y oid lo que os dijere, con mucha diligencia; mirad que no se os olvide nada de lo que os dijere, veis aquí estas joyas que le presentéis de mi parte, que son todos los atavíos sacerdotales que a él convienen."[5]

As Cortés and his army moved inland from the coast toward the Aztec capital or Tenochtitlán, many Indians thought them to be *teules*, or gods (Díaz Del Castillo 1963, pp. 116–17). These tribes lived under Aztec domination, and whether the Spaniards were *teules* or men, they presented the potential for liberation from this dominion. The Totonacs and the Tlaxcalans, for example, "were bitter enemies of the Aztecs, who exacted tribute from them and seized their young men to die on the altars of Huitzilopochtli" (Parkes 1969, p. 45). They complained that Motecuhzoma's tax collectors took away their jewelry and raped their handsome wives and daughters (Díaz Del Castillo 1963, p. 110). A predisposition to freedom from Aztec rule and willingness to convert to Christianity gained Cortés allies as he marched to Tenochtitlán.

His arrival there in November 1519 was hailed by Motecuhzoma as signaling the return of the great lord Quetzalcóatl. He explained that the Aztecs knew they descended not from the inhabitants of this land "but from strangers who came to it from very distant parts; and we also hold that our race was brought to these parts by a lord whose vassals they all were, and who returned to his native country" (Blacker and Rosen 1962, p. 43). They also believed that "those who descended from him [Quetzalcóatl] would come to subjugate this country and us . . . and according to the direction from which you say you come, which is where the sun rises, and from what you tell us of your great lord, or king, who has sent you here, we believe, and hold for certain, that he is our rightful sovereign. . . . Hence you may be sure that we shall always obey you, and hold you as the representative of this great lord . . . you will be obeyed and recognized, and all we possess is at your disposal" (ibid., p. 43). However, the greed of the Spaniards and poor judgment on the part of Pedro de Alvarado, who in Cortés's absence massacred several thousand defenseless Indians as they celebrated a religious festival in honor of Huitzilopochtli, the sun god, precluded a peaceful takeover (Leon-Portilla 1962, pp. 74–76). The Aztecs revolted against this assault on their persons and religion and fiercely defended their capital. Eventually the Spaniards were routed, and Cortés lamented the defeat of his troops as he cried at the foot of the *árbol de la noche triste* ("tree of the Night of Sorrows") in Tacuba. The downfall of Tenochtitlán finally came on August 13, 1521, but only after a fierce struggle and with the aid of the Tlaxcalan, allies who warmly received the defeated Cortés, nursed his men back to health, and joined him in a renewed siege on the Aztec capital. With the demise of Tenochtitlán, the pacification of the remainder of Mexico was inevitable.

Mexico, or New Spain, was unified into a colony of Spain and administered by a viceroy of the king. It remained a colony for approximately 300 years, until independence was obtained in 1821. The newly independent nation, however, was besieged with problems and internal turmoil which facilitated the eventual annexation of Mexico's northwest territories by the United States. The next half century was to be a chaotic period in Mexican history, characterized by fiscal insolvency, internal conflict, and numerous revolutions. Liberals called for the institution of a liberal democracy patterned after the United States, with local autonomy; conservatives, for a strong centralized government which retained the power of the church and the army; reactionaries, for a complete return to Spanish rule (Parkes 1969, p. 181).

Mexico's northern territories were isolated and sparsely populated. Prior to 1823 there were probably fewer than 3,000 white settlers in the Texas territory (ibid., p. 200). The United States had acquired Florida from Spain in 1819, but the Transcontinental Treaty did not include Texas within the boundaries of the United States (Acuña 1972, p. 10). Anglo Americans believing that Texas rightfully belonged to the United States clamored for annexation and made abortive invasions into the territory as early as 1819. The unstable Mexican government, leery of her expansionist northern neighbors, opted to encourage Anglo settlement by awarding cheap land grants to United States citizens. Mexican federalists hoped this policy would help the government retain control over its distant province (Parkes 1969, p. 200), but it proved to be a serious blunder that paved the way for annexation. The influx continued, and by the end of the decade there were about 20,000 American settlers and 2,000 slaves (Acuña 1972, p. 11). Slavery being virtually nonexistent outside of her Texas province, Mexico abolished this practice in 1829, with the intent of discouraging further Anglo immigration. But the law was circumvented by Anglo slave owners, who freed their slaves and proceeded to sign them to lifetime contracts as identured servants (ibid., p. 12). Conflict intensified when the Mexican government attempted in 1830 to prohibit all American immigration (Moquin 1971, p. 138). The move was met with resistance, and Americans continued to come into Texas in defiance of the Mexican government. Believing themselves to be racially and morally superior, arrogant Anglo settlers refused to obey Mexican laws and regulations. The renewed tensions gave impetus to the movement for Texas independence, and in 1835 war broke out between Texas and Mexico. Official hostilities ended with a convincing victory by Texas in the Battle of San Jacinto on April 21, 1836, but the status of Texas remained unsettled. Mexico refused to recognize the Treaty of Velasco, signed by Santa Anna in exchange for his freedom, or to recognize the independent Lone Star Republic. In the United States opposition to her admittance into the Union grew among Northern abolitionists, who feared that Texas would become a slave state.

The Texas revolt was to set the stage for a full-scale war between Mexico and the United States. The conflict had generated intense hatred of the Mexicans. "To the early American settlers, the Mexicans were lazy, shiftless, jealous, cowardly, bigoted, superstitious, backward, and immoral" (McWilliams 1968, p. 99). The Anglo-American considered himself to be racially, culturally, and morally superior to the Mexican (Brack, 1973, p. 63). The Mexican War came then to be colonially motivated and justified by an expansionist philosophy which saw the appropriation of surrounding territory as the manifest destiny of a superior, chosen Anglo-Saxon race (Acuña 1972, p. 21). By the early 1800s the belief that Americans were destined to settle and rule over the entire area that lay between the Eastern and Western coasts was deeply ingrained. Some even believed that this dominion would extend northward to the Arctic Circle and southward to Tierra del Fuego (Meier and Rivera 1972, p. 56). John O'Sullivan, editor of the *Democratic Review* and a leading exponent of this doctrine, stated in 1845, "The Anglo-Saxon foot is already on its borders. Already the advance guard of the irresistible army of Anglo-Saxon emigration has begun to power down upon it. . . . A population will soon be in actual occupation

of California, over which it will be idle for Mexico to dream of dominion" (Gossett 1963, p. 310). Tension between the two nations mounted,
and when Texas was admitted into the Union in 1845, Mexico saw this
as the first step in the annexation of other Mexican provinces and broke
off diplomatic relations with the United States. The United States coveted the entire rich, unused Mexican territory which was to become the
American Southwest. In 1845 President Polk made an unsuccessful
attempt to purchase California. When this effort failed, he provoked
war with Mexico by sending General Zachary Taylor, "Old Rough and
Ready," to protect the Texas border (Meier and Rivera 1972, p. 64).
The location of the border, however, was disputed; the United States
claimed that it was at the Rio Grande and Mexico that it was 150 miles
north, at the Nueces River. When Taylor moved his forces across the
Nueces to the Rio Grande, Mexico considered this an invasion and proceeded to arrest some American dragoons. Polk prepared a war message, and on May 13, 1846 Congress officially declared war. Given the
numerical and military superiority of the United States, however, the
outcome of the war was never really in doubt.

The official end of the war was marked by the signing of the Treaty
of Guadalupe-Hidalgo and its ratification by the American Senate on
March 10, 1848. Mexico, facing the prospect of a total takeover, ceded
more than half her territory (including the present-day states of Arizona, California, New Mexico, Utah and Nevada, and parts of Colorado) in exchange for $15 million. The Mexican government was con-
cerned with the fate of its citizens, however, and fought to insure that
the land, property, and political rights of Mexican citizens who would
be incorporated into the United States would be maintained. But provisions of the treaty designed to protect land titles and water rights of
Mexican citizens and to guarantee them "the enjoyment of all the rights
of citizens of the United States according to the principles of the Constitution" (Acuña 1972, p. 29) were either ignored or grossly violated
(Moquin 1971, p. 181). Their rights were not honored, and in the aftermath of the war Mexicans living in the Southwest territory (Chicanos)
became a colonized or conquered people, rendered politically and economically powerless and having a foreign culture and language imposed
by force. The Chicano "found his lands gone, his religion seriously challenged, and himself a citizen of a country whose language, laws, and
social customs he did not understand" (Meier and Rivera 1972, p. 72).
In short, he became a victim of cultural genocide.

The parallels between the colonization of the American Southwest
and the conquest of Mexico are striking. Both the conquering Spaniards

and the Anglos saw native culture and institutions as inferior and sought to supplant them with their own; both gained control through the use of military force; both rendered the conquered peoples politically and economically powerless; and both conceived their mission to be divinely ordained. In addition, a prevailing ethic was that they saw themselves as chosen people who were subjugating an inferior race and culture. Yet there are also important differences between the two conquests. The conquest of Mexico exemplifies the "classic" type of colonialism, in which a distant land is subordinated by a foreign power; the Southwest conquest was an "internal" type in which contiguous territory is acquired.[6] Another difference is that classic colonialism allows for more continuity between the pre- and postconquest societies. Thus native leadership and elites remain largely intact, although they come under foreign control, and native institutions are modified but retained (Moore 1970, p. 466). In Mexico, "where possible or expedient, or where they could be closely regulated, native political and social practices were incorporated and retained. . . . In the process local native rulers served as intermediaries between the dominant Spanish society and the subordinate Indian society" (Gibson 1966, p. 149). In internal colonialism, on the other hand, native elites are deposed from power, and native institutions are completely destroyed. Finally, the "classic" colony is recognized formally and legally, while the "internal" colony has only an informal existence.

Chicanos today are not formally colonized. They constitute an internal colony within the territorial boundaries of the United States. The internal colony is a de facto one, with formal and legal equality but informally excluded from the legal-political system (Barrera, et al. 1972, p. 483): "Internal colonialism means that Chicanos as a cultural/racial group exist in an exploited condition" (ibid., p. 485). Chicanos are powerless, lacking control over critical social institutions which have a direct impact on them. Barrio businesses are generally owned by outsiders, and the schools, political system, and other institutions are also controlled and administered by outsiders.

Should a Chicano who is Anglo in appearance adopt the culture and values of that society, he might escape colonial subordination. "However, this would not produce a noncolonized Chicano, but a noncolonized non-Chicano. Thus the apparent semi-permeability of the colonial barrier for Chicanos is illusory, since there is no escape from the colonial status for an individual *as a Chicano*" (ibid.). Many Anglo-Americans reject the idea that Chicanos are colonized because *formally* they have the same rights as other citizens, and there are enough examples of Chicano success stories to perpetuate a myth of equality. However, the low visibility of internal colonialism makes it not only more insidious but perhaps more oppressive than classic colonialism. The latter renders native culture and institutions dependent and sub-ordinate, but they are nonetheless retained. The effects of internal colonialism are more devastating, precisely because the existence and legitimacy of native institutions or culture are not recognized. Informal mechanisms destroy the native way of life. One of the most effective mechanisms of destruction is benign neglect. The culture, values, and language of Chicanos have no formal or legitimate standing within American society. Throughout history Chicano culture and institutions like *la familia* have had to resist the onslaught of the schools and other public institutions which serve as instruments of the dominant group. Chicanos have been punished in school for speaking their native tongue or for expressing familial or cultural values that run counter to dominant Anglo values.

Chicanos constitute a disadvantaged and exploited internal colony within the territorial boundaries of the United States. They are also descendants of a colonized Mexican nation. This colonial heritage is critical to understanding not only the status of Chicanos as a people but also the status of Chicanas. As a colonized woman the Chicana faces problems and forms of oppression not experienced by noncolonized women.

Who Is the Chicana?

Since the word "Chicana" is the feminine of "Chicano," it is necessary to define both before we can characterize Chicanas. We will use "Chicano" to designate persons of Mexican descent living in the United States. Other terms such as "Mexican," "Mexican-American," "hispano," and "latino" are also in use, but "Chicano" is rapidly becoming the preferred term. While it has not gained wide public exposure until recently, the term is certainly not new. For many years its use was largely limited to Chicanos. Some argue that its origins are ancient, deriving from the Nahuatl for "Mexican" or "Aztec." A less elevated but perhaps more plausible interpretation is that it is a distorted or Americanized version of "mexicano." The Chicano, like a *pocho*, was a tainted or contaminated *mexicano*. The word seems to have had a paradoxical meaning like "nigger" or "queer," pejorative when used by outsiders and positive when used by insiders. Significantly, it is a term that has been adopted by Chicanos themselves. Just as black Americans selected "black," a previously pejorative term, as the rallying point for the black movement and as a source of pride and dignity, so Chicanos have self-consciously chosen Chicano. One of the unstated goals of the *movimiento* is restoration of pride in and respect for the word "Chicano." The movement is thus a movement of *Chicanismo* or *carnalismo* (brotherhood).

Another common term, "Mexican-American," connotes middle-class respectability and is perhaps more palatable to Anglos than "Chicano" because it lumps such persons with other hyphenated American groups like Irish-Americans, Italian-Americans, and German-Americans, thereby reinforcing the belief that American society is a melting pot of diverse ethnic groups. "Chicano," on the other hand, underscores the uniqueness of this group. Unlike immigrant groups who entered American society voluntarily, Chicanos' entrance into the United States was imposed. Terms such as "hispano" and "latino" are euphemistic and fail to differentiate Chicanos from other Spanish-speaking people. While some New Mexicans trace their ancestry to the original Spanish colonists, for many years the use of "Hispanic" or "Spanish" was a way of saying that one was European and Caucasian, not to be confused with Chicanos, whose heritage was predominantly Indian. These terms, in other words, provided ways for Chicanos to assimilate, ways to become "noncolonized non-Chicanos."

We will use the term "Chicana" to denote a woman of Mexican ancestry living in the United States, whether she refers to herself as Mexican, Mexican-American, *latina*, *hispana*, or whatever. However, we do not wish to suggest that Chicanas are homogeneous or uniform, for there is great diversity among them. In terms of ethnic identity they range from those who see themselves as *mexicanas*, even though raised and perhaps even born in the United States, to those who see themselves as "Americans" (sometimes called "coconuts," in that they are said to be brown on the outside and white inside). Similarly, some Chicanas are bilingual while others are monolingual, either in English or Spanish. There are also generational differences. Third- and fourth-generation women tend to become more Americanized, although many, especially the college educated, are rediscovering their Mexican-Indian roots. Another source of variation is the degree of commitment to or acceptance of the traditional female role. While some Chicanas accept their traditional role and eschew any affiliation with feminism, others are deeply committed to feminist ideals and seek to improve woman's condition. Some Chicanas are homemakers, others work, and still others are on some form of public assistance. There are also urban-rural, educational, and economic differences. The more affluent, college-educated, urban, feminist, third- or fourth-generation Chicana provides a sharp contrast to her impoverished, less educated, rural, traditional, first-generation *hermana* (see Cotera 1976, pp. 4–5).

Despite their diversity, Chicanas share a number of important characteristics. The Chicana is a woman (1) of Mexican descent, (2) living in the United States, (3) culturally neither Mexican nor American but influenced by both societies, and (4) from a colonized minority. An overriding characteristic shared by Chicanas, in addition to their Mexican heritage, is a sense of marginality in an Anglo-dominated society. The essence of being Chicana is that one is not fully Mexican or American. Internal colonization means that Chicanas are free to be Mexican or American but not Chicana, since Chicanos are a nonentity in colonial America. In other words, she may be Mexican (i.e., foreign) or American—a noncolonized non-Chicana.

The Triple Oppression of Chicanas as Colonized Women

Perhaps the unique characteristic of the Chicana is in the nature of her triple oppression. Chicanas suffer more than the double oppression of women who are members of a colonized group; they are also internally oppressed. As noted earlier, Chicanas are part of an economically and politically exploited colony. They are victims of attempted cultural genocide as the dominant group has sought insidiously to destroy Chicano culture and render its institutions subordinate and dependent. Chicanos, however, have resisted assimilation, and, as we shall show, women have played a critical part in this resistance. The second form of oppression results from their gender. As women, Chicanas experience the universal oppression that comes from being female. Although references to female-dominant matriarchies are common, in reality such societies are rare, if not nonexistent. Despite vast cross-cultural differences in the status accorded women, in most societies, past and present, they have been subordinate to men (see Rosaldo and Lamphere 1974, p. 13). Even in matrilineal society, "the woman is never anything more than the symbol of her lineage. Matrilineal descent is the authority of the woman's father or brother extended to the brother-in-law's village" (Lévi-Strauss 1969, p. 116). Thus, although group placement runs through the female line in matrilineal descent groups, authority still runs through the male line (Schneider and Gough 1961, p. 7). Finally, Chicanas carry an additional burden of internal oppression by a cultural heritage that tends to be dominated by males and exaggerates male domination over women (see Vidal 1971, p. 6; Flores 1971b, p. 3; and Nieto-Gómez 1974, p. 34).

The issue of *machismo* is a complex and sensitive one for Chicanos. All too often it has served as a useful myth for social scientists to perpetuate stereotypical depictions of Mexican-Chicano culture (Sosa Riddell 1974, p. 156; and Baca Zinn 1976, p. 19). The term has also been distorted by popular usage, which tends to equate it with male chauvinism. Our intent is not to reify the concept or to perpetuate additional stereotypes and misconceptions but to argue that the origins of male dominance in the culture are external and emanated from forces imposed via colonization (Sosa Riddell 1974, ibid.; and Baca Zinn 1975, p. 22). We argue, moreover, that regardless of its origins and varied interpretations, the problem of male dominance in Chicano culture is real and must be faced directly. Because of its complexity and importance, the concept of *machismo* will be discussed more fully in ensuing chapters.

The oppression of Chicanas, as colonized women, is much more pervasive than that of nonminority women or Chicano men. The effects of this oppression are not additive. Their socioeconomic oppression, as we will see, for example is greater than would be predicted from the cumulative effects of race and gender.

Two

Cultural Heritage I Mexico

The involuntary entrance of Chicanos into United States society came with the signing of the Treaty of Guadalupe Hidalgo in 1848, when the "American Southwest" was created, supplanting what was formerly Aztlán or northern Mexico. As members of a colonized group, Chicanas have not commonly identified with the cultural mainstream of Anglo-American society. Though the dominant society has sought to obliterate Chicano culture and heritage, contemporary Chicanas recognize that their roots are in Mexico, not in the United States.

This chapter examines the historical and cultural roots of the Chicana in pre-Columbian and colonial Mexico. If Chicanos as a group have been generally bypassed by American historians, Chicanas have been slighted even more, because they do not have a formally recognized role in the historical and cultural process. Stereotypical images of Chicanas emerge from the pages of American history as sultry, flashing-eyed señoritas or loose women and saloon keepers.[1] Histories of Mexico have proved to be more generous in their inclusion of women, but references to them remain few and far between.

The purpose of this chapter is not to present a history of the Chicana or systematically to document her contribution to history. Rather, our goal is to present an overview of the cultural heritage of the Chicana in a historical context. One of our theses is that a number of present-day cultural mandates which impinge on the contemporary Chicana originated in ancient Indian and Mexican culture.

Some cultural expectations of Chicanas date back to Aztec models— such as being the heart of the home, bearing and rearing children, being clean and tidy, dedicating oneself to a husband, and preserving one's respectability in the eyes of the community. Restrictions such as being protected and sheltered in childhood and adolescence, developing finesse in sewing and embroidery, and perceiving a formal education as superfluous have antecedents in the colonial period. Marked departures from traditional feminine roles begin with the war of independence, when *heroinas* first emerged and were recognized, and culminate in the revolution of 1910, with extensive female participation in areas outside the home. The impact of the revolution on traditional female roles was so significant that it brought about the genesis of a broadly based "movimiento feminista." Discussion of the revolution is therefore reserved for the chapter on Chicana feminism. In this chapter we isolate a number of feminine models who served as exemplars and precursors of this later movement, examining first the role of women in pre-Columbian Mexico.

The Role of Women in Aztec Society

A rigid social structure, a strict moral code, and the concept of dualities in Aztec mythology and religion are all ancient but significant contributions to the Chicana's cultural heritage. Pre-Columbian society in Mexico had reached a high evolutionary state just before the conquest, and whether the society was a military democracy of warlike clans with tribal links, as Bandelier (1879) suggests, or a more sophisticated sociopolitical system, as Manuel Moreno (1971) proposes, its organization can be characterized as rigid and its outlook strict. Aztec society was a stratified yet collective enterprise into which individuals were born, to which they responded, and from which they derived rewards and reprisals. Compliance with assigned class roles thus determined personal merit in the collective community.

The *Florentine Codex* is a pictographic document that attests to delineations of roles and behavior in Aztec society. A whole array of people are described, from noblewomen and merchants to weavers, cooks, and common women. Accompanying illustrations of modes of dress, hair arrangement, and adornments reveal a person's station in life. But what the codex most reflects is rigidity and strictness of social expectations by outlining the behavior or attitude one should assume in carrying out one's duties. These are not simply descriptions of duties but, rather, systematic appraisals of what constitute appropriate and inapproriate comportment for various class and social roles. A distinction is made, for example, between a good and a bad noblewoman: "The good noblewoman, the beloved noblewoman [is] highly esteemed, good, irreproachable, faultless, dignified, brave; . . . very much hers are goodness, humanity, humanness, the human way of life, excellence, modesty, the fullness of love. . . . [She is] perfect, faultless. The bad noblewoman [is] bad, wicked, evil, ill, incorrigible, disloyal, full of affliction, quite besmirched, quite dejected. [She is] haughty, presumptuous, arrogant, unchaste, lewd, debauched." Similarly, the good and the bad weaver are differentiated: "The good weaver of designs is skilled—a maker of varicolored capes, an outliner of designs, a blender of colors, a joiner of pieces, a matcher of pieces, a person of good memory. She does things dexterously. The bad weaver of designs is untrained—silly, foolish, unobservant, unskilled of hand, ignorant, stupid. She tangles [the thread]; she harms [her work]—she spoils it. She ruins things scandalously; she scandalously ruins the surface of things" (Sahagún 1961, pp. 50–51). Because of her high status, the noblewoman is vested with abstract human qualities like goodness, excellence, and modesty, while the lower-ranking weaver is praised for the quality or fineness of her weave and design—virtues linked to the more tangible qualities of her skill. These descriptions appear not only to preserve class distinctions but also to reflect a ranking of individual qualities which was class based.

Regardless of social class, women participated at all levels of Aztec society, though their representation was often governed by expectations that drew on their domestic attributes and skills. Noblewomen were worthy in regard to their concern for less fortunate fellow beings, for their good deeds or "volunteer work," if you will. Lower-class weavers, spinners, and cooks contributed to the more basic and mundane of society's needs (Hellbom 1967, p. 301). The status of the *curandera* (healer) approached a more esoteric plane, given her special knowledge and skills, which were capable of producing medicinal wonders. Perhaps the highest status in the domestic realm was accorded the *partera*, or midwife. Her role will be discussed in greater depth later, but the scope of her skills should be noted here. The respect she was given arose from the unique combination of skills she possessed; these were not only obstetrical and medicinal, in the administration of drugs for easier labor and delivery; but also spiritual, for the invocation of gods in cases of imminent fatal childbirth, and priestly, for the performance of baptismal rites to recently born children.

The role of women was not limited to domestic concerns, however; they participated in areas of vital importance to the Aztec social structure. In the area of the military, for example, women were generally not warriors, but they did accompany armies to battle and served as cooks and carriers of supplies. It was not unusual for their ranks to be almost as numerous as those of the armies themselves (Peterson 1959, p. 158). Another group of women affiliated with the armies were the *auianime*, who served the warriors as courtesans. Their vocation was distinguished by their decoration and dress—they painted their faces, wore their hair long and loose, and dressed in colorfully embroidered clothing. On the "high feast of the dignitaries," the *auianimes'* attire and adornments became even more lavish as they joined the warriors in a great sacred dance held at night (Soustelle 1970, p. 46).

Women also participated actively in the religious sphere of society. Male priests occupied the most privileged ranks on the religious scale (Vaillant 1966, p. 192), but women were certainly not excluded from the rituals of the priesthood. In fact little girls, like little boys, were started on the long and arduous path to the priesthood while they were still infants. "Some twenty or forty days after her birth, a girl might be brought to the temple by her mother; the woman would give the priest a censor and some *copal* (incense), and this would establish a reciprocal agreement. But it was only when she was a grown girl (*ichpochtli*) that the novice would go into religion, with the title of priestess—or literally 'woman priest,' *ciuatlamacazqui*" (Soustelle 1970, pp. 54–55).

The education a young girl received in a temple was not unlike that of a convent. Secular feminine arts like sewing and embroidery were emphasized, with cloaks for priests and the idols in the temples coming from their handiwork. Religious guidance and instruction were provided by elderly priestesses. All members of the temple participated in daily religious rituals.

The active participation of women in religion is consistent with the structure of Aztec mythology. The genesis of the Aztec universe is feminine. Coatlicue, the awe-inspiring "lady of the serpent skirt," was the creator and destroyer of all matter and all form. From her Zeus-like promiscuity sprang the innumerable gods and goddesses of Aztec mythology. Coatlicue originally embodied a universe that was feminine, but according to myth she was miraculously impregnated by a ball of feathers that dropped through space (ibid., p. 102). From this propitious occurrence came her most powerful offspring, Huitzilopochtli, the sun god. His birth countered the feminine dominance, and the Aztec universe assumed a dual nature. War, the hunt, and abstract natural manifestations and functions fell in the male domain, while the earth, agriculture, fertility, rain, and corn remained in the feminine sphere.

The division of the universe into male and female realms is reflected in the Aztec calendar; almost half of the eighteen months contained feast days devoted to feminine deities or cults. Ceremonies conducted on these feast days were generally administered by priestesses and celebrated primarily by women.

Three of these months honored important goddesses of the pantheon. The third month was dedicated to Coatlicue. Offerings of flowers were made to her during this ritualistic celebration. In the eleventh month the great goddess Toci, also known as "our grandmother," was worshiped. A woman symbolizing Toci was offered as a sacrifice, and warriors marched in display before the emperor (ibid., p. 247). In the seventeenth month homage was paid to the old goddess Ilamatecuhtli, and again a woman dressed entirely in white and personifying her was sacrificed. Mock battles in which young men attacked women with bolsters were also a part of this feast day.

Three other months celebrated the importance of maize in Aztec society. During the fourth month offerings of flowers and food were made to Chicomecoatl, goddess of maize, with processions of girls carrying consecrated ears of corn to her temple. Tribute was paid to Xilonen, goddess of young maize, in the eighth month. The eleventh month honored Chicomecoatl again. Her priestesses are described thus: "Each carried ears of maize wrapped in rich cloth on her back; their faces were painted, their arms and legs adorned with feathers. Singing, they went in procession with the priests of the same goddess; and at sunset they threw handfuls of colored maize and calabash seeds to the crowd, who struggled and scrambled for them, because they were a token of wealth and plenty for the coming year" (ibid., p. 55).

The remaining months contained feast days for other earth and vegetative goddesses. In the thirteenth month five women representing agrarian deities were sacrificed in ceremonies. Celebrations dedicated to other goddesses of the earth and vegetation were also carried out during the eleventh month. These goddesses were depicted with brooms in their hands, which they used to sweep clear the path of the gods. Holy places were swept, fires lit, dances held, and mock battles took place between female healers and courtesans.

Finally the seventh month, with rites for Uixtociuatl, goddess of salt water, and the fourteenth, celebrating Mixcoatl, god of hunting, included feast days in which women participated. In celebrations honoring Mixcoatl, mothers went to his temple in the morning and presented their children to elderly priestesses, who took them in their arms and danced with them.

That nearly half of the calendar should be devoted in some way to feminine deities or cults indicates the importance of not only goddesses in the Aztec pantheon but also the part priestesses and women in general played in religion (a striking contrast to the subsequent Christian religion, where women were conspicuously absent). The concept of dualities or the union of opposites with resultant tensions or harmony was not limited to mythology, religion, and the natural sphere, however, but was crucial to all of Aztec culture. "All things were based on male and female elements that gave birth to the gods, to the world, and to man. Celestial and natural phenomena were attributed to eternal struggles between hostile deities. This accounted for night and day, light and dark, life and death, growth and decay, good and evil, sickness and health" (Peterson 1959, p. 126).

When the concept of dual spheres is applied to the social realm, a sharp separation of male from female becomes apparent, with role expectations revolving around one's gender. Moral pressures by the collective society so impinged on the individual that adherence to one's role elicited praise while deviation was condemned or punished. Whether one was a high-ranking noblewoman or a lowly slave, this rigidity of expectations was heightened by a sober outlook that saw life as laden with affliction, labor, and misery—all to be borne with stoicism.

Thus the worth of the female of whatever class, like that of other members of the society, derived from how well her designated role was carried out. Personal harmony with her role occurred when it was well executed, tension when it was not. The ideal for the female was to embrace her role and adopt an attitude of passive endurance in the face of life's demands. To help her along, a prevailing familial ethic of strictness governed her upbringing; from birth to death, ritual exhortations were recited that emphasized her feminine role. Social mores were also an ever present force, as were her immediate family and extended relatives who constantly surrounded her. They were present at all critical transitions of the life cycle, including births, baptisms, marriages, announcements of pregnancy, and deaths.

When a girl was born, the *partera* cut the umbilical cord, and as she did so, she recited the following:

Habéis de estar dentro de casa, como el corazón dentro del cuerpo,
no habéis de andar fuera de casa no habéis de tener costumbre de ir
a ningua parte: habéis de ser la ceniza con que se cubre el fuego del
hogar; habéis de ser las trébedes, donde se pone la olla; en este lugar
os entierra nuestro señor; aquí habéis de trabajar, y vuestro oficio
ha de ser traer agua, y moler el maíz en el metate; allí habéis de sudar
junto a la ceniza y el hogar.[2]

The umbilical cord was buried near the hearth, symbolically linking the
newborn with her life's vocation. Not only was the home defined as a
woman's place, but she appears as a kind of Cinderella figure destined
to the drudgeries of housekeeping.

The female baptismal ceremony that followed birth began before
dawn, as relatives gathered in the patio of the parent's home. The
accoutrements of two feminine trades, spinning and weaving—a spin-
dle and a shuttle—were placed in the center of the patio along with a
tiny skirt and smock, a *huipil*. The child was held up to the rising sun
by the *partera*, doused with water to insure purity from carnal desires,
and offered to the goddess of fresh water, Chalchiuhtlicue. From this
goddess of verdure and growth the baby girl was to inherit the desired
attributes of liveliness, alertness, and diligence in her duties (ibid.,
p. 633).

Parental guidance was always integral to her upbringing. When she
came of age, her father and mother each recited a set of exhortations
to her. The father outlined her roles in marriage and the home and
dwelled on her function as the propagator of a noble race. The mother's
exhortation counseled her on the behavior she was to demonstrate both
in the home and in public. These exhortations are remarkable both for
their meticulous detail in describing the duties of the daughter and as
literary phenomena that reveal the Aztec love of rhetoric. Their tone
has a rare, warm quality that momentarily displaces the more typical
sobriety of the Aztec character. The daughter is called a "precious
gem," a "rich feather," and a "beloved dove." The lyricism of these
metaphors falls short of sheer poetics, however, because it is grounded
in the real world, where joy is not free of sadness and rest is not unen-
cumbered by affliction. The father reminds her that worldly affliction
can be eased if a pattern or a divine order is seen in life and roles assigned by the lord are assumed. The pains of childbearing, for example,
might then be balanced by joy, just as laughter and dreams provided a
necessary balance to more essential eating and drinking when man was
created. "Nuestro señor nos dió la risa, el sueño, el comer, y el beber

con que nos criamos y vivimos; diónos también el oficio de la generación con que nos multiplicamos en el mundo; todas estas cosas dan algún contento a nuestra vida por poco espacio, para que después nos afligamos con continuos lloros y tristezas."[3] Though this exhortation may have been an insiration for the young Aztec woman, compliance with the demands of her reproductive function was far from simple. She was to fulfill it with a nobility and generosity of character that would be a tribute to her ancient forebears. Not only was maternity to be a noble endeavor, daily chores like grinding corn and making chocolate —general preparation of all food and drink—was to be done with grace and delicacy.

The mother's exhortation focused on personal dress, behavior and demeanor. Cleanliness of body, clothing, and mind was urged, as were an honest face and bearing. These two virtues paid public homage to her revered ancestors and helped her hold a man. The virginal purity of a freshly scrubbed face and clean, simple, clothing were preferred to the painted faces, attire, and behavior of loose women.

> Mira también hija que nunca te acontezca afeitar la cara, o poner colores en ella o en la boca por parecer bien, porque esto es señal de mujeres mundanas y carnales; . . . las desvergonzadas que ya han perdido el pudor y aun el seso, que andan como locas y borrachas; . . . para que tu marido no te aborrezca, atavíate, lávate, y lava tus ropas . . . porque si cada día te lavas y también tus ropas, decirse ha de ti que eres relimpia y que eres demasiado regalada.[4]

Personal honor in this world, as it derived from the virtues of honesty and cleanliness, was a concern more of the mother than of the father. What others thought, the public at large, was an immediate preoccupation. The highest womanly virtues in Aztec society were virginity and fidelity—virginity until marriage and thereafter fidelity to one's husband, ending only with death. The ultimate disgrace that could befall a woman in the mother's eyes, indeed in the society as a whole, was adultery. Adulterers were punished publicly by being stoned to death (Bonilla García 1959, p. 265). The severity which adultery was dealt with probably arose from the fact that marriage was regarded as a sacred institution. It served to propagate a noble race, and it was through this institution that women most fully achieved their destined roles.

Within marriage, reproductive abilities accorded the woman special sanctity. The frighteningly difficult ("espantablemente dificultoso") path of life her father had described to her became a reality for the

Aztec woman in pregnancy and birth. And to assist her on this path was the venerated *partera*. Throughout the early stages of pregnancy the advice and aid of several *parteras* were enlisted. The expertise of these ancient midwives is astounding, and while old wives' tales may seem quaint to us today, they reveal a knowledge that is not at all quaint. *Parteras* cautioned "the newly impregnated one" about things that are now commonplace—not to work too hard or too much, not to run, not to lift heavy objects, and to avoid frightening situations that might cause her to abort (Sahagún 1946, 1:590). In the seventh or eighth month, family and relatives of the mother-to-be gathered to settle on a particular *patera* and officially engaged her for delivery of the baby.

Because of its association with birth, midwifery was so exalted that it was regarded as a divine vocation. The "venerated woman" was asked to "hagáis . . . vuestro oficio y facultad pues que nuestro señor os ha hecho maestra y médica, y por su mandate ejercitáis este oficio" ("exercise your powers and perform the vocation our lord has made you a master and physician of, and through his will, perform it": ibid., pp. 584–85). Having been summoned and officially engaged, the midwife ceremoniously accepted pleading humility and disclaiming that she belonged to the special class of midwives. "Yo que soy una vieja miserable y malaventurada; no sé qué os ha movido a escogerme a mí, que ni tengo discreción ni saber, ni sé hacer nada agradable a nuestro señor, pues soy boba y tonta, y viven hoy, y florecen muchas siervas de nuestro señor, muy sabias, prudentes, experimentadas y muy amaestradas, a las cuales ha enseñado nuestro Dios con su espíritu e inspiraciones, y las ha dado autoridad para ejercitar este oficio."[5] In accepting her services, family and relatives accepted the instructions and will of God, for whom, the *partera* declared, she was but a mere instrument. Success or failure of a pregnancy and its ensuing and delivery was transferred into his hands through this means. In addition to her spiritual endowments, the midwife possessed exceptional terrestrial powers, given the fact that, although pregnancy and birth were a very public process, they nevertheless retained an element of mystery to which only the midwife had access. Her skilled hands could enter the mysterious womb, straighten the fetus, and bring it forth. In cases of difficult labor, her medicinal knowledge could create concoctions to facilitate it. When a fatal end was imminent, her priestly role could be assumed as she invoked the gods to spare the dying woman; and when delivery meant inevitable death for the mother and the midwife determined that the child was dead in the womb, she would cut the baby up with an obsidian knife and take it out to save the mother. If relatives objected, she recited prayers over the dying woman and left her alone in an isolated room. So it was that the difficult path of worldly life a woman began in the *partera's* hands might also end in them.

Significantly, women who died in childbirth enjoyed a special kind of immortality in Aztec culture. They were called *mocihuaquetzque,* or "valiant women," who were perceived to have fought a fierce battle equivalent to that of the warrior in the field, and as such they shared residence in a heavenly realm set aside only for warriors and themselves. While the loss of these women was lamented, it was accepted philosophically, if not with a certain amount of joy, because they would be canonized as *ciuateteo* who brought honor to their kin. *Ciuateteo* were *mocihuaquetzque* elevated to celestial ranks as goddesses. This indicates that like marriage, as we have mentioned, the reproductive process was more than functional in Aztec society, it was sacred. The entire reproductive process from conception to parturition was accompanied by prayers and invocations to deities associated with it. Successful births were greeted with feasting, exhortations and celebrations. Thus the fulfillment of a woman's most essential biological function reaped her the highest rewards the society could offer. Even in failure, she was sanctified.

Death in childbirth relieved the Aztec woman of her most difficult worldly burden. The toil and travail of this life were blissfully left behind as she died "the good death" and was carried to a paradisiacal new life where the midwife urged her to awaken: "Depertad pues, y levantaos hija mía, que ya es de día, ya ha amanecido, ya han salido los albores de la mañana, ya las golondrinas andan cantando y todas las otras aves. Levantaos, hija mía y componéos; id a aquel buen lugar, que es la casa de vuestro padre y madre el sol, que allí todos están regocijados, contentos y gozosos, ídoos para vuestro padre el sol, y que os lleven sus hermanas las mujeres celestiales."[6]

Deviation from Aztec Norms of Feminine Virtue: Two Examples

We have seen that the rigid Aztec social structure outlined a woman's role from birth to death based on her class, her skills, or a life's vocation in religion or in the home. If a woman performed her duties and functions well, she was rewarded by her family and the society as a whole. But if she performed them poorly or otherwise deviated from social norms, she was in a position to be judged and punished. This rigid social mandate left little room for deviation.

Aztec norms of feminine expectation have remained surprisingly intact to the present day. They are relevant for Chicanas because they suggest that prescribed roles for women in the culture are essentially inflexible. The following section isolates two females of Aztec origin, La Malinche, a historical figure, and La Llorona, a figure in folklore, as examples of females who deviated from expected norms, had moral judgment passed on them, and survive as burdensome cultural forebears of Chicanas.

La Malinche

La Malinche was a young Aztec woman who served as Hernán Cortés's translator and concubine during the conquest. She persists in Mexican and Chicano culture as an infamous emblem of female transgression and treachery. The basic historical facts that she mated with Cortés, produced a son, and aided him in the conquest as his translator have been blurred by damning cultural judgments that label her a whore, the mother of a bastard race of *mestizos*, and a traitress to her country. However she is depicted, Malinche represents deviance, and as a symbol of damned femininity, she has become a cultural burden to subsequent generations of *mexicanas* and Chicanas. The intent of the following discussion is to reexamine her role in the conquest and to contrast the popular folkloric view of her with the view that emerges from historical accounts. Specifically, the discussion will seek to determine whether she warrants the labels of whore, unnatural mother, and traitress.

One persistent indictment of La Malinche in folklore, concerning the fact that she was Cortés's mistress or whore, implies active volition on her part, but this need not have been the case. Paz (1961), a modern-day commentator on the topic, suggests that Malinche's sexual transgression derives precisely from passive volition on her part, an openness or willingness to be violated. Whether active or passive, history does not ascribe volition to Malinche in becoming Cortés's mistress; she was presented to him as a slave along with nineteen other women when he arrived on the coast of Mexico.

Although as a slave Malinche occupied the lowest rung in Indian society, she was not born to this position. Malinalli Tenepal (her Aztec name) was of noble lineage born into the family of rich and powerful *caciques* (chiefs) from the province of Coatzalcualco. Her mother was widowed while Malinalli was still a child, but as an aristocrat and a woman, the daughter should have rightfully inherited her deceased father's title and properties. The mother remarried, however, giving

Tenochtitlan.

Fig. 1   Tenochtitlan: Malinche and Cortés. Courtesy
of the Bancroft Library, University of California.

birth to a son whom she preferred as an heir, so Malinalli was given to a
group of Mayan traders from Xicalango who took her south and sold
her as a slave to the Tabascans. It was the Tabascans who made a gift
of her to Cortés. "To be sure, it must have been a very painful, traumatic and confusing experience to have gone from the drastic transition
of Aztec princess to Mayan slave" (Del Castillo 1974, p. 59). This
would appear to be the case if one considers that she was only eight
years old when she was thrust into an alien environment among the
Tabascans and barely fourteen when Cortés acquired her (Rodriguez
1935, p. 20).

Malinalli's birthright suggests that she was more than an ordinary
slave at the time of the conquest, as do the names by which she was
known. Malinalli was a name probably given for the day of the calen-

dar on which she was born. Another name, Malintzin, has been considered to be a corruption of "Marina" to "Malin," with "tzin" added to it. "Tzin" was a reverential ending used by the Mexica Indian tribe and indicates that she was held in some reverence by them. Her Christian title, Doña Marina, reinforces the idea of high regard, because in Spanish "Doña" before a first name is a title indicating respect. Her last name, Tenepal, is possibly her familial name and has been explored thoroughly by Gustavo Rodriguez.[7] His findings are significant because they suggest that her last name denotes her unusual abilities as a speaker and a linguist (ibid., pp. 7–8).

When put in the context of the period in which she lived, it is clear that Malinche was a gifted young woman whose imposed bondage deprived her of an aristocratic birthright. On the basis of her names, it is also evident that she was held in high esteem by Indians and Spaniards alike. The label of whore given her by folklore might also be reconsidered in this historical context. Had she been the despicable creature Mexican and Chicano culture claim she was, she would have embodied characteristics of the common harlot as the *Florentine Codex* describes them: "The carnal woman is an evil woman . . . perverse; . . . a brazen, a proud, a dissolute woman of debauched life; a fraud—gaudy, fastidious, vain, petty. . . . She goes about haughtily, shamelessly—head high, vain, filthy, given to pleasure" (Sahagún 1961, p. 55). None of these characteristics are attributed to La Malinche by historians or eyewitness accounts. Bernal Díaz, a *conquistador* who was present when she was given to Cortés as one of twenty slaves, records a first impression of her as "a most excellent person" (Díaz Del Castillo 1963, p. 80). His reaction betrays a response to her total bearing as a person rather than simply to her femininity, which would certainly have caught his attention had she been the debauched woman she is supposed to have been.

Díaz's positive appraisal of her character is supported by her part in an incident that took place in 1523, two years after the final fall of Tenochtitlán. Díaz, Doña Marina, and a group of men accompanied Cortés on a missionary expedition that took them into the province of her origins. The *caciques* of the region were summoned for instruction in the holy faith, among them her mother and her brother. Díaz says, "It was easy enough to see from the strong resemblance between them that Doña Marina and the old lady were related. Both she and her son were very much afraid of Doña Marina; they feared that she had sent for them to put them to death and they wept." But she showed no bitterness toward either one, demonstrating instead great benevolence and

generosity. "She comforted them, saying that they need have no fear.
. . . She told her mother that when they had handed her over to the
men from Xicalango, they had not known what they were doing. She
pardoned the old woman, and gave them many jewels and some clothes.
Then she sent them back to their town, saying that God had been very
gracious to her in freeing her from the worship of idols and making her
a Christian" (ibid., p. 86).

The generous quality Marina exhibited on this occasion is also acknowledged by the historian Prescott (1873, 1:293–94): "Her open,
expressive features indicated her generous temper." Other qualities he
ascribes to her are that "she possessed uncommon personal attractions"
and that she had a "lively genius." Bernal Díaz was in constant contact
with her during the course of the conquest and after. She apparently
related to him that she was a deposed aristocrat, and whether this or a
more general impression of her prompted him to say that "she was truly
a great princess, . . . as was very evident in her appearance" (Díaz Del
Castillo 1963, p. 82), descriptions of her nature and disposition are consistently positive. Perhaps the overriding impression we might gather
from these accounts is that Marina possessed uncommon attributes in
being "good looking, intelligent and self-assured" (ibid.).

Another popular condemnation of Doña Marina is that as Cortés's
invaluable translator and cohort, she was largely responsible for the
downfall of Mexico. As such, she has been called a traitress to her
country. "Malinchismo" is a term commonly used in Mexico today to
denote selling out to foreigners, and the subject of her betrayel continues to be controversial in modern-day culture. As late as 1970 an
eminent Mexican novelist, Carlos Fuentes, dedicated to her a slender
but emphatically negative volume, *Todos los gatos son pardos.*[8] Amparo
Ochoa, a folksinger of "la nueva canción mexicana," also includes a
song by Gabino Palomares, "La maldición de Malinche," in a recent
(1975) album which has enjoyed great popularity. Three stanzas from
the song illustrate a self-indictment by Mexicans in this century for
opening their doors to foreigners, yet the curse that originates in
Malinche is ultimately seen as infecting the culture, so that she is once
again held accountable for the chains Mexico has assumed in inviting
foreigners into its land.

> Se nos quedó el maleficio
> de brindar al extranjero
> nuestra fe, nuestra cultura,
> nuestro pan, nuestro dinero. . . .

Hoy, en pleno siglo viente!
nos siguen llegando rubios
y les abrimos la casa;
y los llamamos amigos. . . .

Oh! Maldición, de Malinche!
enfermedad del presente,
cuándo dejarás mi tierra?
cuándo, harás libre a mi gente![9]

In addition to being given the enduring label of traitress, La Malinche represents a form of deviation with regard to her having produced *mestizo* offspring in her union with Cortés. The mixing of Indian with Spanish blood evokes bitterness in the minds of Mexicans and Chicanos on several counts. The most obvious is that the humiliation of conquest by physical force is heightened by the humiliation of sexual possession of Indian women by the Spaniards. More difficult to deal with is that because Marina's liaison with Cortés was illegitimate, the origin of *mestizaje* is therefore illegitimate. The wrath Malinche suffers thus derives from her being the mother of a bastard race. Historically and culturally, the fact of illegitimacy cannot be remedied. This has given rise to the impotent rage of succeeding generations which Octavio Paz describes in a classic pathological study of the Mexican psyche, *The Labyrinth of Solitude* (1961). His work emphasizes the intense negativity with which La Malinche is regarded and stresses her role as the violated mother, or La Chingada. Her passive receptivity, her willingness to be violated are given special attention, leaving little doubt that such passivity is even more deplorable than an active seduction would have been. This point is particularly critical for Chicanas because its cultural manifestation is that as members of the "tainted" sex and as symbolic daughters of La Malinche, their sexuality, whatever its form, is stigmatized. If Malinche is considered in a religious context, she is transformed into a negative image of woman and becomes a Mexican Eve. Her opposite, on the other hand, is La Virgen de Guadalupe, who embodies the most virtuous feminine attributes: piety, virginity, forgiveness, succor, and saintly submissiveness. Both are images of motherhood, but La Malinche is seen as selfish and rejecting, while Guadalupe is giving and nuturant. A polarized perspective of women thus emerges, whereby only La Malinche as supreme evil and La Virgen as supreme good are possible. Chicanas inherit this polarity; the ideal of virginity until marriage and saintly docility thereafter are general cultural norms, and deviations from this ideal are viewed as moral lapses.

Revelations of historical data on the role of La Malinche in the conquest will probably not temper the severity with which she continues to
be treated in Mexican and Chicano culture. But they can be significant
for contemporary Chicanas and *mexicanas* who bear the cultural
brunt of judgments passed on her. La Malinche should be reconsidered
as the remarkable woman she has been documented to be, by virtue of
her personal character and attributes, and viewed as positively as she
was in her own time. The move to resurrect her as a model of inspiration
rather than condemnation has already begun. Two women have begun
the task of reappraisal: a *mexicana*, Juana Armanda Alegría (1975),
and a Chicana, Adelaida R. Del Castillo (1974).

Alegría's work is basically a psychological assessment of Malinche as
a human being. She begins by querying how it is possible that, given the
paucity of historical information about her, La Malinche continues to be
an object of discussion. Alegría attributes this to the mystery that surrounds her true role in the conquest. Malinche participated in a short
seven years of Mexican history; her origins are still subject to debate,
and within a few years after the conquest she disappeared again. Alegría
contends that interest in her arises from her role as a negative symbol
and an example of "lo que *no se debe hacer*" ("what *shouldn't be
done*", p. 71). This reinforces a one-dimensional, stereotypical image
of Malinche as mistress and traitress that limits estimations of her as a
total person. Alegría sets out to explore the character and motives of
Doña Marina in light of her circumstances as a slave or, better, a trade
commodity who passed from one set of hands to another. As an object
in transactions, Alegría asks, "¿Por qué exigerle entonces tanta con-
vicción? La mentalidad de un esclavo se condiciona a obedecer a su amo,
y el amo de Marina era Hernán Cortés, no había razón para desobede-
cerlo."[10] Marina's obedience to Cortés was not based on meekness or
passivity, however. It is viewed as an intelligent response to an alienating experience. Marina was cut off from her own Aztec people at an
early age; she lived among the Tabascans, a group foreign to her, and
was given to an even more alien group, the Spanish. In view of these
shifting and alienating environments, it is not farfetched to conclude
that "ella no tenía por qué ser fiel ni por que guardar lealtad a nadie.
Seguramente fue fiel a sí misma en el momento en que las circunstancias
le fueron propicias y puso su inteligencia al servicio, no tanto de Hernán
Cortés, sino más bien de los hechos históricos que le tocaron vivir."[11]
Thus Malinche's extraordinary abilities were able to flourish. Her lack
of loyalty to any one group reflects personal strength rather than
bitterness at being a woman without a country, so to speak. The end

result was that as a neutral party she became a mediating force between adversaries, both of whom esteemed her. Her role was thus positive and instrumental.

Alegría's appraisal of Malinche as an active, intelligent, and sympathetic mediating force in the conquest successfully combines historical fact with psychological motive. The result is that we see Malinalli as an almost organic entity in which two languages, two cultures, and two races, met and merged.

Del Castillo's study of La Malinche also focuses on a motive for her participation in the conquest. Her perspective is religious rather than psychological. Doña Marina's participation in the Conquest of Mexico was a manifestation of her faith in a godly force—the prophecies of Quetzalcoatl. It is because of this faith that she sees the destruction of the Aztec empire, the conquest of Mexico, and as such, the termination of her indigenous world as inevitable" (Del Castillo 1974, p. 71).

Del Castillo contends that a general knowledge of the prophecies, sympathy with outlying tribes with whom she lived, and anticipation of relief from oppression were all factors that predisposed Marina to aid Cortés in the actual overthrow of the empire. In addition, Marina was a newly converted Christian at the time of the conquest, so it is not hard to believe that she saw the new religion as more humane than what preceded it. Bernal Díaz attested to her dedication to Christianity in his report of her gratitude for being freed from the adoration of idols. All in all, the image Del Castillo offers of La Malinche is one of religious mysticism that bridges the pagan and Christian worlds; she sees her as a mediator who tempered destruction and mitigated violence in the course of the conquest.

These reinterpretations of Marina's role in the conquest suggest that it may have been more positive than negative. There are a number of other points that support a favorable view of La Malinche. Among them is the allegation that she was the mother of an entire bastard race of *mestizos*. This is clearly symbolic rather than actual. The son she gave birth to as a result of her liaison with Cortés was recognized as legitimate; Gustavo Rodriguez's monograph on Doña Marina includes a family tree that traces Marina and Cortés's legitimate offspring through the twentieth century (1935, p. 58). On this same theme, *mestizaje* did not originate with Doña Marina; it was occurring elsewhere during the conquest with the birth of children to other *conquistadores* and *indias*. In fact the phenomenon predates Cortés's arrival; Gonzalo Guerrero, a shipwrecked Spaniard, is recorded by Bernal Díaz already to have had a family with an Indian woman when he met him (Díaz Del Castillo 1963, pp. 60–61).

The idea of Malinche as a traitress to her country should also be reconsidered. Mexico at the time of the conquest was not the unified republic it is today but a conglomerate of tribal city–states in which no national identity existed. The ready allegiance so many tribes gave to Cortés on his march to Tenochtitlán attests to the autonomy of the tribes. Prophecies of doom in Aztec mythology itself also moved imminent destruction of the empire out of the reach of human forces. They evidence an ironic predisposition to conquest that the tribes, rather than Malinche, facilitated when they allied themselves with the Spaniards. Other factors to be taken into account are the military superiority of the Europeans (Gibson 1966, p. 35), their missionary zeal (Prescott 1873, 1:267–68), and their notorious greed for gold. With or without Marina, the conquest of Mexico was inevitable, and what emerges from this discussion is that a female historical figure had her role lifted from its proper time and place, was made a cultural scapegoat, and was blamed for a tragic clash between cultures. Social judgments of La Malinche's role will undoubtedly persist, however, as they do for a folkloric figure who also has her origins in Aztec Mexico, La Llorona.

La Llorona

La Llorona, or the Weeping Woman, is a mythological figure whose existence in Mexican-Chicano culture dates back to pre-Columbian times and persists through modern times. Various interpretations of La Llorona reflect varying attitudes toward women. In pre-Hispanic Mexico, Sahagún (1946, 1:414) records that sounds of wild beasts or a woman's cries heard at night were considered ill omens by the ancient *agoreros* (diviners). The cries foretold poverty or death for the individual who heard them and were often the culmination of an astrological forecast that accompanied the bad sign a person had been born under. Another early interpretation is offered by Alfonso Caso (1958, p. 54), who traces La Llorona to Cihuacoatl, the patron of the *ciuateteo*, sanctified women who died in childbirth. On days of the calendar dedicated to them, they descended to the earth wailing and moaning in the night air. They appeared at crossroads and were considered ill omens that could prove fatal to women and young children. As Cihuacoatl, La Llorona "is said to carry a cradle or the body of a dead child in her arms and to weep at night at the crossings of city streets. In times gone by, people knew that she had passed that way when they found in the market the empty cradle with a sacrificial knife laid beside it" (ibid.).

Sahagún also links La Llorona with Cihuacoatl and describes the latter as appearing "often . . . as a woman dressed in court robes; it was also said that she groaned and cried out in the night air" (1946, 3:25).

A final pre-Columbian reference to La Llorona is again made by Sahagún. Included in the eight omens of doom the Aztecs had received prior to the arrival of Cortés was one, the sixth, in which anguished voices, like those of women, were heard in the night air: "Oh, my children, we will be lost! . . . Oh, my children, where shall I take you!" (ibid., p. 16).

In the colonial period, La Llorona left her former station at the crossroads, assumed a human female form, and moved into the streets of Mexico City. She was seen on fully moonlit nights walking slowly through silent, lonely streets, emitting penetrating and prolonged moans. She would stop, drop to her knees, and cry. As she cried, she terrified those who saw and heard her: "Not a few of the valorous and strong conquistadores, who themselves had been the fright of death itself, became mute, pale, and cold like marble in the presence of that woman" (González Obregón 1936, p. 18). La Llorona's forlorn solitary wanderings often attracted followers. The boldest ones who ventured forth took full advantage of the moonlight and followed at some length behind her, helplessly watching as she entered, became submerged, and finally disappeared beneath the waters of a nearby lake; they knew neither whence she came nor where she was going.

González Obregón adopts the court robes Sahagún assigned Cihuacoatl, but in the colonial period a thin white veil covered La Llorona's face, and she was given other qualities. She was not only seen walking through the streets but flying through the air, standing on rooftops, walking though niches and crannies, and bathing or disappearing into water. In time, during this period, La Llorona came to be associated with crimes of passion, and her wanderings usually led her to a local cemetery, where she threw herself at the foot of a cross and disappeared into the walls surrounding the cemetery or into vaults and crypts.

The Weeping Woman as mother also came to be transformed into the Weeping Woman as widow, who cried for her orphaned children. Other associations were with the virginal bride who died on the eve of her wedding and brought a garland of white roses to the bridegroom who would have fathered her unborn children. She was also the wife who died in her husband's absence and returned to bring him the final kiss of farewell he had been denied. As a disgraced woman who was killed violently by a jealous husband, she came back to protest her innocence. In addition to being the echo of an ancient deposed goddess or a host of women in sad predicaments, La Llorona has been directly associated with La Malinche. A popular version is that, powerless to keep Cortés in Mexico after the conquest, Malinche protested his leave-taking by stabbing and throwing their young son from a balcony and later cried out with bitter regret as she roamed endlessly through the countryside. In one version she laments the loss of Cortés, but in others she, like Cihuacoatl, laments the passing of the Aztec empire, and her weeping is that of betrayal, of a penitent traitress.

The legend of La Llorona has persisted not only through time but through space as well. Migrations to the north of Mexico, today the Southwestern United States, carried the myth into Chicano culture. Among other states, California and Texas have unique oral interpretations of who La Llorona is and what she represents. In California, for example, she is a woman who killed her three children so she might continue her wild life. When she died, she was unable to account for them to God, so she was sent on a painful, eternal search for them. An Austin version also depicts her as a woman who disposed of her two children by drowning them because she did not want them. Other Texas interpretations present her as a seductive siren who is followed along a river or through the streets, only to turn around and terrify her followers with an eerie face or frightening cry (Castañeda Shular, Ybarra-Frausto, and Sommers 1972, pp. 105–8).

Whatever maybe the cultural origins of the myth of La Llorona, all versions consistently present her as a female who strayed from her proper role as mother, wife, mistress, lover, or patriot. In every interpretation she is a woman who regrets her transgression or bemoans having been denied the fulfillment of her role; in all instances she returns to lament her fate mournfuly. Whether she is enticingly seductive or a terrifying figure, La Llorona persists as the image of a woman who willingly or unwillingly fails to comply with feminine imperatives. As such, a moral light is cast on her, and she again reflects a cultural heritage that is relentless in its expectations of feminine roles.

The Colonial Period: An Overview

Before discusing the role of women after the conquest, an outline of this period is in order. The colonial period (1521–1821) spans the greatest number of years in Mexican history and is marked by the replacement of an ancient stratified but collective social structure with a rigid and oppressive new one. Among the most important colonial institutions were the church, a caste system, *encomienda, repartimiento,* and *haciendas.* Life as the preconquest Indian had known it was virtually eradicated as foreign religious, social, and political structures were imposed by the conquering Spaniard. In addition, the attitude of the

Europeans toward the New World inhabitants insured that the new systems would keep them in a subservient position (Hellbom 1967, p. 301), often through coercive means.

The church of this period was the "purified" church of the Catholic monarchs Ferdinand and Isabella. Early fifteenth-century problems of clerical privilege, corruption, and deplorable standards of conduct had been eliminated, and a new religious nationalism prevailed on the peninsula. As a result, missionary zeal transferred to New Spain bordered on religious expansionism. In addition, the Christian Humanism of Erasmus was at its height in Spanish universities, so that the pagans of America represented much more than potential converts: "They were to be civilized, taught, humanized, purified, and reformed" (Gibson 1966, pp. 71–72). Bartolomé de Las Casas, a friar and thinker of his day, steadfastly defended the Humanism of Erasmus as well as the "noble savage" concept Columbus had introduced in Europe; he considered the Indians rational beings endowed with all the human capacities of free men. For Las Casas, they simply stood in the darkness of a pagan religion and needed only to be led into divine light. Las Casas's polar extreme was Gonzalo Hernández de Oviedo, who saw the natives as naturally lethargic, vicious, melancholic, and shiftless. "Their chief desire was to eat, drink, worship heathen idols and commit bestial obscenities" (Hanke 1935, p. 20). Oviedo and his group looked on these characteristics as well as the pagan practice of sodomy with such distaste that they regarded the Indian as a creature no higher than a "dirty dog" (ibid., pp. 19–20). The significance of this heated controversy and its final resolution cannot be overstated. It meant not only that the nature of the Indians' very essence was being questioned but that under the guise of Humanistic Christian principles, ensuing exploitation of terrifying dimensions would be justified.

It is not surprising, then, that the first order of business the Twelve Franciscans who followed Cortés into Mexico took upon themselves was to destroy temples and religious sites, terminate pagan rites, and burn codices that contained any reference to the ancient religion. On the foundations of razed temples, Indian labor began to build Catholic churches and monasteries (Vaillant 1966, pp. 267, 271). The Christian church became the hub of newly founded religious communities and Catholicism a primary mechanism of social control. The communities later extended to surrounding towns, where outlying chapels were established. Administration of the church was carried out by an exclusively male European clergy who usurped the earlier functions of priests and priestesses. Mass conversions through baptism began imme-

diately, although the process of Christianization became gradual thereafter. The Indians were initally allowed only the sacraments of baptism
and matrimony, with holy orders denied them altogether. "The doors
of the priesthood were closed to the Indians. The synod of 1555 for-
bade the ordination of mestizos, Indians, and Negroes, and, in 1570, one
reads in the *Códice Franciscano* that the sacrament of [admission to]
the Order is not administered to the Indians, even for minor orders,
because they do not yet have the necessary qualifications" (Ricard
1966, p. 230). The missionary church of the sixteenth century might be
characterized as eager to swell its ranks with converts while exerting
total control over subsequent privileges of conversion. The prevailing
ethic of Christian expansionism during this period is notorious for
attitudes that all too often went hand in hand with inhumane acts,
despite the presence of singular exceptions like Bartolomé de Las Casas
and Bernardino de Sahagún—missionaries who did practice a truly enlightened and Humanistic Christianity. Generally, the methods of conversion in the Spanish Catholic church were coercive, so that "Indians
who refused to accept Christianity were punished, sometimes by death"
(Gibson 1966, p. 73).

The religious zeal that theoretically sought to make the less than
human heathen a worthy counterpart to the European Christian also
infiltrated the social and political realms. A rigid caste system was im-
plemented, in which the pure bred who were born in Spain *(penin-
sulares)* occupied the highest positions and received the greatest privileges in society and government, while *castas*, who represented a mixture of Indian and Negro blood, and imported Negro slaves occupied
the lowest rungs of the social ladder. Aztec slaves in pre-Columbian
society, though lowly, could earn their freedom, produce free offspring,
and perform menial but significant tasks that contributed to the society
as a whole. A sense of individual worth and input into the collective
were replaced in the new order by levels of exclusion in a system so
rigid that neither upward mobility nor individual worth was recognized.

By the second half of the sixteenth century, Erasmian thought had
fallen into disrepute, and his writings were officially condemned in
Spain. The heated controversy over the Indian as a rational and free
agent had been won by his adversaries, and the hitherto temporary
institution of *encomienda* became firmly entrenched in the New World.
Encomienda, whereby indigenous laborers were placed at the disposal
of Europeans, sprang from a secular dichotomy similar to the religious
one. Monarchical imperialism, like Christian expansionism, perceived
its goal in the New World to be the acquisition of tribute-paying sub-

jects. Tributes were but a meager source of revenue for the royal coffers, however; a richer source lay in the natural wealth of the new land, and to extract that wealth a large source of labor was necessary. The attitude that viewed Indians as inferior beings came into direct conflict with a royal dictate that declared them free subjects, and because they clearly represented the needed labor source but were free subjects, they could not be legally obligated to work. Individual natives or entire tribes had refused to pay tributes to the crown, however, and this resistance came to be readily punished with sentences of enforced labor for *encomenderos*. Strict attention continued to be paid to the fact that Indians were technically "free," but *encomenderos* eventually practiced a legally sanctioned form of semivoluntary slavery. The "dirty dog" view of the pagans continued, and as *encomienda* spread it was sanctioned and granted multifunctional authority as a "service" to Indians, because it was designed "to civilize them by encouraging orderly habits of industry" (Gibson 1966, p. 52).

Encomienda reached its height in the 1530s and 1540s. Its decline coincided with a tragic native phenomenon—depopulation. The European conquerors who entered the New World brought with them diseases such as smallpox, typhoid, and measles, to which indigenous inhabitants had no immunity. As a result, even casual contact between the groups spread deadly epidemics. The native population was so drastically reduced in the wake of these epidemics that it is estimated to have declined from about 25 million in 1519 to approximately 1 million by 1605 (ibid., p. 63).

Depopulation created such a severe cutback in the labor force that the "voluntary" institution of *encomienda* was replaced by *repartimiento*. This was a formal allotment system whereby an employer applied to local authorities for a specified number of workers. Workers were obtained from a community labor pool composed of a percentage of able-bodied native males. Contracts were drawn up and entered into by both parties. The employer agreed to provide humane treatment for his workers and pay a given wage; employees in turn agreed to work for a designated period of time. This form of "free contract labor" prevailed until about 1630, when it degenerated into an unqualified form of peonage that typified another colonial institution, the *hacienda*.

The phenomenon of depopulation had not only depleted the supply of labor so that natives were exploited; it also caused a change in native land occupation. Large tracts of Indian land were left vacant by the deadly epidemics, open to acquisition by the Spanish. A move to acquire these lands legally was made by issuing land grants, allowing mergers with contingent property, and permitting outright purchases. Once access to these lands was gained, economic survival had to be insured, so *haciendas* were built on them. These contained dwellings that provided housing for those who worked it. *Haciendas* were basically a secular version of church communities, with large numbers of natives serving the *hacendero* and his family. These self-contained social microcosms, where workers were allowed to cultivate their own parcels of lands in exchange for labor, have often been likened to the medieval feudal system, and understandably so. The *hacienda* system made the *peon* a modern-day serf, given that *haciendas* established in the colonial period survived into the twentieth century. Much of the grass roots support for the revolution of 1910 issued from these landless *peones*, who were no longer able to tolerate the *hacienda* system.

The Role of Women in the Colonial Period

Since the role of women in Mexico's colonial period is little documented, it is necessary to extrapolate and interpret from available historical accounts and social commentaries.

As noted, pre-Hispanic society incorporated women at all social levels, though their roles were rigidly defined by social class and cultural expectations. Its replacement with an entirely new European system and institutions that perpetuated limited feminine roles resulted in the displacement of women regardless of race or class. Though a wide institutional gap existed between them, a poor, rural *india* shared with the *española* of the upper classes the prevailing norm of exclusion from participation in the new system. The universal function of women during this period was to serve in the home as procreators, housekeepers, wives, and mothers.

The immediate establishment of church communities in the New World signaled the end of the intricate and close type of family system which had been the heart of the Aztec woman's domestic life. Clustering of large numbers of Indians in and around churches and monasteries transferred the locus of daily activity from the family hearth to the church altar, and an alien altar at that. The major familial events in an Aztec woman's life—birth, baptism, and marriage—became submerged in a Christian context. Daily masses, rituals, and annual church feast days gained priority as the focus of her life. The advent of Christianity also meant that women were no longer priestesses, though they continued to perform many of the same ceremonial tasks in their capacity as servants to the clergy. Putting fresh flowers in churches, sweeping them, and embroidering vestments and altar cloths became lay functions that had formerly been priestly ones in the temples. The strict demands of Christianity were generally so pervasive that they even displaced the role of parents in the family. The moral stoical upbringing Aztec children received through parental guidance and exhortations was replaced by impersonal Christian dogma and mandates that carried penance or eternal punishment for transgressions. Individual work aimed at the collective good and honoring one's ancestors gave way to the quest for divinely mandated individual salvation.

Institutions like *ecomienda* and *repartimiento* further eroded the familial roots of the old society. The Indian male represented the primary source of labor necessary to successful colonization of the New World. As such, he suffered European labor demands so taxing that they curtailed and even eclipsed his responsibilities to his family and the Indian community. His former role in sharing in the upbringing of his children was transformed into a peripheral one, given the long work hours demanded of him. The outcome of this role displacement was that in the lower Indian classes the woman's domestic role became multifaceted and required more stoical endurance than ever. The woman's role was especially taxing in rural villages and urban barrios, where Indian populations were most concentrated and where the labor supply was most numerous.

The institutions of the church, *encomienda*, and *repartimiento* were not the only new phenomena in the colonial period that contributed to the evolving role of the Indian woman. Another important factor was intermarriage with Spaniards with its resultant *mestizaje*. Just as Indian males provided a ready supply of labor, Indian women had been and continued to be a source of female companionship for the Spaniard, whatever its form. Their accessibility was enhanced by the scarcity of European women both during and after the conquest. It has been documented that a number of Spanish women actually accompanied the *conquistadores* (O'Sullivan-Beare 1956; and Ortega Martínez 1945), but their numbers were few. In the aftermath of the European takeover, Hernán Cortés became sensitive to casual unions that sprang up in the course of the conquest and issued an edict proclaiming that the men who served under him should arrange to bring their wives from Spain within a prescribed period of time. The edict may have been an effort to reestablish former legal bonds or a response to pressures exerted by the church and crown; whichever is the case, it stands as an imposed corrective measure for excesses. This apparent concern to rectify wrongs through legal means was more a European preoccupation than an Indian one. The Spanish religious and legal concept of marriage introduced in the New World differed greatly from Indian concepts and practices. The primary intent of Indian folk ceremonies was to insure lines of descent and inheritance in a tribe rather than to grant legitimacy to a union (Borah and Cook 1966, p. 953). As such, the fact that Indian chiefs gave their own daughters or those of other noble tribal members to the *conquistadores* with tribal consent indicates that they sanctioned such liaisons.

Despite its casual origins, intermarriage became very common after the conquest, given the continuing scarcity of Spanish women. But while its incidence increased and was ostensibly not frowned upon, the offspring of these unions suffered from discrimination through exclusion from certain privileged positions in the social order. "Spaniards tended to lump mestizos, mulatos, and free blacks as undesirables, especially as their numbers increased . . . all were excluded from the priesthood, . . . from the trade guilds, . . . and, as far as possible, from all social position" (Liss 1975, p. 142). Thus, though for the first time in history black, brown, and white elements of the human race intermingled, the worth of their offspring was still proportionate to the amount of European blood they inherited.

Interestingly, while Indian women as a group were in greater supply than Spanish women and might have been a less desirable "commodity," the latter shared in being slighted once their procreative functions had been fulfilled. The respect and fidelity a Spanish woman was initially accorded as the preferred woman who mothered the privileged upper classes often waned quickly. It was not uncommon for men to exercise an informal right to maintain two separate households, one legitimate, the other not. Other common grounds of exclusion shared by *indias* and *españolas* were the universal denial of participation in religion, government, and education. The bonuses a wealthy woman might have by virtue of her class, such as instruction in music, French, and finesse in embroidery and lace making, were not bonuses at all; they were but pastimes for a girl until she became of age and was eligible for her true vocation—marriage. Ironically, the lives of aristocratic women of the colonial period were as restricted to the home and its confines as they had been for young Aztec women.

*Madame Calderón de la Barca: An Eyewitness Account
of the Times*

The published letters of Madame Calderón de la Barca (1931), the English wife of a Spanish minister, contribute significantly to our understanding of the role of women in colonial Mexico, in that they provide an extensive and detailed account of social and cultural life in the years 1839–40. (Although technically her observations occur after the colonial period, they suggest that the social systems and mores of that period were still very much intact.) Madame de la Barca's observations focus for the most part on the highest social classes and often reflect European aristocratic arrogance and class prejudice, but she traveled widely and commented on a broad cross section of the population.

Madame de la Barca's medium, personal correspondence, is informal, yet the scope of her commentary is greater than what is typically found in letters from abroad. Her two-year stay in Mexico produced a wealth of first-hand information on a variety of subjects, including landscape, landmarks, cuisine, customs, hospitality, manners, modes of dress, and the general social and political conditions that served as a prelude to the war of independence.

It is also rare that a feminine eye has provided a personal view of a historical period; perhaps Madame de la Barca's greatest service is that her letters contain insights into the lives of women in the period that might not be found in more formal historical texts, her class biases notwithstanding. Our purpose here will be to draw specifically on her observations on the role of women in the caste system, marriage, and convents, which offered a religious and educational alternative to marriage.

Within a matter of months of her arrival in Mexico, we note the pervasive caste system, which virtually equated social worth and rank with skin color and ancestry, invading Madame de la Barca's descriptions of feminine beauty. She makes a clear and calculated distinction between the beauty of Mexican women of the upper classes and the beauty of lowly Indian women. Her observations reflect an attitude of European disdain that was already commonplace in Mexico. She begins by boldly asserting that one is struck by the comparative scarcity of true beauty in Mexico and proclaims that her own pure English beauty is rare in this foreign land: "The brilliant complexion and fine figure of an Englishwoman strike every one" (p. 98). The compliments she initially pays Mexican women are quickly followed by a hard look at their defects. "The beauty of the women here consist in superb black eyes, very fine dark hair, a beautiful arm and hand, and small, well made feet. The defects are, that they are frequently too short and too fat, that their teeth are often bad, and their complexion not the clear olive of the Spaniards, nor the glowing brown of the Italians, but a bilious-looking yellow" (ibid.). In cases where sveltness was preserved and one was endowed with white teeth and a fine complexion, a *mexicana* could be "extremely handsome." *Mexicanas* in the provinces outside the city of Mexico, like *españolas* outside the city of Madrid, were more likely to embody the desired characteristics she describes and so in her estimation were "the handsomest women in Mexico."

Interestingly, when her eye turns to common Indian women, she merges their total bearing with their physical features. For the most part, she finds these women to be "very plain, with an humble, mild expression of countenance, very gentle, and wonderfully polite in their manners to each other; but occasionally, in the lower classes, one sees a face and form so beautiful, that we might suppose such another was the Indian who enchanted Cortés; with eyes and hair of extraordinary beauty, a complexion dark but glowing, with the Indian beauty of teeth like the driven snow, together with small feet and beautifully-shaped hands and arms, however imbrowned by sun and toil" (p. 99). The whiteness of "teeth like the driven snow" which she celebrates along with the sun-drenched browness of their limbs is again neutralized by her English pride, however. It is "more than probable," she reflects, that the blood of intermarriage runs in the veins of these remarkable Indian beauties. Surely somewhere in the past their progenitors united with descendants of the conquerors to produce such loveliness. She thus hints directly that pristine Indian beauty is not possible without some prior mingling with European blood.

By the end of her stay, Madame de la Barca became more generous about *mexicanas*, applauding the unusual wormth of their hospitality and paying homage to the fact that marital transgressions were unknown to them, either in thought or deed. On the point of native beauty, however, she did not yield, despite the fact that she continued to come upon women in remote areas who made the same impression on her. It was in the outlying areas that Indian culture was preserved and kept most intact, indicating that the probability of intermarriage might be negligible.

The caste system not only determined Madame de la Barca's criteria for beauty; it also delegated hierarchical roles executed by *indias* on the lowest levels and aristocratic *mexicanas* on the highest. A classic relationship in which these polarities were evident is that of mistress and servant. Madame de la Barca herself exemplified this relationship during her brief stay. She was struck by a young Indian girl who was "rather pretty" and "very intelligent," took her into her household, gave her discarded silk stockings and satin shoes to wear, and attempted to have her taught to read. Her efforts were misguided and unsuccessful, however, not only because of obvious class differences but because education was something generally denied all women and was not valued, given the domestic expectations of the colonial female. Moreover, nowhere in the social structure could an educated *india* of the lower classes have been accommodated. Had the naive but well-meaning Englishwoman succeeded, she would have been an anomaly.

Like Madame de la Barca, *criollas* were mistresses of large, elegant homes and employed a houseful of servants. There was a notorious problem in acquiring and keeping "good" servants in Mexico City at the time, primarily because Indian servants lacked what their European counterparts prided themselves in, loyalty to their masters. Servants exhibited a form of passive resistance to their overseers by being predictably lazy, slow, slovenly, and unreliable in the execution of their duties. Their own well-being took precedence over their mistress's, and a not uncommon practice was to work for a period of time to earn wages which then financed a vacation of an equal period of time, "para descansar ("in order to rest"). The tension and disharmony of mistress-servant relationships helped reinforce and perpetuate the unfavorable views that the upper classes already held of the lower classes. The conflict experienced in city households carried over into rural households on the *haciendas*.

On a visit to one *hacienda* in particular, Madame de la Barca observed a duplication of lack of respect between masters and servants. But whereas in the city servants were passively defiant, here it appears that a conscious alienation was sensed between the *hacendero* and members of his household. The community typically assembled in the evening in a large hall for entertainment.

> It must be supposed that in this apparent mingling of ranks between masters and servants, there is the slightest want of respect on the part of the latter; on the contrary, they seem to exert themselves, as [if] duty bound, for the amusement of their master and his guests. There is nothing republican in it; no feeling of equality; as far as I have seen, that feeling does not exist here, except between people of the same rank. It is more like some remains of the feudal system, where the retainers sat at the same table with their chief, but below the salt. [Pp. 156–57]

The alienation or detachment people exhibit here while adhering to prescribed roles pervaded all aspects of society and impinged particularly on young women. The universal norm for colonial women of all social classes was to marry, procreate, and raise children. For aristocratic women this imperative proved especially alienating, because their entire life preceding marriage was a preparation for this role. If a young woman found life at home uneventful, she might very well anticipate that marriage itself would be uneventful. This being the case, Madame de la Barca observes that "it appears to me, that amongst the young girls here there is not the desire to enter upon the cares of matrimony, which is observed in other countries" (p. 164). Lack of enthusiasm for marriage was heightened by the general absence of matchmaking efforts and a scarcity of social occasions or other opportunities for young people to meet and court. It might also be speculated that given the rigidity of the caste system, the "right" match, or perhaps a "brilliant" one, was what parents sought for their daughters. Under these circumstances, the function of marriage may have been largely social and economic, minimizing personal and emotional considerations. Also, despite the fact that matrimony and maternity were the major expectations colonial society had of women, if a girl had passed her prime and had chosen not to marry, she was viewed without censure. Madame de la Barca observes that women who showed "the ravages of time" made no attempt to conceal their age and that "the opprobious [sic] epithet of 'old maid' is unknown" (ibid.).

One fairly common alternative to marriage open to aristocratic women was to become a nun and enter a convent. This appears to have been an attractive alternative, as much because it was a choice freely made as because it provided a social event that centered around the young woman. The ceremony which took place upon entrance into a convent was celebrated with all the ostentation and pomp of the ball of the season or a wedding itself. Its elaborateness was crowned by the girl herself. Madame de la Barca describes the dress and demeanor of a sixteen-year-old girl on one such occasion: "She was arrayed in pale blue satin, with diamonds, pearls, and a crown of flowers. She was literally smothered in blonde [lace] and jewels; and her face was flushed . . . for she had passed the day in taking leave of her friends at a fête they had given her, and had then, according to the custom, been paraded through the town in all her finery" (p. 192). The church in which the ceremony took place was as richly decorated as the girl: "Beside the altar, which was a blaze of light, was a perfect mass of crimson and gold drapery; the walls, the antique chairs, the table before which the priests sat, all hung with the same splendid material" (p. 193). The ceremony marked a dramatic transition from the worldly sphere into the spiritual one. Hymns were sung, and the novice, ringed by nuns dressed in black robes, was then queried by a bishop as to her chosen vocation. Later, she shed her profane dress and was draped with a black cloth, symbolizing that "she was now dead to the world" (ibid.).

Madame Calderón de la Barca was at first appalled by the frequency with which young women embraced the holy sisterhood and was prompted to say that it was the "saddest event that can occur in this nether sphere" (p. 189). She later assumed a more objective stance and considered that such a course was not unnatural, given the circumstances of a girl's existence.

> Yet the frequency of these human sacrifices here is not so strange as might at first appear. A young girl, who knows nothing of the world, who, as too frequently happens, has at home neither amusement nor instruction, and no society abroad, who from childhood is under the dominion of her confessor, and who firmly believes that by entering a convent she becomes sure of heaven; who moreover finds there are a number of companions of her own age, and of older women who load her with praises and caresses—it is not, after all, astonishing that she should consent to insure her salvation on such easy terms. [Pp. 189–90]

Her assessment of the worldly life versus the religious one reflects prevailing views and practices concerning the holy vocation of service to God in lieu of service to a man on earth during this period.

Convents were heavily populated not only because they offered a religious alternative to marriage or provided on escape from the real world but also because they were a place to escape *to*. Convents were attractive during the colonial period because they served a special function overlooked or neglected by the secular realm—they provided women with educational opportunities.

Genaro García (1910, pp. 17–18) records that during this time the education of women was limited to memorizing catechism, reading and writing poorly, learning embroidery, eating delicately, dressing fashionably, walking with a dignified bearing, and dancing and singing. He adds that in 1790 only six *colegios* were open to women, and a mere one-eleventh of the female population was educated. Fifty years later, when Madame de la Barca wrote, things had not changed significantly. Except for a few "brilliant exceptions" who, she confesses, rise up before her like "accusing angels," she notes that, "generally speaking, . . . the Mexican Señoras and Señoritas write, read, and play a little, sew, and take care of their houses and children. When I say read, I mean they know how to read; when I say they write, I do not mean that they can always spell; and when I say they play, I do not assert that they have generally a knowledge of music" (p. 221). The minimal education she describes concurs with what García observed. It confirms that a

more traditionally academic education was apparently considered superfluous or at best a rudimentary supplement to the feminine arts.
Moreover, as stated earlier, education was not universally bestowed
but mostly limited to the aristocratic classes. Although *mestizas* had
been admitted to the Colegio de San Juan Letrán, founded between 1536
and 1539, it was considered an "asylum" for them, "so they could get
husbands" (Liss 1975, p. 60). *Indias* probably received little, if any,
formal education. The disparity between education available to upper-
class women, however limited, and that available to *indias* reinforces
a class structure that doubly oppressed the latter as women and as
lower-class citizens.

In addition to providing educational opportunities for aristocratic
women, convents of the time were devoid of traditional austerity,
though a few orders did conform to this norm. Madame de la Barca
touches on what typically passed within the walls when she remarks
that female companionship and the praises and caresses of older women
were found there. Recent accounts of what convents were like describe
them as far from austere and suggest as well that the mistress-servant
relationship carried into religious confines. "Un convento femenino en
la América Colonial era un lugar santo, pero alegre; devoto, pero entre-
tenido. Cien o doscientas monjas lo habitaban. Cada una con su criada
y muchas con su esclava . . . y con niñas educandas. Había pues chismes,
dimes y diretes, ir y venir de criadas, juegos, y algarabía de niñas.[12]

De la Maza also comments that cells were like little houses or apart-
ments, each with its own living room, bedroom, and kitchen. He cites
an 1862 source, Ramirez Aparicio, who was surprised to discover that
these comfortable little houses were a far cry from "la austeridad del
claustro" ("the austerity of the cloister") or "el rincón donde oculta sus
lágrimas el religioso" ("the humble corner where a cleric hid his tears").
Ezquiel A. Chávez (1975, p. 36) agrees that a convent "tenía que ser
considerado no sólo como casa de alejamiento de las inquietudes mun-
danas, y de virtud, y de oración, sino también como centro de cultura
superior, y de amor a lo más puro de las letras y de las humanidades
latinas, y como albergue de prestigio."[13] Not only were convents centers
for companionship and for the study of the humanities, they were not
closed to the outside world; nuns had regular days when visitors were
allowed to come to their cell windows.

These more accurate reports, counter the suggestion that a girl "was
dead to the world" when she embraced the holy sisterhood; it appears
that she could lead a fulfilling existence within its congenial and stim-
ulating walls.

Sor Juana Inés de la Cruz: "La Décima Musa"

Perhaps the most prodigious and famous woman to emerge from the colonial period in Mexico was Sor Juana Inés de la Cruz, a gifted young woman who chose life in a convent to pursue intellectual and poetic endeavors.

Sor Juana was born Juana Inés de Asbaje y Ramírez de Cantillana in a farmhouse at the picturesque foot of the two volcanoes outside Mexico City, in a town called San Miguel de Nepantla. She was born on the twelfth day of November in 1651. Her father was a *vizcaíno* from the town of Vergara (Chávez 1975, p. 4), and her mother was the daughter of Spanish parents from Yacapixtla, Nueva España (García Naranjo 1906, pp. 564–65). Juana was a child prodigy likened to Mozart. It is said that at the age of three she accompanied her sister to her lessons, deceived the teacher into thinking she was older, and was thus taught how to read: "A los cinco añõs había aprendido a leer y a escribir, contar y hacer todas las menudencias de labor blanca" ("by the age of five she had learned to read, write, count, and do intricate needlework," ibid., p. 565). Her eagerness to learn was so great that at the age of seven she entered a contest for which a book was the prize. Verses were submitted to celebrate the feast day of the Sacred Sacrament, and her *loa,* a short dramatic poem, took the prize. Moreover, her verses were publicly applauded for meeting all the poetic qualifications of that poetic form. Her embryonic facility in metrics and rhyme, manifested so early in life, eventually became fully developed and established her as a poetess of such stature in Mexican letters that she came to be known as "La Décima Musa," the tenth muse.

Juana de Asbaje's ardor for learning continued. She became aware that in Mexico City there existed a university where arts and sciences were taught. The fact that she was a female and would be barred from admission did not dampen her youthful spirit; she asked her parents to dress her as a boy and take here there. She was not enrolled in the university, but at the age of ten she was sent to Mexico City to live with her grandfather. He gave her access to books she delightedly consumed. He also instructed her in grammar and then engaged a tutor, Don Martín de Olivas to teach her Latin. To their amazement, it took the young girl only twenty lessons to gain full mastery of the language. The ease with which Juana absorbed knowledge can be attributed to her natural endowment of a fine mind but also to the personal intensity she exhibited in dedication to the learning process. While still at a tender age she began to shun the trivialities of everyday life and set intellectual goals for herself. A curious exercise she would practice was to cut three or four inches of her hair off, "impondiénose de que si cuando volviese a crecer hasta allí no sabía tal o cual cosa que me había propuesto deprender . . . me lo había de volver a cortar ... que no me parecía razón que estuviese vestida de cabellos cabeza que estaba desnuda de noticias."[14] Juana's statement combines youthful intensity with a disdain for locks as the crowning glory of femininity. Her preference for a head filled with knowledge and denuded of hair anticipates the seriousness with which she approached her life as a scholar and writer in a convent as opposed to life as a charming, worldly woman.

By the time she was thirteen, Juana's accomplishments were of such renown that she was invited to the palace of the local viceroy, Don Antonio Sebastian de Toledo, the marqués de Mancera. His wife, Doña Leonor Carreto, is credited with "discovering" Juana.

Juana's relationship with the marquesa has not been explored in depth other than to point out that her protegeé dedicated a number of poems to the marquesa when she died. The marqués was to stage an event, however, that confirmed Juana's intellectual powers and helped establish her national fame. He assembled a group of forty scholars from a number of disciplines, including theology, mathematics, history, and the humanities, to test her formidable knowledge by asking her numerous questions. Her performance at the age of seventeen was astounding: "Ella contestó cumplidamente a todos. Y es que la cultura y el talento de Juana Inés depertaban sospechos y temores. Como nunca habían visto fenómeno igual, los teólogos andaban pensando si toda equella sabiduría, o más bien, aquel insólito afán de conocer, sería 'infuso,' es decir, dado por Dios—o por el Diablo—o 'adquirido.' "[15] The mixed reaction Juana received from the assembly of male scholars anticipates conflicts she was to have with three clerics who oversaw the convent she entered.

Her motivation to become a nun is perhaps the one point of debate concerning her life. Some commentators contend that she chose the sisterhood because she had been disappointed in love (Chávez 1975, pp. 17–25; and Le la Maza 1967, p. 17); others argue that her confessor repeatedly urged her to enter the cloister (González Obregón 1900, p. 260); and still others like a clergyman, Diego Calleja, perceived her as excessively virtuous, making the religious life a natural choice (García Naranjo 1906, p. 566). Perhaps the truth lies in the all-important fact that Juana Inés was such a rarity in her time. Her exceptional intellectual gifts and spirited nature had no place in the mundane life of her native village or in the artificial atmosphere of the court, where she was

the object of incredulous scrutiny. The choice she made was undoubtedly made knowingly and for "conveniencia y no por religión; buscaba en el cláustro, como ella misma lo dice, un lugar donde pudiese estar alejada del matrimonio sin mortificar para nada su decencia ni sufriera menoscabo su reputación."[16] García Naranjo reflects on the social pressures Juana may have experienced in making her decision. She was, after all, a beauty (by all historical accounts), came from a respectable family, was skilled in needlework, played the lyre, wrote admirably, and possessed all the social graces with which a stay at court would have invested her. In sum, she was a highly desirable and eligible young woman. Despite this, it appears that any awareness she may have had or her social extraordinariness did not prevail over the allurement a convent represented as a refuge for pursuing educational interests and writing poetry. The fervor with which she pursued these secular arts once she was in the cloister, however, fanned ongoing conflicts with male superiors who eventually pressured her into abandoning these enterprises altogether. Her confessor and two archbishops contributed to this conflict.

Antonio Núñez de Miranda served as Juana's confessor while she was in residence at the palace of the marqués and continued in this capacity when she entered the convent of San Jerónimo. Juana made a forthright confession to him that religion had taken a back seat to education and writing in her decision to embrace the holy sisterhood. This not only alarmed him, it apparently unleashed his fanatic proclivity to save souls. He saw hers as potentially lost and severely reprimanded her profane inclinations. He personally considered literature to be a corruption of the honesty of youth and proposed that comedies, novels, and romances be banned from the cells of noviates, especially noviates like Juana, who not only consumed them eagerly but wrote them as well. De la Maza asserts that "his point of view was correct, but not in this peculiar case of a muse robed in a Jeronimite habit" (1967, p. 39).

Another cleric who imposed on Sor Juana's life was the archbishop of Mexico, Francisco de Aguiar y Siexas, an ascetic and well-known misogynist who banned women from his residence when he took office. The archbishop not only refused to have female housekeepers and laundresses, he destroyed furniture women had touched and tiles they had walked on. His aversion to the feminine sex carried over into a general intolerance of all diversion (which was banned in all towns under his jurisdiction) including verse, the theater, and books. Aguiar y Seixas's aceticism was obsessive, to the point that gilded or jeweled holy objects used in churches were disposed of, with the proceeds going as alms for the poor. When he died in 1698, his generosity had brought his archdiocese into such indebtedness that many of the 4,000 volumes Juana had in her library were sold to offset debts (ibid., pp. 43–46).

By this time in her clerical career, Sor Juana's secular interests were under continual attack, and her beloved library had been severely depleted. The archbishop of Puebla, Manuel Fernando de Santa Cruz, was to administer a final blow to her enduring dedication to the arts and sciences. Santa Cruz had grown so concerned over the seepage of secular influences into convents that he suggested banning the "infernal" visits of outsiders. Juana's lifeline to the outside world came by way of these visits; she had constantly received at her cell window national and international luminaries who had spread her fame. Santa Cruz's suggestion was like a death knell.

This was but the beginning of his impatience with Juana's fame, however, though it was tempered in 1690 when she wrote a response to a moving sermon she had heard. The sermon was delivered by a Portuguese priest, Vieyra, who posed the question of man's greatest refinement when God created him. She answered that God had given him none, so that man was able to enjoy everything spontaneously and without retribution. Her insistence on applauding the rational, sensate side of man as opposed to his religious, spiritual one incited the archbishop to write an anonymous rejoinder. In a famous letter addressed to "Sor Filotea de la Cruz," he pointed to Santa Teresa de Avila as an exemplar of what a life devoted to God should be and proceeded to denounce the joy Juana took in learning. "Letras que engendran elación (soberbia) no las quiere Dios en la mujer. . . . Vuestra Merced cautiva el entendimiento que es el más arduo y agradable holocausto que puede ofrecerse en las de la religión . . . lástima es que un tan grande entendimiento de tal manera se abata a las rateras noticias de la tierra y no desee penetrar lo que pasa en el cielo, y ya que se humilla al suelo, que no baje más abajo, considerando lo que pasa en el infierno."[17] This vehement attack silenced Sor Juana for a number of months, but when she was heard again, it was via the brilliant "Respuesta a Sor Filotea," which made a formidable defense of women, of culture, of study, of scientific pursuits—of all that comprised the "rateras noticias de la tierra" ("vile earthly knowledge") which had suffered the archbishop's attack. She rebuked his condemnation of worldly sciences by asking how God's earthly wonders were to be understood if not with the aid of logic, physics, the natural sciences, and geometry. She asserted that all of these formed ascending rungs of a ladder that led to perfect knowledge, to knowledge of God.

Sor Juana's stubborn refusal to be deprived of the pursuit of knowledge and writing was further reinforced by examples she cited of female writers and thinkers in the church. She reasoned that if her own pursuits were prohibited, would they not also be prohibited for other women? The "Respuesta" marks the high point of Sor Juana's religious career and stands as a milestone in advancing the rights of women to educational and intellectual opportunities.

Heroinas in the War of Independence

The war of independence was instrumental in transforming traditionally feminine and maternal virtues like devotion, self-abnegation, and protectiveness into patriotic, national ideals. At this critical juncture in Mexican history when the first real efforts to overthrow an outdated, feudal system were made, women were praised publicly for exerting as much effort in the cause of independence as in their domestic endeavors. Tributes to their contributions abound and are typically rendered in superlatives. "Durante la guerra de insurrección, las mujeres mexicanas recorrieron nuestras ciudades y campos de batalla, como diosas protectoras, ya anunciando el génesis de nuestra independencia, ya avivando con su amor un amor más grande y santo; ora sorprendiendo con hazañas que rayaron en lo fabuloso, derramando su propia sangre, no contentas con haber ofrecido la de sus hijos."[18] The activities of women did in fact range from being "protective goddesses" to spilling their own blood. The Mexican penal code during this turbulent period did not exempt dissident women from prison or firing squads. *Insurgentes* and *realistas* alike are known to have imprisoned and killed women (G. García 1910, p. 99).

Perhaps the single most important woman to be recognized as a *heroina* in the fight for independence is Doña María Josefa Ortiz de Domínguez, also known as "La Corregidora." Doña Josefa and her husband Manuel were *criollos* who belonged to a literary and social group in Querétaro that recognized King Ferdinand but opposed being governed by *gachupines*, the Spanish power elite in Mexico. Their group included a military officer, Ignacio Allende, and a humanitarian priest, Miguel Hidalgo y Costilla. The group advocated the overthrow of the local viceroy, worked to gain the support of other *criollos* who shared their sentiments, and finally proposed to make a public declaration of independence at a local fair held in December 1810. Three months before the proposed announcement, their plans were found out, and thirteen of the conspirators were arrested. Doña Josefa's complicity was not discovered, however, and on the eve of September 16, 1810, she sent emissaries to alert Hidalgo about the arrests. Her warning compelled him to make a momentous decision—he made a famous call to arms from the town of his parish, "El grito de dolores," and chose to lead an armed rebellion against the Spanish.

La Corregidora's dedication to the idea of independence is said to have been embodied in another *heroina*, Leona Vicario, as early as 1808, when she was only nineteen years old. Leona was also a *criolla*, but unlike many women of her class, she was formally educated. She also possessed a highly spirited personality whose zealous devotion to independence won her historical recognition. Her efforts for the cause began immediately after "El grito," with her defiant attacks upon the church and the clergy who condemned insurrection and threatened participants with excommunication and damnation. They denounced the insurgents, "haciéndolos aparecer como bandidos de la peor especie, herejes sacrílegos, tigres anhelosos de beber la sangre humana, furias salidas del infierno . . . excomulgándolos para ponerlos fuera del seno de la iglesia y entregarlos á la condenación eterna."[19] Similarly, they set upon terrorizing relatives of insurgents as well as anyone who sympathized with or aided them in their efforts.

Censorship of thought and action, however, did not deter Leona in her unusual contributions. She began by making unsuccessful attempts to correspond with Hidalgo and Allende and then turned to developing a correspondence with the wives of insurgents and ultimately with a temporary junta in Zitácuaro. Her efforts were so notable that after a time she expanded the lines of communication and became known as "el conducto por donde se comunicaban los patriotas de México con los insurgentes" ("the channel through which Mexican patriots communicated with insurgents," Lizardi 1955, p. 9). Despite the informal nature of her "dispatch service," it appears to have been effective and highly sophisticated, with an elaborate code system built into it. Her success with the printed word found another outlet in a press which produced the work of the patriotic insurgents (González Obregón 1900, pp. 636–37).

Leona Vicario's unwavering dedication to liberation culminated in two remarkable feats of self-sacrifice. One of the couriers in her "postal service" was intercepted by the *realistas* and implicated her. She was forced to flee Mexico City in such haste that all her belongings were left behind. When she returned she was apprehended, tried, and sentenced to serve a jail sentence at the Colegio de Belén. However, the threat of prison or more severe measures never moved her to divulge the name of her cohorts.

Whatever belongings she may have salvaged in her flight from Mexico City went, along with all her jewels, into a personal fund she used to finance a remarkable undertaking—the building in 1813 of a cannon factory in Tlalpujahua. Leona not only financed this enterprise but also recruited expert armorers who served the viceroyalty to conduct the construction of cannon and firearms, paid for all the metal used in production, and even maintained the workers and their families from her own resources. The factory was so successful that the firearms it made were said to be "as perfect as those of the Tower of London" (G. García 1910, p. 106). In addition to quality firearms, as many as ten cannon were produced daily. Her generosity was so widely known that Morelos, an insurgent leader who succeeded Hidalgo, offered to subsidize her endeavor. She accepted the regular source of revenue he made available to her but only drew funds from it once.

Leona Vicario's dedication to independence, like that of countless other *heroinas*, is a milestone in the role women have played in Mexican history. For the first time the *patria* categorically acknowledged the unique contributions of women to the common good, far away from the bonds of domesticity.

Three

Cultural Heritage II The American Southwest

A basic thesis of this book is that a full understanding of the contemporary Chicana can only be gained through an examination of her colonial heritage in Mexico and the United States. This chapter examines the Chicana's heritage in the Southwest when the area was a Spanish-Mexican colony and after the American takeover. Our task in part is to demythicize the Chicana so as to depict her not as passive or ahistorical but as a moving force in the shaping of history and the development of the Southwest. We therefore focus on women who transcended conventional norms and refute stereotypical characterizations of Chicanas as either women of questionable virtue or as passive, dependent saintly figures.

Women in the Colonial Southwest: Precursors of the Chicana

Spanish colonization was not limited to the Aztec empire but extended to remote areas beyond its southern (Guatemala) and northern (Buachichiles or Zacatecas) borders. By 1543 Spanish explorations had reached from the western shores of South America to Oregon (Bolton 1908, p. 3). Not long after the conquest of New Spain the Spanish ventured into territory that was to become the American Southwest. In 1528 Cabeza de Vaca, part of the ill-fated Narváez expedition, was shipwrecked on an island near Galveston. He and the other survivors, naked and in tears, were fed and cared for by friendly Indians. De Vaca records, "They sat down beside us and cried, too. I cried all the harder, to think people so miserable had pity for us. . . . These simple Indians were the first relenting of nature to us in months and months. That evening, for fear we might die on the way, the Indians made fires at intervals along the path to their village. . . . That night and many nights after we slept beside them on the oyster shells which floor their huts, wrapt in hides against the cold winds from the sea" (Long 1936, pp. 13–14). De Vaca lived among the Indians for six years, learning their language and customs and gaining fame as a medicine man. He and his shipmates Dorantes, Castillo and Estevan, a black Moor, traveled westward until they came upon a Spanish slave-hunting expedition on the Gulf of California. De Vaca finally reached Mexico City in July of 1536.

Other expeditions followed. Fray Marcos de Niza's account in 1539 of Zuñi pueblos, believed to be the fabled cities of Cibola, led to the authorization the following year of Francisco Vásquez's famous search for the seven cities of gold (Swadesh 1974, pp. 10–11; and Villagrá 1933, pp. 53–54). On June 27, 1542 Juan Rodríguez Cabrillo sailed from the port of Navidad (near Manzanillo) on an incredible voyage along the coast of California (Bolton 1908, p. 13). Although the voyage was to cost him his life, the expedition returned to Navidad on April 14, 1543, after having discovered the bays of San Diego and Santa Monica and describing in detail the ports, bays, and islands they encountered. California was especially alluring to Cabrillo not only for its promise of unfound riches or of a strait that would link the Pacific and Atlantic but also because of the widely held belief that it was a mythical island populated by Amazon women who were capable of reproducing themselves. Cortés himself encouraged the exploration of California "because I am informed that down the coast . . . there are many provinces thickly inhabited by people and containing, it is believed, great riches, and that in these parts of it there is one which is inhabited by women, with no men, who procreate in the way which the ancient histories ascribe to the Amazons" (ibid., p. 3).

Despite the number of early expeditions, the first permanent settlements in the Southwest did not come until 1598, when Don Juan de Oñate founded two Spanish colonies near Santa Fe. Earlier expeditions by Rodríguez and Espejo had stimulated great interest in conquering and settling New Mexico, so that near the end of the sixteenth century there was considerable competition for the position of adelantado of New Mexico (ibid., p. 201). A contract making Oñate governor, adelantado, and captain-general of New Mexico was finally secured in 1595.

Oñate, husband of the granddaughter of Cortés and great-granddaugh-
ter of Motecuhzoma, was a member of one of the most prominent and
wealthy families of New Spain. With an expedition consisting of eighty-
three wagons and carts, more than 7,000 head of cattle, and 400 men, he
moved directly northward toward what is today El Paso and up the Rio
Grande. On April 30, 1598 Oñate formally took possession "of all the
kingdoms and provinces of New Mexico, on the Rio del Norte, in the
name of our Lord King Philip. There was a sermon, a great religious
and secular celebration, a great salute, and much rejoicing. In the afternoon a comedy was presented and the royal standard was blessed"
(ibid., pp. 202–3). Similar ceremonies were enacted at each pueblo,
pledging loyalty to the king of Spain (Swadesh 1974, p. 12). Oñate
continued to "pacify the land" in the name of the king. When the
pueblo of Okeh was renamed San Juan de los Caballeros (in honor of
his men) and Yuquequnque was renamed San Gabriel, the first permanent European settlements in the Southwest were established.

However, the Spanish colonization of the Southwest met with considerable resistance. Oñate dealt severely with Pueblos who resisted the
missionary program. When encountering resistance at Acoma, "Oñate
retaliated by burning the pueblo and killing a large number of the Indians. For those who survived, he ordered one foot amputated from
each man over twenty-five years of age and imposed a fine of twenty
years of personal service. The men between twelve and twenty-five
years escaped with twenty years of service. All the women over twelve
years of age were likewise doomed to twenty years of servitude"
(Dozier 1970, p. 47). This was to serve as a warning to others who
would not submit to Spanish rule. Countless other atrocities and abuses
were also committed against the Pueblos.

Since conversion of the Indian was critical to pacification, missions
were erected within or near Pueblo settlements. The early New Mexican
colonists were able to establish a number of settlements, and by 1769
they had founded forty-eight missions (Forrest 1929, p. 17). The missions were imposing walled structures built with Indian labor under the
supervision of the friars. The missionaries sought not only to exploit
Indian labor but to destroy indigenous beliefs and values and to supplant them with their Catholic counterparts (Dozier 1970, p. 50).

Though the Pueblos assumed the outward trappings of Christianity,
they privately bore much resentment and hostility about the suppression of their beliefs. The organization of Pueblos into relatively au-
tonomous and independent political units almost precluded an organized rebellion, but such a collective effort was finally realized in the

Pueblo revolt of 1680. Many colonists and friars were killed and missions destroyed as the Spaniards were driven from New Mexico (Bancroft 1886, p. 18). It is interesting to note that some Mexican Indians and *mestizos* were sympathetic to the revolt and not only joined it but in some cases were actually leaders in it (Dozier 1970, p. 60). The area was subsequently reconquered by Don Diego de Vargas in 1693–94.

Settlements in Arizona, Texas, and California did not come until much later. California remained unsettled from 1542 until 1769, when Fray Junípero Serra reached San Diego. Perhaps the most notable and arduous of the Spanish expeditions took place in 1774, when Juan Bautista de Anza marched across the desert from Tubac, Arizona, to San Gabriel. In a subsequent expedition the following year from Culiacán in Sinaloa, de Anza accomplished an even more incredible feat, reaching the bay of San Francisco.

It was in California that Spanish colonization was most extensive—twenty-one missions across the state, four presidial towns (military forts: San Diego, Santa Barbara, Monterey, and San Francisco), and the two pueblos of San Jose and Los Angeles were founded. In Texas, primary settlements were limited largely to San Antonio, Goliad, and Nacogdoches, although twenty-five missions were also established throughout the state (McWilliams 1968, p. 26). Thus Spanish explorations covered a vast area, although, with the exception of the mission system along the coast of California and a few settlements in New Mexico, stable population centers were few and far between.

Colonization was impeded not only by a shortage of manpower and a hostile environment but by Indian resistance. The pacification of borderland Indians proved to be especially difficult and was never fully achieved. Spanish colonization, based as it was on the *presidio*, mission, and *hacienda* system of enforced peonage, was virtually impossible to implement, except among the more sedentary Pueblo Indians of New Mexico. Even the sedentary coastal tribes of California had to be brought to the missions, because they did not live in villages (ibid., p. 30). This system, which called for the Indians to be subjugated by the military, converted by the clergy, and exploited by the *encomendero*, had been effective in central Mexico but was actively resisted by nomadic and propertyless borderland tribes such as the Apache and Comanche (Webb 1931, pp. 88–89).

The pattern of Spanish settlement of the Southwest was to have a profound impact not only on their relations with the conquered Indians but on the status of pioneer women and on relations between the sexes.

Unlike the *conquistadores* of central Mexico, many of the Southwest colonists were accompanied by their wives and families. Of the 400 men in the Oñate expedition, some 130 made the journey with their families (Bolton 1908, p. 202). Women were also encouraged to join their husbands on the famous second de Anza expedition. It is a tribute to de Anza and members of the expedition that on this long journey from the interior of Mexico to the bay of San Francisco the only death was that of a woman in childbirth; as many as eight children were born during the journey (Bancroft 1886, pp. 259–60).

Though the Spanish officially discouraged fraternizing with Indian women, the rule was frequently violated, resulting in numerous unions between Spaniards and Indians. Much of the hybrid population, however, was the result not of voluntary unions but of the traffic in Indian slaves (McWilliams 1968, p. 67). It was not uncommon for Indian women to be forced into household service and for illicit relations to emerge between them and their masters. The official Spanish attitude toward fraternization is intriguing because, although the colonists were defined as Spanish or white, many were mixed descendants of Cortés's soldiers and Indian women (Dozier 1970, p. 52). A large number of Tlaxcalan Indians accompanied the Oñate expedition, and significantly, with the founding of Santa Fe in 1610, a separate barrio was set off for these Indian colonists. As a reward for their alliance with Cortés in the subjugation of the Aztecs, the Tlaxcalans had been promised a share of territories in the colonization of Mexico's northern territories (Swadesh 1974, p. 12). With the passage of time, the proportion of the population with pure Spanish blood declined accordingly. The settlers who reconquered New Mexico under Diego de Vargas in 1693–94 were called *españoles mexicanos*, indicating that they were born in Mexico and were at least partly descendant from Mexican Indians (ibid., p. 21). The Pueblo Indian population remained stable, but the *mestizo* component increased rapidly (McWilliams 1968, p. 68). The roots of the Chicano in New Mexico and other Southwestern states are thus mixed.

The fact that many of the early settlers were of Indian or mixed blood meant that they occupied the lowest position in the caste structure. Frequently they were lured to the expeditions by the promise of a better life on the frontier. De Anza's followers, known as "los pobres," were bold and courageous, and their tenacity, as they marched across the desert with children in arms, was undoubtedly motivated by their quest for a better life. Captain de Anza selected recruits from poor areas in Sinaloa and Sonora, reasoning with Viceroy Bucareli that most were "submerged in the direst poverty and misery, and so . . . would

most willingly and gladly embrace the advantages which your Excel-
lency may deign to afford them" (Bolton 1930*a*, p. 206). The new
recruits were dazzled with new outfits. The women were issued two
new linen jackets, three chemises, three petticoats, two skirts, two pairs
of Brussels stockings, high-heeled shoes from Spain, and six yards of
bright ribbon to adorn their hair; the men received three good linen
shirts, three pairs of cotton underwear, a new sombrero, two cloth
jackets, two pairs of boots, and a fine leather jacket, making them
"soldados de cuero" (ibid., p. 221). Each family was also provided with
eight blankets and four mounts well equipped with fine bridles and
saddle bags. Finally, to avert the squandering of cash on gambling,
arrangements were made for payment to be made in clothing and
necessities.

From the onset, then, the population of the Southwest settlements
was divided into two groups, *los pobres* and *los ricos*. The division was
part of a caste system which placed lighter complexioned and more
European-looking persons in privileged positions. In New Mexico *los
ricos* obtained massive land grants and established great estates in the
Rio Abajo section, while *los pobres* either worked as *peones* on these
large estates or attempted to eke out a living on small grants (Twitchell
1925, pp. 162–63). The rich lived isolated within their *haciendas*, while
the existence of the far more numerous poor was precarious. Theirs
was a subsistence pastoral life which depended on hard work, perse-
verance, and the establishment of bartering relations with friendly
Indians for survival.

Life on the frontier was not only difficult and austere, but settlements
were isolated from the mainstream of Spanish-Mexican society. The
isolation was both geographical and cultural. There was little time or
concern, even among *los ricos*, for the development of "cultural" or
aesthetic tastes. The social life of most communities revolved around
family and church activities. According to one observer,

> Each community held a great fiesta on its patron saint's day. On
> that day, church services and processions were carried out in all the
> humble splendor that was within the means of the community.
> Public markets offered delicacies and other goods for sale or barter.
> Horse races, *corridas de gallo* and other games, dances, serenades,
> and banquets were the order of the day. . . . Musicians and poets vied
> with each other in regaling the populace with their offerings. Im-
> promptu songs and poems, about important events and persons,
> were recited and dedicated to visitors. . . . These *fiestas* constituted
> the most important social events of the year [G. J. Sanchez 1967,
> pp. 7–8].

Education typically took place in the home or at a local parish as children were instructed in church doctrine. The need for literacy was not great, since the culture was transmitted orally, and it was especially rare among women, who had little use for reading and writing in their daily lives. Gregg (1954, p. 141) comments on this: "Female education has, if possible been more universally neglected than that of the other sex; while those who have received any instruction at all, have generally been taught in private families. Indeed, until very lately, to be able to read and write on the part of a woman, was considered an indication of very extraordinary talent."

The frontier conditions in the border lands made the maintenance of traditional Spanish institutions and customs difficult. Especially difficult to enforce was the concept that the woman should occupy a subordinate and protected status. Adherence to a rigid sexual division of labor, in which the man was responsible for economic production and the woman for bearing and rearing children, was a luxury that could not be maintained in a subsistence economy. Women were actively involved in activities outside the home such as tending grazing herds and butchering and skinning animals, as well as planting, irrigation, and harvesting crops (Swadesh 1974, pp. 178–79).

Pioneer women performed multiple functions and were frequently knowledgeable about midwifery and plant medicine. "They were their own doctors, dressmakers, tailors and advisers" (Cabeza de Baca 1954, p. 60). While wealthier or older women were exempted from the more rigorous physical tasks, they would specialize in "handiwork, herbal medicine and midwifery, or reading for purposes of religious observance" (Swadesh 1974, p. 179). The wife of the *patrón* occupied an especially important place in the social structure of the Llano in New Mexico. "The *patrón* ruled the *rancho*, but his wife looked after the spiritual and physical welfare of the *empleados* and their families. She was the first one called when there was death, illness, misfortune or good tidings in a family. She was a great social force in the community— more so than her husband. She held the purse strings, and thus she was able to do as she pleased in her charitable enterprises and to help those who might seek her assistance" (Cabeza de Baca 1954, p. 60).

There can be little doubt that the pioneer women of *la raza* made invaluable contributions to the development of early Spanish settlements. They provided comfort and emotional support and performed tasks that were necessary to survival in an otherwise hostile environment. Yet the deeds of these women are seldom documented by historical accounts. The achievements that are recorded are mostly those of members of the rich social class and little information is available on the contributions of those common, ordinary women who served as the backbone of the colonization and provided Chicanas with a rich cultral heritage. The pioneer women of Aztlán remain an enigma, mythicized as either beautiful and romantic Spanish señoritas or women of questionable virtue. According to Dakin (1963, pp. 2–3),

> Women in the Spain-oriented parts of the world were seldom enlightened by education, endlessly child-bearing because of religion, not protected by law—having no rights, only "privileges." They suffered unacknowledged hardships and indignities. The memory lingers, from random reading, of Indian girls roped by Spanish soldiers and dragged into housewifery in a mud hut (a California *adobe*).
>
> They remained embryonic, spiritually and mentally—the poor Indians used for pleasure and infected with disease by soldiers and sailors exploring, conquering, colonizing along the Pacific Coast; the Spanish and Mexican women who followed their men over the trails blazed by missionaries, trappers and other inland explorers. Such as these, known in Mexico City as *las pobres* ("the poor ones"), formed the mission communities and populated the *presidios* of Alta California. Custom sheathed them. Few protested, and fewer are remembered.

It seems fitting, then that "the first woman to emerge as an individual in the Far West," (ibid., p. 3), María Feliciana Arballo y Gutiérrez, was an aristocrat but the widow of a common soldier in Captain de Anza's second expedition. Doña Feliciana, known as the "merry widow" of the expedition, was recognized by de Anza himself as an important morale booster (for a discussion of her, see ibid., pp. 1–11; and Bolton 1930a, pp. 312–13). Young Feliciana had married a soldier named Arballo at the age of thirteen and given birth to a daughter, Tomasa, at fourteen and another daughter, Eustaquia, two years later. Her husband died as preparations were being made for the expedition, but she was determined to make the trip without him. The captain agreed to her request: "Undaunted, the young widow placed Eustaquia on the saddle in front of her, Tomasa behind; and answered roll call. . . . She astonished the crowd of colonists and onlookers, including her own close relatives, by announcing that she would take her husband's place—play father and mother to their little girls—carry out the orders of their King, where it lay within her power, on the 1,600-mile ride to Spain's northernmost frontier; and afterwards in the colony to be founded on the shore of San Francisco Bay" (Dakin 1963, p. 7). Though the pretty and vivacious widow charmed and encouraged her fellow travelers, she apparently proved to be a thorn in the side of de Anza's chaplain, Father Font, who was very concerned about her effect on the men. His attitude is revealed in a diary entry of December 17, 1775, after a fandango with much singing, dancing, and drinking to celebrate the Christmas season and the return of men feared dead: "At night, with the joy at the arrival of all the people, they held a fandango here. It was somewhat discordant, and a very bold widow who came with the expedition sang some verses which were not at all nice, applauded and cheered by all the crowd" (Bolton 1930b, p. 138). Father Font continued to be distressed by the drinking and celebration of the colonists, but it is to de Anza's credit that he recognized the importance of these emotional outlets and came to the defense of the "merry widow" when her escort at the fandango attempted to chastise her. As the disgruntled Franciscan records, "The commander, hearing of this, sallied forth from his tent and reprimanded the man because he was chastizing her. I said to him, 'Leave him alone, Sir, he is doing just right,' but he replied, 'No, Father, I can not permit such excesses when I am present.' He guarded against this excess, indeed, but not against the scandal of the fandango, which lasted until very late" (ibid.).

Doña Feliciana did not reach her final destination. When the colonists stopped to rest and get supplies in San Gabriel, she fell in love with a young soldier, Juan Francisco López, who had come to California with Father Serra in 1769. He courted the widow and persuaded her to marry him and give up her journey north. Doña Feliciana lived a full and happy life, devoting herself to domestic duties and the housemothering of young Indian girls in the mission dormitory. Her descendants were to become prominent and distinguished citizens of Alta California. Her daughter Eustaquia married a young soldier, Jose Maria Pico, and gave birth to seven daughters and three sons. Two of these sons, Don Pio and Don Andrés, became governors of the state.

In comparison to the lot of *las pobres*, life for women of the *ricos* was relatively comfortable and secure, but they too faced problems of adjustment on the frontier. Even *los ricos* lived under constant fear of Indian attack, and while attempting to emulate the genteel life of the leisure class in Spain and Mexico City, they were forced to sacrifice and make do without many customary luxuries. Two upper-class contemporaries of Feliciana Arballo, Doña Eulalia Fages and Doña Concepción Argüello, provide an interesting contrast in the life-styles of the two social classes.

Doña Eulalia, wife of Don Pedro Fages, governor of California, came from a well-to-do aristocratic family which was heavily influenced in its values and life-style by the French refinements introduced into New Spain society by Viceroy Le Croix. The fact that her family was well bred and influential may have contributed to the rapid rise of Don Pedro (Bancroft 1886, p. 390). Her educated upbringing and training were consistent with her breeding, and she had perfected the many graces of drawing room society.

Don Pedro, on the other hand, was a seasoned veteran of the Sonora Indian wars, an explorer, and a bear hunter. Whether it was his experience as a hunter or his gruff manner that earned him the title of "El Oso" (The Bear) is not clear, but there is no doubt that his values and life-style were very different from those of his aristocratic young bride. He had courted the beautiful and much younger Eulalia during one of his many visits to Mexico City. By marrying Don Pedro, Eulalia was unwittingly exchanging a palace in Mexico City for an adobe governor's mansion in Monterey.

Shortly after being appointed governor in 1782, Don Pedro asked his wife to join him in the *provincia*. Eulalia agreed to make the journey at the urging of her family and some of their influential friends, but only after being assured that California was not totally barbaric (ibid., p. 389). The governor, seeking to provide a fitting home, set about designing and constructing a "mansion" of adobe mud bricks, a clay tile roof, and pine. He also planted an orchard and vineyards.

When Doña Eulalia entered San Gabriel in 1782, only six years had elapsed since the small community had been dazzled by the "merry widow" of the de Anza expedition. San Gabriel was also dazzled by the beauty of Eulalia, but unlike Feliciana, who charmed the community with her warmth and friendly spirit, *la gobernadora* appeared to be a shrew. "Entering San Gabriel, she perched precariously on a side-saddle. She wore a flowing habit of green velvet, a matching hat with plumes, and a sour expression on her face. . . . She disturbed the *padres* all along el *Camino Real* from Loreto . . . to Monterey" (Dakin 1963, p. 13). The lady's disposition had apparently not changed throughout the trip, as she complained incessantly about the ruggedness of the terrain and trails and the poor accommodations at local missions. Upon her arrival at Monterey, her reaction to the governor's mansion was equally severe. The adobe house might have been appropriate for servants, but it was found to be totally inadequate by the first lady. The nakedness of the Indians also upset her, and she proceeded to clothe them with her own and her husband's clothing (Bancroft 1886, p. 390). The first lady's dislike for these primitive conditions and her quick temper did not abate with the passage of time or the birth of her second child, and when the governor refused to let her and the children return to Mexico City to visit her mother, she promptly went on strike, locking him out of the bedroom and refusing to speak to him for three months. When this tactic failed to move the governor, she shocked the populace and mission priests by claiming that her husband was infatuated with a beautiful Indian servant named Indizuela and demanded a divorce—a practice almost unheard of. Though the mission priests determined that her charges were unfounded and there were no grounds for divorce, she continued to press for a return to Mexico City. Unable to control his headstrong wife and embarrassed by her public outbursts, Don Pedro turned her over to the local mission priests. The priests were also unable to placate Doña Eulalia, and during her stay at Mission San Carlos "the records relate that her outbursts of fury, some of which evidently took place in the sacred precincts of the church itself, finally brought threats of flogging and irons" (N. van de G. Sánchez 1929, p. 15). But these threats and charges that she was "possessed" did not daunt Eulalia, and she resorted to other tactics. Shortly after inviting her husband back into the bedroom in September 1785, she sent a request to the judicial court at Guadalajara that her husband be replaced as governor because of poor health; Don Pedro had the communique intercepted before it reached its destination (Dakin 1963, p. 19). Her various other schemes foiled, Doña Eulalia tried a bizarre plan. She intended to escape on a French ship with a young officer who had been overwhelmed by her beauty, but El Oso got wind of the plan and interceded before it could be carried out. In the end Doña Eulalia had her way; Don Pedro resigned the governorship in 1790 and returned to Mexico City shortly thereafter.

Lest our judgment of Doña Eulalia be too harsh, a number of factors should be taken into account in evaluating the actions of the infamous first lady of California. First, we should keep in mind that her journey to California was not totally voluntary and that the frontier conditions encountered would be difficult for anyone to endure, but especially a person of her breeding. Second, since Don Pedro was governor, the mission priests and historians have tended to be sympathetic to his view of their marital discord. Third, Don Pedro has been lionized as an affectionate, henpecked husband, but there is reason to believe that he was not without fault. Who is to say that her charges of infidelity with the beautiful Indian girl, whom he had brought from Colorado, were unfounded? Why did he steadfastly refuse to let his wife visit Mexico City?

A more sympathetic view would suggest that Doña Eulalia was not a shrew but a highly spirited and independent female who resisted enforced bondage and used every means at her disposal to effect her freedom. The testimony of Captain Nicolás Soler, an old family friend who was asked to attempt to arbitrate the dispute, supports the view that Doña Eulalia's treatment was not appropriate for a person of her station. While admonishing her for immoderate actions and not restraining her wrath, Soler was also quick to point out that "the lady whether guilty or not should not, in consideration of her position and breeding, be subjected to such indignities" (Bancroft 1886, p. 392). In short, it appears that Doña Eulalia was adamant in the defense of her wifely rights and persistent in her desire to return to Mexico City. It seems ironic that a man who could tame the frontier and subdue bears was not up to the challenge of a spirited female.

At about the same time that Doña Eulalia was returning to Mexico City to live out her life in relative obscurity, Doña Ignacia Argüello gave birth to a daughter, Concepción, who was to become a symbol of feminine virtue in Alta California. Her benevolent nature brought her the title of "La Beata"—The Blessed One. Doña Concepción was born into a prominent family; her father, Don Jose Dario Argüello, served as comandante of the port of San Francisco and was acting governor of the province.

During this period visits from foreign powers were officially discouraged by the Spanish government but were welcomed informally, and the ports of Alta California were popular stop-off points and sources of badly needed supplies for foreign vessels (Dakin 1963, p. 26). The Argüello household entertained visiting dignitaries, and Doña Ignacia was renowned as a warm and gracious hostess. So it was that on April 8, 1806, a Russian ship from Sitka, Alaska, commanded by Count Nikolai Petrovitch Rezánov, sailed into the port of San Francisco seeking badly needed supplies and food for her starving and scurvy-ridden crew. The Russians, who had taken a calculated risk by entering a foreign port unannounced, were overwhelmed by the reception of their Spanish hosts. The ship's doctor, Georg von Langsdorff, was impressed not only by their hospitality but by the warmth shown among members of the Argüello family, noting in his journal that "mutual esteem and harmony glowed without diminution in the conduct of this kindly family, who knew scarcely any other diversions or pleasures than those resulting from family joys and domestic happiness" (ibid., p. 36). The Russians were impressed with the entire family but were especially enchanted by the most beautiful and intelligent of the daughters, Concepción. Though only fifteen, Concha dazzled the visitors with her youthful beauty. According to Langsdorff, "she was lively and animated, had sparkling, love-inspiring eyes, beautiful teeth, pleasing and expressive features, a fine form, and a thousand other charms, yet her manners were perfectly simple and artless" (N. van de G. Sánchez 1929, p. 24).

Even the dashing forty-two-year-old count could not resist her youthful charm. In the next few weeks the recently widowed Rezánov courted Concha daily. One must wonder, however, if he was inspired in his courtship of the young California maiden only by romantic ideals. Again according to Langsdorff, "He conceived the idea that through a marriage with the daughter of the comandante of the Presidio de San Francisco a close bond would be formed for future business intercourse between the Russian American Company and the provincia of Nueva California. He therefore decided to sacrifice himself by wedding Doña Concepción, to the welfare of his country, and to bind in friendly alliance both Spain and Russia" (Dakin 1963, pp. 37–38).

Concepción fell in love with the count and quickly acceded to his proposal of marriage, though her father was less easily persuaded. In fact, had it not been that Concha was her father's favorite and persisted in the match, Don Jose might never have agreed. Differences in religion precluded an immediate marriage, but the count managed to get betrothal papers signed before departing for Russia. The marriage would take place if papal permission could be obtained. Concha gave Rezánov a locket with a strand of her hair to wear around his neck as the two lovers bid farewell and vowed eternal fidelity.

This romantic tale was to have a tragic ending. The count never reached his destination, meeting his death in Siberia as a result of a fall from a horse. The weeks, months, and years passed with Concha waiting faithfully for his safe return. Not until thirty-six years after the count's departure did Concha receive word of his untimely death, but she could be consoled by the fact that he had kept his vow and was said to have spoken her name in his last breath (ibid., p. 41). Though constantly pursued by suitors, she was to remain true to her lover throughout her life, leading an exemplary life of devoutness and charity, always helping the poor and the sick, those less fortunate than herself.

The second climactic moment in Concha's life came on April 11, 1851, when at the age of sixty she was admitted into the Dominican order as a novitiate, assuming a new name, María Dominica, and a new life (ibid., p. 55). Perhaps it was fitting that when La Beata took her final vows on April 13, 1852, she became California's first nun. Doña Concepción died five years later (December 1857) and was buried within the walls of the peaceful, tree-shaded convent cemetery. A simple inscription adorned the brown stone cross on her tomb (N. van de G. Sánchez 1929, p. 29): "Sister María Dominica, O.S.D."

From the preceding it is clear that each of the three women highlighted here, though very different from the others, was outstanding in her own right. While these women caught the fancy of contemporary chroniclers and of historians (two because they were *ricas* and the other because she was the only widow on the de Anza expedition), the contributions of many other notable women have not been recorded. There is reason to believe that life for most women in urban *presidios* was fairly routine, but what of women on the ranches and in the plains? According to Walter Prescott Webb (1931, p. 505), a prominent Texas historian, "The Great Plains in the early period was strictly a man's country.... Men loved the Plains ... men developed a hardihood which made them insensible to the hardships and lack of refinements. But what of the women? Most of the evidence, such as it is, reveals that the Plains repelled the women as they attracted the men. There was too much of the unknown, too few of the things they loved. If we could get at the truth we should doubtless find that many a family was stopped on the edge of the timber by women who refused to go farther." Webb's statement is more significant as a revelation of his own biases than as a statement about the contributions of pioneer women, but it illustrates the persistence of the myth of the frontier as an exclusively male domain. This myth is perpetuated by the public and historians alike.

An article on "Great Women of California" appearing in the September 1949 issue of the *Historical Society of Southern California Quarterly* listed twenty-eight outstanding women, but only two, Doña Eulalia and Doña Concepción, were from the period of Spanish-Mexican provincial rule (Hunt 1949). The biases of research of this sort are inherent in the norms of selection. Hunt used newspaper accounts and "tradition" as the basic criterion for inclusion. Not only was literacy low and there were few newspapers in the colonial period, but after the conquest, Anglo-American society was insensitive to the perpetuation of Spanish-Mexican traditions. "Traditions and popular reports grew up as verbal recognition of the activities of the women of those days but there were no newspapers or books to record their deeds, and the traditions are now lost or perhaps have descended in some manner to the present third and fourth generations" (Bowman 1957, p. 150). Fields of activity for women were extremely limited; literary works were the domain of the padres, the theater was not well developed, and education was mostly open to men. By and large, then, "only the field of philanthropy was open to the women—serving their neighbors in time of childbirth, sickness, or catastrophe" (ibid.).

Another index of prominence which can be employed is land-grant activity. Those who believe that the frontier was exclusively a man's world would be surprised to find that women did participate extensively in the acquisition and maintenance of land grants. In order to obtain a grant, it was necessary to submit a petition with a *diseño* of its location; provide information about the need of the petitioner, his stock, and his capacity to occupy the land; and then actually occupy the land with stock and a house (ibid., p. 152).

Bowman (p. 165), using norms of size, occupation, claim before the American tribunals, and the granting of a United States patent, has discovered that a number of Spanish-Mexican women in provincial California played an important part in the acquisition of land grants. Using these criteria, he isolates twenty-six outstanding women of this period. Of the sixty-six women associated in one way or another with provincial land grants, twenty-two were successful in eventually obtaining a United States patent after the American conquest. These women acquired 355,000 acres of land, or more than 41 percent of all the patented lands granted to women. This constitutes more than 3 percent of the acres granted and more than 4 percent of the patented lands.

Perhaps it is worth isolating one of the most prominent of these women. Juana Briones de Miranda was born on January 9, 1796 at Monterey or Carmel. Dissatisfied with her domestic life, she petitioned the bishop for permission to live apart from her estranged husband, a soldier in the San Francisco *presidio*. She successfully acquired a grant at Rancho Purisima Concepción in Yerba Buena (San Francisco), built an adobe house on the property (still in use), cultivated the fields, and oversaw her stock. "Her social services included assistance to deserting seamen, providing milk, vegetables, and Yerba Buena tea to callers, serving her neighbors in sickness and childbirth" (ibid., p. 163). Widely known as Juana Briones or the Widow Briones, she gained prominence for her philanthropic activity and for being the only female householder in Yerba Buena. She lived at Rancho Purisima Concepción until she moved to Mayfield in advanced years. She died on December 3, 1889 and was interred in an unmarked grave in Menlo Park Cemetery.

These women are without doubt prominent representatives of their sex. What is most noteworthy about them, perhaps, is that they succeeded—sufficiently to be included in Bowman's list, despite the stringent and limiting norms he employs. To be included, a grantee had to obtain legitimacy for the grant from the American tribunals, and the grant had to be patented. Significantly, though all of the women included initiated their land-grant petition during the provincial period, the patents were not obtained until well after the American occupation of the Southwest. Since numerous legal and extralegal mechanisms were employed to defraud Chicanos of their land after the American takeover (Acuña 1972), only women who successfully resisted the land grab are included. These women are thus truly exceptional.

Women after the American Takeover of the Southwest: Birth of the Chicana

If the achievements of Hispanic women are difficult to document during the colonial period, they prove to be even more elusive after the American takeover of the Southwest. The Anglo conquest transformed Mexicans from a colonizing to a colonized people and brought about the almost total disruption of a way of life. Power and control of major social institutions shifted from the Mexican to the Anglo-American. Treaty provisions guaranteeing the protection of land titles, water rights, and the cultural and religious autonomy of displaced Mexican citizens were either ignored or wantonly violated. Life that had once centered on the *presidio, rancho,* rural village, or collective now revolved around towns and cities and was motivated by a capitalistic ethic which stressed individualism and competition rather than collectivism and cooperation. In New Mexico, life centered on the rural village and required cooperation among settlers; water rights and pasture lands were communal. "An interdependency existed among the villagers, with the settlers relying on each other for entertainment and assistance in building their homes, tending crops and animals, maintaining the village, and caring for the sick and the aged, as well as in burying the dead" (Acuña 1972, p. 60). This pastoral, communal life was supplanted by one that measured individual worth by the accumulation of land and capital. The net result was that a few unscrupulous capitalists gained control of the economy, territorial government, and the legal and judicial system. The ensuing land grab is well documented and needs only to be mentioned here (see ibid.; McWilliams 1968; and Rendon 1972). Legal and extralegal means were used to establish powerful large-scale land, cattle, and mining rings which controlled the wealth of the Southwest territories.

With the exception of a few *ricos* who entered into collusion with Anglo capitalists, Chicanos found themselves a landless and impoverished people exploited economically and politically. They provided much of the cheap labor in the construction of railroads, mining, and the development of agriculture. This exploitation was not simply political and economic but physical as well; beatings and lynchings of Chicanos were common occurrences in the fields and mines.

Chicanas were not exempted from abuse. "Juanita" of Downieville, California has the questionable distinction of being the only woman lynched during the gold rush. The lynching of a woman appears to have been a bizarre event indeed, for women were a scarce and coveted commodity in the mines:

> Miners hacking out the wealth of the California Mother Lode treasured a scratched and bent tintype portrait of a woman as they would a solid gold nugget. When a white woman came to the mines, anything could happen as the miners came from miles around just to get a glimpse of her and follow her around. . . . In the gold rush camp of Downieville, it is said that as the first woman to enter the area was seen ascending the trail, the miners streamed up the hill to meet her and picked up the mule, rider and all, carrying them both triumphantly into town. [Secrest 1967a, p. 5]

Why, then, was Juanita hanged? The answer undoubtedly lies in the fact that she was not a white woman but a Mexican, an inferior and subhuman species.

Before the influx of Americans, Mexican miners from the state of Sonora had staked out important claims in the southern region of the California mines. Conflict between Mexicans and Anglos had culminated in war, but with the cessation of formal hostilities, the conflict, rather than subsiding, appears to have intensified. "The ease and swiftness of the victory over Mexico and the conquest of California had bred in the Americans a measureless contempt for all things Mexican" (McWilliams 1968, p. 129). With the admission of California to the Union in 1850, the legislature promptly passed the Foreign Miner's Tax. The bill levied a tax on all foreign miners but in reality was aimed at eliminating the competition of Mexican miners. The act formally legitimated hostility toward Mexicans, and shortly after its passage thousands of Anglo miners stormed into Sonora, California, "firing at every Mexican in sight" (ibid., pp. 127–28). The camp was burned, dozens of Mexicans were lynched during a week of rioting, and most of the miners abandoned their claims. It was an ambience such as this which prevailed during the lynching of Juanita on July 5 of the following year.

While a number of questions concerning the lynching remain unanswered, enough information is available to reconstruct the events preceding her death (see Secrest, 1967a). First, it appears from contemporary accounts that the woman's name was actually Josefa, although she has come to be referred to popularly as Juanita. Josefa lived in a small cabin with a slightly built man named José. It is not clear whether he was her husband or lover, but their relationship was certainly monogamous, and there is no reason to impugn Josefa's character or to suggest that she was sexually permissive. George Barton, a witness to the trial and lynching claiming to know her well, remarked that "the Mexican woman was a plain person, about 23 or 25 years of age, neat and tidy in dress and person, quiet in demeanor, and like all her race had raven-black hair and a dark complexion, and lived with her husband, or protector, on Main Street" (ibid., p. 29). Another resident of Downievile, J. J. McClosky, claimed that she "was about 26 years old, slight in form, with a large, dark, lustrous eye, that flashed at times . . . like a devils [sic] . . . all agreed that her character was good" (ibid.). Another contemporary described her as "rather low of stature, stout built, with raven tresses that flowed freely over her neck and shoulders—black eyes, teeth regular and of pearly whiteness. She might be called pretty, so far as the style of swarthy Mexican beauty is so considered" (ibid., p. 8). These eyewitness accounts are important in that they reflect Anglo prejudices and stereotypes. Dual standards of beauty were employed, and Josefa was considered attractive, for a Mex.

Whether attractive and of good character of not, Josefa seems to have drawn the attention of a number of miners who were envious of her paramour. One man who was said to have been particularly interested and to have pursued her for some time was a popular miner named Fred Cannon. On July 4, 1851 a glorious celebration was held commemorating the first Independence Day since California had become a state. Partying, drinking, and riotous behavior continued into the night. What happened next is disputed, but Cannon and two of his drunken cronies, Lawson and Getzler, found themselves in front of Josefa's cabin. Cannon's account was that he leaned against the door and accidentally fell into the room; Josefa's was that he broke the door down and tried to make advances toward her. Whatever the truth, Cannon put a scarf around his neck, and the drunken miners left the cabin laughing.

The next morning Cannon went with Lawson to obtain some medicine from Dr. Hunter, who happened to live next door to Josefa, and was confronted by the small Mexican who demanded payment for his door. In the ensuing argument, José is said to have refused to fight the larger, athletic Cannon. At this point Josefa, speaking in rapid Spanish, pushed between the two men and asked Cannon to hit her instead. Cannon reputedly called her a whore and other bad names. José managed to lead her into the house as she yelled at Cannon, daring him to come into the house and call her those names. As Cannon rushed the door, the enraged Josefa grabbed a knife from a table and stabbed him in the chest.

Many in the angry, drunken mob wanted to hang them immediately, but it was decided instead, in the words of a crowd leader, to "give 'em a fair trial first—and then hang 'em." Despite the protestations of a lawyer named Thayer, who was beaten and pummeled by the mob, and Dr. Cyrus D. Aiken, who claimed that Josefa was pregnant and should be spared, she was found guilty and sentenced to hang in two hours from the Jersey Bridge. José was acquitted but told to leave town within twenty-four hours. Josefa was brave and defiant even as death neared. According to a *Pacific Star* correspondent,

> At the time appointed for the execution, the prisoner was taken to the gallows, which she approached without the least trepidation. She said, while standing by the gallows, so I was informed, that she had killed the man Cannon, and expected to suffer for it; that the only request she had to make was, that after she had suffered, that her body should be given to her friends. . . . This request was promptly complied with [and] she extended her hand to each of the bystanders immediately around her, and bidding each an "adios senor" [sic], voluntarily ascended the scaffold, took the rope and adjusted it around her neck with her own hand. [Secrest, 1967a, p. 25]

The lynching of Josefa was not an isolated event, as much violence was perpetrated against Mexicans in the aftermath of the war. Lacking the protection of the legal and judicial system, a number of Chicanos took the law into their own hands. Those who attempted to right injustices against their people came to be known as Chicano Social Bandits, feared and labeled as outlaws by Anglos and helped and admired by Chicanos. Two of the most famous of the California bandits, Tiburcio Vásquez and Joaquín Murieta, turned to a life of crime after witnessing countless abuses against Mexicans. They were especially concerned with protecting the honor of Mexican women. According to Vásquez, "my career grew out of the circumstances by which I was surrounded. As I grew up to manhood, I was in the habit of attending balls and parties given by the native Californians, into which the Americans, then beginning to become numerous, would force themselves and shove the native born men aside, monopolizing the dance and the women. This was about 1852. A spirit of hatred and revenge took possession of me. I had numerous fights in defense of what I believed to be my rights and those of my countrymen" (Truman 1874, p. 14).

Although Vásquez is best known for his exploits as a horse thief and robber who terriorized Anglos for a quarter of a century and gained the respect and admiration of his people, he was also known as a ladies man, and women were a determining force in his life. According to Hoyle (1927, p. 4), "in all those counties where he operated, he had the moral support and physical aid of his countrymen, and especially his countrywomen." Vásquez was good-looking and daring; one of his early exploits was an ill-fated attempt to run away with Anita, the daughter of a rancher in Monte Diablo County. The escape was foiled by the girl's father, but she was shot, and Vásquez escaped in the ensuing gunfight (May 1947, p. 125).

It seems apt, then, that a woman should have played a principal role in his capture and prosecution. When Tiburcio and his gang terrorized the state between 1873 and 1874, his first lieutenant was a Chilean named Abdon Leiva. The Chilean suspected but could not prove that Tiburcio and his wife Rosario were romantically involved. When Leiva finally caught the indiscreet pair, he wanted to shoot Vásquez but feared retaliation from other gang members; instead, he gained revenge by turning himself in to the authorities, implicating Vásquez, and informing them of his whereabouts. Tiburcio is said to have kept Rosario until he tired of her and then left her to die in the wilderness. Though she was pregnant and alone, she managed to make it to town after a four-day walk, and she and Leiva were to serve as important prosecution witnesses during Tiburcio's trial in San Jose. When Ben Truman (1874, p. 26), editor of the *Los Angeles Star*, asked the captured bandit in 1874 if he felt a woman had anything to do with his capture, he responded, laughing, "No; I never trusted one with information that could harm me." His affinity for women was to continue until the end. Women sent him flowers and were frequent visitors to his cell in the San Jose jail; he sold cards with his picture and a brief biography. On March 19, 1875 the noted bandit was hanged.

Despite the success and relatively long tenure of Tiburcio Vásquez's criminal career, it was Joaquín Murieta who was to gain fame as the most notorious of the Social Bandits. That Joaquín gained infamy as the Robin Hood of the West is intriguing, not only because his career was short-lived, spanning a brief two-year period, but because very little is actually known about his life. A great deal has been written about Joaquín, but many accounts are mythical or fictionalized and exploit stereotypes and romanticized notions about Mexicans and the old West (J. H. Jackson 1948, p. 176).

The first account of his life was that of John Rollin Ridge (Yellow Bird), *The Life and Adventures of Joaquín Murieta*, published in 1854, only one year after the bandit's alleged death at the hands of Harry Love and the California Rangers (Ridge 1955). Ridge was a half-Cherokee journalist who came to California in 1850, and sympathized with the exploited Mexicans. The small book was a detailed and vivid account of his life, written firsthand as if the author was an eyewitness to many major events. It depicted Joaquín as larger than life, an epic hero acting to override injustices against Mexicans in California (Nadeau 1974, p. 13). For many years the Ridge biography was accepted as accurate and authoritative, despite his own admission that only "in the main, it will be found to be strictly true."

According to Ridge, Joaquín was born in Sonora "of respectable parents and educated in the schools of Mexico" (p. 8). Disgusted with his countrymen and positively disposed toward the Americans, Joaquín set off to seek adventure in the Golden State. We first hear of him in the spring of 1850, placer mining on the Stanislaus River. Though only eighteen, the energetic young Mexican was respected and loved by those who came in contact with him and quickly developed a successful mining claim. "He had built him a comfortable mining residence in which he had domiciled his heart's treasure—a beautiful Sonorian girl, who had followed the young adventurer in all his wanderings with that devotedness of passion which belongs to the dark-eyed damsels of Mexico" (ibid., p. 9). His life of bliss was interrupted, however, by a band of lawless, desperate men who "visited Joaquín's house and peremptorily bade him leave his claim, as they would allow no Mexicans to work in that region . . . they struck him violently over the face, and, being physically superior, compelled him to swallow his wrath. Not content with this, they tied him hand and foot and ravished his mistress before his eyes" (ibid., p. 10). The embittered Joaquín and his heartbroken mistress retreated to the northern portions of the mines, hoping to find peace and happiness on a small farm. But once again he was driven from his house and land by a group of unprincipled Americans. Though angered, Joaquín did not seek revenge, turning instead to dealing *monte*. It was not until his half-brother was hanged by an angry mob at Murphy's Diggings that Joaquín's character changed drastically and he began a life of crime. He then "declared to a friend that he would live henceforth for revenge and that his path should be marked with blood" (ibid., pp. 12–13).

Other versions differ from Ridge's account. According to Richard Mitchell (1927, p. 39), Joaquín's companion was not raped and killed by angry miners, although they did force him from his claim. She was shot, but it was by Joaquín himself, who was angered after she had left him for a settler named Baker. Her wound was not fatal, however, and she lived to tell of the shooting (ibid., pp. 68–69). Remi Nadeau (1974, p. 24) goes one step further by denying the existence of such a companion and asserting that Ana Benitez was the only woman linked to Joaquín by available records. Accounts making reference to "Rosita," "Carmela," and other women are fictional, according to Nadeau.

Ana Benitez was a 22-year-old woman who came to Los Angeles from Santa Fe and was Joaquín's mistress by her own admission and the testimony of others (Secrest 1967b, pp. 8–9). On the night of November 7, 1852, General Joshua H. Bean, brother of the famous Judge Roy Bean, was ambushed and killed as he returned from attending the *maromas* (a Mexican circus featuring rope dancing) in San Gabriel. Joaquín had also attended and was alleged to be responsible for the crime, although the identity of the assailant(s) was never established. The motive for the crime was also unclear, but the general was apparently making things too hot for outlaws in the area and was said to have been drunk the night of the *maromas* and to have insulted some Mexican women. Joaquín managed to escape apprehension, but six Mexican men and Ana were arrested for the crime. Throughout the trial Ana insisted on Joaquín's innocence, swearing that he had been with her the night of the shooting, and implicated a man named Cipriano Sandoval. She alleged that Sandoval had confessed the murder to Joaquín and her the day after the shooting. The angry crowd was not to be denied and voted to hang Sandoval, Reyes Feliz (a member of Joaquin's gang and Rosita's brother), and Benito Lopez (who had no involvement in Bean's death but made the mistake of confessing to two other murders) (Nadeau 1974, p. 26).

The last woman linked to Joaquín was Rosie Martínez, proprietor of a fandango hall and saloon in the town of Hornitos. Hornitos was a Mexican mining town where the bandits found refuge among their own people. "During these periodic visits, Rosie would lock the doors to her place and the outlaws would take over, freely availing themselves of liquor and women. The musicians would play and the outlaws and Rosie's girls would revel for several days and nights, dancing on the red tile floors until they were exhausted. They then would retire to the cribs upstairs. At the first hint of danger, the outlaws could flee from the saloon, using a tunnel in the basement that led to a house across the street" (Secrest 1967b, p. 28).

Although Rosie Martínez has gained notoriety through her affiliation with Joaquín Murieta, she was not uncharacteristic of Mexican saloon keepers and fandango dancers. Such women have generally been dismissed as loose women of questionable virtue, but they undoubtedly fulfilled essential functions in mining camps and towns of the Old West; they provided warmth and comfort for the men and were valued and respected.

A perusal of American descriptions of Mexican women, on the other hand, reveals a curious ambivalence toward them. They simultaneously appeared coarse and unladylike and fascinating and incredibly seductive. When compared with their puritanical, unadorned, and sedate Anglo counterparts, Chicanas appeared dazzling, flamboyant, free, and uninhibited. The stereotype of the Mexican male as lazy and shiftless had its analogue in the unkempt and sexually permissive female (For an excellent discussion of Anglo attitudes toward Mexicans, see Robinson 1963; and R. Paredes 1975). An eyewitness report on the discovery of gold in California in 1848 remarked that "the men are generally lazy, fond of riding, dancing and gambling. . . . The women will gamble as well as the men. The men are mostly addicted to liquor. The women are, or may be generally considered handsome, with dark, fascinating eyes and good features; the better kind very courteous, but, in general, indolent; they dress rich and costly, are addicted to fandangoing and gallantry, but not much coquetry; sociable, kind, and good-natured, beautiful and extravagant, and chiefly overkind; but of this I am no judge" (McMurtrie 1943, p. 4).

A similar ambivalence is detected in the firsthand observations of Josiah Gregg in New Mexico (1954, pp. 153–54): "The females, although many of them are about as broad-featured as the veriest Indian, not unfrequently possess striking traits of beauty. They are remarkable for small feet and handsome figures. . . . The belles of the ranchos and villages have a disgusting habit of besmearing their faces with the crimson juice of a plant or fruit called *alegría,* which is not unlike blood. . . . A country beauty will often remain in this filthy condition for a whole fortnight, in order to appear to advantage at some favorite feast or ball . . . the cheeks look as fresh and ruddy as the natural darkness of their skin will permit."

Anglo puritanism was shocked by half-naked children and the flimsy attire of native women, who appeared immodest without the benefit of undergarments, petticoats, bustles, or bodices (McWilliams 1968, p. 131). Their dress consisted of no more than a loose white chemise and *enaguas,* or brightly colored flannel petticoats, and a *rebozo* (shawl). According to Gregg (1954, p. 152), "uncouth as this costume may appear at first, it constitutes nevertheless a very graceful sort of undress —in which capacity it is used even by ladies of rank." The *rebozo* was viewed as the most fashionable item in female wearing apparel, but there was objection to its use because one could easily conceal pistols, knives, and other weapons (ibid., p. 152). Women were also typically adorned with fancy jewelry (Twitchell 1925, p. 162).

Anglos were horrified by the affinity demonstrated by Mexican women for smoking and gambling. Even the loveliest and most refined ladies would smoke *puros* or *cigarros*, and it was not uncommon for cigarettes to be passed around the parlor or the dinner table (Gregg 1954, pp. 170–71). Señoritas would be seen whirling around the dance floor with a *cigarrito* in their hand, and it was fashionable for them to be outfitted with fancy cigarette holders. Gambling was a popular pastime among women of all social classes. Of the multitude of games, *monte* was probably the favorite among men and women. Another game that was attractive to women was *chuza*, a game played with little balls which was faintly similar to roulette (ibid., p. 169). The love of gambling was said to be so great that it constituted

> a distinguishing propensity of these people . . . that passion for gambling, which in Mexico more than anywhere else—to use Madame Calderon's language—"is impregnated with the consti-tution—in man, woman, and child." It prevails in the lowly hut, as well as in the glittering saloon; nor is the sanctity of the gown nor the dignity of station sufficient proof against the fascinations of this exciting vice. No one considers it a degradation to be seen frequent-ing a *monte bank*: the governor himself and his lady . . . the gay caballero and the titled señora . . . while the humbler ranchero, the hired domestic and the ragged pauper, all press with equal avidity to test their fortune at the same shrine. [Ibid., p. 168]

One of the most notorious and succesful *monte bank* dealers of the Old West was Gertrudes Barcelo, popularly nicknamed "La Tules" (see Twitchell 1925, pp. 338–39; and Gregg 1954, pp. 168–69). A native of Taos but unable to make a living in that town, she moved to Santa Fe and tried her hand at *monte*. After several unsuccessful years, her luck took a turn for the better, and she was able to accumulate several hundred dollars and open her own bank. She soon gained fame as the best *monte* dealer in Santa Fe and established a successful gambling house. Her beauty, charm, and skill made hers the most popular estab-lishment among the elite of Santa Fe society. "Magnificent pier-glass mirrors adorned the walls, brussels carpets, brought from the 'states,' covered the *adóbe* floors" (Twitchell 1925, p. 338). As she gained fame and fortune, she gained acceptance in the highest social circles and came to be known as Señora Doña Gertrudes Barcelo. Her upward social mobility was so rapid that at one point La Tules was Governor Armíjo's mistress and reputed to be "the power behind the throne" (ibid., n. 610).

La Tules was not without opposition, however, as many Anglos were disgusted with the way she and women like her were accepted by high society. Susan Magoffin, a contemporary observer, was aghast to find at one such gathering that not only did women smoke and dance with the men but that La Tules was there and was liked and accepted by everyone, even though she owned and managed the biggest gambling hall in Santa Fe (Robinson 1963, p. 78). She further described her as "a stately dame of a certain age, the possessor of a portion of that shrewd sense and fascinating manner necessary to allure the wayward, inexperienced youth to the hall of final ruin" (Drumm 1926, pp. 120–21).

According to these early accounts, the Mexican fascination for gambling was exceeded only by their love of dancing. Dancing was a way of life for the native population; from the lowliest fandango to the finest *baile*—"from the richest nabob to the beggar—from the governor to the ranchero—from the sobrest matron to the flippant belle— from the grandest *señora* to the *cocinera*—all partake of this exhilarating amusement. . . . But what most oddly greets, and really outrages most Protestant ears, is the accompaniment of divine service with the very same instruments, and often with the same tunes" (Gregg 1954, p. 170). The fandango was apparently a mechanism for minimizing class differentials and intensifying ethnic solidarity. Inhibitions and restrictions were so much lowered that, according to one eyewitness, "it was not anything uncommon or surprising to see the most elaborately dressed and aristocratic woman at the ball dancing with a *peón* . . . an old man of 80 or over, dancing with a child not over 8 or 10. . . . I have never seen anything lascivious, or any want of decorum and self-respect in any woman in a *fandángo* [sic], whatever might be her reputation for virtue outside. I have known of disorders and serious brawls in *fandángos,* but it was almost invariably where Americans and whisky were found in profusion" (Twitchell 1925, p. 238).

These observations suggest that many Anglos experienced severe cultural shock when confronted with the customs, values, and mores of the native population. To the God-fearing Anglo-American the Mexican appeared lazy, self-indulgent, and immoral. The Mexican's love of riding, gambling, parties, and fandangos was at once incomprehensible and repulsive. The female's flamboyance, charm, revealing attire, and love of gambling, dancing, and smoking were viewed as marks of permissiveness and degeneracy. The Chicana proved to be an elusive and seductive creature, nonetheless. Anglo fascination for Mexican women was a source of conflict between the two groups, and Mexican men were quick to uphold the honor and virtue of their women.

While Chicanas appeared deviant to the Anglo observer, their life-style and mode of dress reflected a successful adjustment to prevailing conditions. Their attire and activities were functional in a frontier society, which precluded the enforcement of traditional mores and a narrow division of labor between the sexes. In addition to the frontier conditions that existed, the American takeover forced many Chicanas to abandon traditional feminine roles. Excluded from traditional occupations and lacking economic security in the home, they took to *monte bank* dealing, saloon keeping, fandango dancing, and the like. Others assumed even less conventional roles. Doña Candelaria Mestas, for example, was a pony-rider mail carrier. During the turbulent 1890s she served her New Mexican community by carrying the mail from Arboles to Rosa (Swadesh 1974, p. 100).

Other Chicanas gained fame as a result of their victimization at the hands of the legal and judicial system. Chipita Rodríguez of San Patricio, Texas, was the only woman in that state to be sentenced to death and executed by the courts (Cotera 1976, p. 60). Although an elderly and respected member of her community, she was charged with the murder of a horse trader named John Savage. The only evidence presented against her by the prosecution was that Savage's body was found near her home. Throughout the trial Chipita insisted on her innocence, but to no avail; she was convicted and eventually hanged on November 13, 1863.

Another Chicana charged with murder in Texas was Mrs. Refugia Robledo (see A. Paredes 1958, pp. 67–73). She became involved in the "Battle of Belmont" because she harbored Gregorio Cortez, the famous Social Bandit, in her home. Gregorio sought refuge when he attempted to elude a posse headed by Sheriff Glover. There were seven persons at the Robledo house: Refugia and her husband Martín, the three Robledo sons (aged thirteen, sixteen, and eighteen), a young boy named Ramón Rodríguez who lived with the Robledos, and Martín Sandoval, a visitor.

The men were sitting on the front porch on the southeast corner of the house when the posse approached from the north and surrounded the premises. In the ensuing gunfight Glover was apparently shot by Cortez, who then ran into the brush along with the other men and the eldest Robledo boy. Mrs. Robledo was left alone in the house with the three other boys, unarmed and at the mercy of the posse. The gang of Mexican bandits now consisted of an unarmed woman and three children. Frightened by the gunfire, Mrs. Robledo and the boys ran back and forth inside the house. Deputy Swift entered the rear of the house and shot at the two men who were "running back and forward" (ibid., p. 70). Swift shot the Rodríguez boy and would have undoubtedly shot the Robledo boys if Refugia had not shielded them with her body. According to the court proceedings, Mrs. Robledo "came in between said party and witness, and he could not shoot again" (ibid.). Refugia was wounded by other members of the posse who fired repeatedly into the house at the "Mexican gang of outlaws."

In addition to the wounding of an unarmed woman and a young boy, the famous Battle of Belmont left two officers dead (Sheriff Glover and Henry Schnabel, owner of the ranch on which the Robledos lived and a member of the posse). Refugia, her husband, their two young sons, and the Rodríguez boy were arrested, and she was promptly charged with the murder of Schnabel, based on the testimony of Deputy Tom Harper, who said he had seen her shoot Schnabel from the window. Harper later changed his testimony, and there is reason to believe that he may have inadvertently shot Schnabel. The charges against Mrs. Robledo were subsequently dropped in an exchange for a "confession" that she saw Cortez kill Glover on the east end of the house and then run around to the west end to kill Schnabel (ibid., p. 90).

Despite the many obstacles faced after the American takeover, a number of Chicanas were to emerge as outstanding personalities before the turn of the century. One of the most extraordinary women of this period was Teresa Urrea, "La Niña de Cabora" (see Gill 1957; Putnam 1963; Rodríguez and Rodríguez 1972; and McWilliams 1968, pp. 199–200). The illegitimate Teresa was born on a ranch near Ocoroni, Sinaloa, on October 15, 1873 (Gill 1957, p. 628). Her father, Don Tomás Urrea, was a wealthy Mexican rancher and her mother a Yaqui Indian named Cayetana Chávez. Teresa was to gain fame as a *curandera* with extraordinary healing powers and as a champion of oppressed Indians under the Díaz regime. At the age of sixteen she had gone to live with her father at Rancho Cabora in Sonora and developed a relationship with an old Indian servant named María. Although María was to play a critical role in Teresa's life, there are conflicting accounts of their relationship (Rodríguez and Rodríguez 1972, p. 51). One account is that María was a *curandera* and that Teresa became her apprentice; another, that she was taught to read by María and went into a trance and cured the servant of paralysis. The trance lasted three months and eighteen

Terecita Urrea. La Sta: Niña de Cabora

Fig. 2 Teresa Urrea. Courtesy of the Arizona
Historical Society.

days, and Teresa was taken for dead but made a miraculous recovery. Her fame as a healer spread quickly as she effected many similar cures. Most of her followers were poor, especially Indians such as the Yaquis and Mayos of Sonora, the Guasaves of Sinaloa, and the Tarahumaras from the state of Chihuahua (Putnam 1963, pp. 250–51).

Even more significant than her healing powers were her social pronouncements against the church and the government. Though attributed with saintly qualities, Teresa remained intensely anticlerical, preaching against the church's exploitation of the poor (Gill 1957, p. 629). She was also extremely critical of the government and its treatment of the Indian. When hundreds of Mexicans came from distant places to see La Niña, she was denounced by the church as a heretic. At the urging of the clergy, Porfirio Díaz ordered troops to arrest her, but they were ambushed before they could reach Cabora by Yaqui Indians who were determined to protect their Saint. This incident signaled the beginning of the "Tomochic War," also known as the "Revolt of the Yaquis" (McWilliams 1968, p. 200).

Teresa's healing powers may have masked an intense radical revolutionary fervor. In a short time she became a symbol of the Indian resistance against the dictatorship of Porfirio Díaz. Especially important was her role in inspiring the revolt of the poor Indians of the mountain villages of Tomochic and Temosáchic.

Tomochic was a small town of fewer than 300 inhabitants, nestled in the mountains of Chihuahua. The townspeople were Tarahumara Indians, known as fierce and independent men with "powerful physiques and black beards" (Putnam 1963, p. 252). Termed fanatical by the established church, they were Christianized and developed a unique religious movement, mixing elements of Catholicism and pagan religion. During a tour of the village, the governor of Chihuahua discovered a religious painting he felt had considerable artistic merit and ordered it removed to the state capital. When the villagers resisted, they were held to be in a state of rebellion, and a punitive expedition was launched against them (Gill 1957, p. 630). In the first encounter with federal troops, the *tomochitecos* lived up to their reputation and emerged victorious. Having heard of Teresita's miraculous powers, the villagers decided to visit La Niña in order to avoid further conflict with *los federales* and receive counsel and inspiration from her (ibid., p. 631). They were pursued by federal troops, and in a second stand on December 27, the *tomochitecos* won another resounding victory.

During the visit to Cabora, the residents of Tomochic placed a guard around Teresita's house. After bearing witness to her curative powers

for four days, they affirmed their belief in her saintly qualities and pro-
claimed her their village saint (Putnam 1963, p. 252). They then returned to Tomochic and placed an image of her in the church.

Growing weary of the rebellion and of Teresa's powers, the government launched its third attack on October 29, 1892. Although outnumbered twenty-three to one (1,500 soldiers to 65 adult male villagers),
the *tomochitecos* fought valiantly for nine days. They succumbed only
after more than 700 government soldiers were killed or wounded and
the village was destroyed (Rodríguez and Rodríguez 1972, p. 56). During the battle countless atrocities were inflicted on the Indian rebels.
Perhaps it was only through their faith in Teresa that they resisted. This
faith sustained them in the belief that by invoking her name with cries
of "Viva Teresa Urrea" and "Viva La Santa de Cabora" they would be
protected and that those who fell in battle would be revived in three
days (Putnam 1963, p. 253).

Women and children were also actively involved in the resistance.
Among the many heroes of Tomochic were two fourteen-year-old boys,
Pedro Medrano and Nicolás Mendía. Medrano died after killing five
government soldiers and Mendía after killing seventeen (Gill 1957,
p. 640). The mother of the Medranos, sixty-eight-year-old Antonia
Holguín, was at the side of her children. When they fell she picked up
a rifle and fought to her own death.

The battles of Tomochic set off a number of other Indian rebellions.
In the spring of 1892 more than 200 Mayon Indians took over the
town of Navojoa, shouting "Viva La Santa de Cabora," and on the
fourth of April 1893 a revolt took place in the town of Temosáchic.
Allegedly inspired by a group of *tomoches* seeking revenge for the
destruction of their village, the movement was led by two brothers,
Celso and Simón Anaya. After gaining reinforcements of 400 men,
they launched an attack on and took the state capital, dealing the
federales a stunning defeat in the famous battle of Casa Blanca (ibid., p.
641). When government reinforcements arrived in May, they abandoned the city and returned to Temosáchic.

As the Indian rebellion grew, Teresita seemed more and more dangerous and subversive to the Díaz regime. The governor of Sonora had
her arrested and taken to Guaymas, but when the Yaquis began to con-
verge on the city, Teresita was released. Finally, in 1892 Díaz ordered
her deported to the United States. The citizens of Nogales, Arizona,
welcomed La Santa, providing her and her father with a furnished house
when they arrived (Putnam 1963, p. 254). Rather than diminishing her
popularity, the deportation appears to have increased it, as Indians from
both sides of the border flocked to her in great numbers.

Once in the United States, she established contacts with deposed Mexican revolutionaries, including Lauro Aguirre, who was intensely anti-Díaz and published two radical newspapers in El Paso, *El independiente* and *El progresista* (Rodríguez and Rodríguez 1972, p. 58). Perhaps influenced by Aguirre, Teresa appears to have grown more militant. She became convinced that liberty had to be obtained in this world, not the next, and that it would only come with the overthrow of the dictatorship (Gill 1957, p. 643).

As pressure from her enemies and the clergy mounted, Don Tomás decided to move his family to Solomonville in eastern Arizona. But at Aguirre's urging, they moved to El Paso after only eight months away from the border (Putnam 1963, p. 255). Shortly after her arrival in El Paso, a group of her followers, Yaquis known as *teresistas*, attacked the custom house in Nogales, Sonora. Crossing over from the American side, they advanced crying, "Viva La Santa de Cabora!" According to the *New York Times* (August 14, 1896), "the main object of the raid was to secure the arms, ammunition, and money in the Custom House . . . they intended to start for the City of Mexico to overthrow the Diaz government." After a battle which left seven Yaquis dead, the invaders were forced to flee into the mountains on the American side. The attack induced fear and panic among the populace on both sides of the border. Conspirational theories of the attack were confirmed when copies of the *Independiente* were received in Nogales, Arizona, and found on some of the dead Indians. These were special editions dated June 8 and July 25, 1896, calling for the overthrow of the Díaz government (ibid.). The attack, not surprisingly, was blamed on Aguirre and Teresa. The *New York Times* (August 20, 1896) reported that "the Mexican Government has already made a requisition on the United States for Lauro Aguirre and Teresa de Cabora, and her father. . . . The Indian prisoners say her father is more to blame than she, as the girl does about as he wants her to. Aguirre is the worst, they say, as he has complete control over Teresa's father. . . . It is estimated by the Mexican officials that he and Santa Teresa by their influence, have caused the death of more than 1,000 people in the last six or seven years." Several other skirmishes took place, and within days it was reported that about 1,000 Yaquis had risen in sympathy with the revolutionary movement (ibid., August 19, 1896).

It was generally assumed, especially by the press, that if Teresa did not mastermind the attacks, she at least gave them her tacit approval. Yet Teresa firmly disavowed any direct connection with the revolt. In a statement issued to the El Paso *Herald* on September 11, 1896 she declared,

"The press generally in these days has occupied itself with my
humble person in terms unfavorable in the highest degree, since in
a fashion most unjust . . . they refer to me as participating in political
matters; they connect me to the events that have happened in
Nogales, Sonora, Coyame and Presidio del Nortre, Chihuahua,
where people have arisen in arms against the government. . . .
I have noticed with much pain that the persons who have taken
up arms in Mexican territory have invoked my name in aid of the
schemes they are carrying through. But I repeat I am not one who
authorizes or at the same time interferes with these proceedings.
Decidedly I am a victim. [Putnam 1963, pp. 256–57]

This disclaimer notwithstanding, the Díaz government continued to feel
threatened by her presence in El Paso and pressured United States officials to remove her from the border. Whether it was as a result of this
pressure or in order to secure Teresa's safety (several attempts had been
made on her life), Don Tomás elected to move to Clifton, Arizona, in
1897 (ibid., p. 258). The remoteness and isolation of this small copper-
mining town made life less hectic for Teresita, but she was still idolized
by Chicano miners as a saint capable of curing the sick and restoring
sight to the blind, as she had been idolized and worshiped in Mexico.

In October 1899 a Yaqui named Guadalupe Rodríguez fell in love
with La Santa and she reputedly with him. Don Tomás predictably
refused to approve of the marriage, for it is unlikely than any man
would have proved suitable to him. Lupe was angered and returned
that evening with a justice of the peace, brandishing a rifle and literally
forcing Teresa into marriage (ibid., p. 259). But Lupe proved no match
for her, and the next morning he is reported to have acted very strangely
and to have started running without direction. He was overpowered by
her followers, who were outraged by this sacrilege, tried, declared
insane, and placed in an asylum (ibid., p. 260).

Teresa's aborted marriage had strained her relationship with Don
Tomás, and within days of the wedding she agreed to go to San Jose,
California, to cure Mrs. A. C. Fessler's daughter, a three-year-old who
was seriously ill and had not been helped by medical treatment. When
the girl made a remarkable recovery, the incident was widely publi-
cized by San Francisco newspapers, who named Teresa the Joan of Arc
of the Indians (ibid., p. 261).

The publicity prompted a group of promoters to seek exploitation
of her commercial value by forming a medical company to tour the
United States. Thinking that she was embarking on a philanthropic
rather than a commercial venture, she signed a contract for $10,000

over a five-year period, with the proviso that she would not charge people for her services. There was, however, no provision to preclude the medical company from charging them.

The remaining years of her life were difficult ones for Teresa. Through her affiliation with the medical company she was transformed from a charismatic spiritual leader to a carnival freak. Teresa was ill at ease in her new theatrical role, especially since she had never really mastered English and was confused by what was transpiring. In January of 1901 when the company went from San Francisco to St. Louis, Teresa wrote to her good friend Juana Van Order of Solomonville, asking that she send one of her children as an interpreter. Juana, a native of Tomosachic, had moved to Solomonville and married John H. Van Order, an English mining engineer. She sent her second oldest son, John, who was not much younger than Teresa and bilingual. Teresita was obviously pleased with him, since he later became her husband (Rodríguez and Rodríguez 1972, p. 64).

The medical company then moved to New York, where Teresa learned that her father was seriously ill, but because she was in the late stages of pregnancy she did not return to Clifton, and he died on September 22, 1902. Hungry for publicity, the antics of the medical company now reached bizarre proportions. Teresa was, for example, entered in a beauty contest and crowned queen (Putnam 1963, p. 262).

By the spring of 1904 Teresa had grown weary of the medical company and returned to Clifton. Her savings from the tour were used to build a large, two-story house that was to serve as a place to nurse the sick and heal the wounded. The San Francisco River flooded in December of 1905, leaving a wave of destruction in its wake. Teresa spent many hours in cold rain and water during the rescue effort, and she contracted a bronchial condition. Anticipating death, she called for her mother, Cayetana, and died within three days of her arrival. According to the medical records, her death was caused by consumption, "but the family and the Mexicans said that she had worn out her spirit in the service of her people" (ibid., pp. 263–64).

Throughout her brief life of thirty-three years and in subsequent years La Santa served as a spiritual symbol for the poor and downtrodden, but she remained nonetheless an enigmatic figure. Was Teresa a radical revolutionary or a victim of circumstances, as her public pronouncements would have us believe? Was she a simple and unassuming faith healer or a sophisticated political leader? In the last analysis, perhaps her personal motivation is unimportant, for regardless of her motives, there can be no doubt that she played a critical role in the shaping of history. Her influence was so extensive that according to one observer, "had she been politically minded and had given the revolution her blessing and personal leadership, the Mexican Revolution might have begun in 1896 rather than 1910" (ibid., p. 256). Teresa Urrea served as precursor not only of the Mexican revolution but of Chicano political movements and remains a symbol of resistance to oppression for contemporary Chicanos. She is thereby a Chicana counterpart to La Virgen de Guadalupe, a symbol of warmth, succor, and hope for the poor, destitute, and exploited.

Another important figure to emerge in this period was Lucy González Parsons, one of the first Chicanas to become involved in and make a significant contribution to the emerging labor movement. A woman of great stature, Lucy has not received proper recognition as an outstanding Chicana. (It is significant, for example, that two major Chicano history texts do not even list her in their indices: see McWilliams 1968 and Acuña 1972).

Lucía González was born in Johnson County, Texas, most probably in 1852. In the fall of 1871 she married a young man named Albert R. Parsons in Austin and moved to Chicago shortly thereafter (Parsons 1903, p. 16). Parsons quickly emerged as a leading figure in the labor movement, and Lucía was his constant companion and collaborator. Even a glance at Parsons's personal correspondence suggests that he held her in very high esteem and that they shared an extraordinary relationship. Lucía was a complete woman and led an exemplary life. She was much more than a loving wife and mother—she was an intelligent companion and a labor organizer and leader in her own right. Perhaps it was a fitting tribute to their relationship that Lucy compiled and edited Parsons's posthumous autobiography.

Albert Parsons was born in Montgomery, Alabama, on June 20, 1848. He was orphaned by the age of five, and his brother William Henry Parsons became his guardian, although Albert was actually raised by a black slave called "Aunt Easter," a woman who was to have a profound influence on his life. At thirteen he joined the Confederate army and fought in a number of campaigns. Parsons returned from the war convinced that he had fought for the wrong side and that blacks should be granted political rights. Settling in Waco, Texas, to work and harvest forty acres of corn, Albert hired a number of ex-slaves as wage laborers. He noted, "I was strongly influenced in taking this step out of respect and love for the memory of dear old 'Aunt Easter,' then dead, and formerly a slave and house-servant of my brother's family, she having been my constant associate and practically raised me, with

Fig. 3   Lucía González. Courtesy of the Labadie
Collection, University of Michigan.

great kindness and a mother's love" (ibid., p. 15). In 1868 he founded
and edited a paper, the *Spectator*, in which he called for acceptance of
the Thirteenth, Fourteenth, and Fifteenth Amendments and Recon-
struction measures designed to uphold the rights of blacks. These political views, not surprisingly, elicited the wrath of many former associ-
ates and of the Ku Klux Klan. The *Spectator* did not survive this hostile
environment, and in 1869 Parsons became a traveling correspondent
for the Houston *Daily Telegraph*. He recalled that "it was during this
trip through Johnson county that I first met the charming young
Spanish-Indian maiden who, three years later, became my wife. She
lived in a most beautiful region of country, on her uncle's ranch near
Buffalo Creek" (ibid.).

In the early 1870s the Parsonses settled in Chicago and quickly became embroiled in the labor struggle. The young journalist and his
bride were interested in the efforts of working people to force the
"Relief and Aid Society" to distribute to the poor vast sums it had

accumulated for relief of the great suffering and poverty brought on by the Chicago fire of 1871. They found support for an accusation that the money had been going to corrupt speculators and not to the poor for whom it was designated. As their involvement grew, they discovered significant parallels between the exploitation of wage laborers by Northern industrialists and the exploitation of blacks by Southern slave holders.

The Parsonses were active not only in labor organizing but in emerging Socialist groups. In 1876 Albert joined the Workingmen's Party of the United States and shortly thereafter was recognized as a leading spokesman for labor. The Workingmen's Party program called for "State control of all means of production, transportation, communication, and exchange" (ibid., p. 17). Unrest and dissatisfaction among working men grew so that by 1877 spontaneous gatherings and assemblies of workers were almost daily occurrences. These peaceable meetings were frequently disrupted by police, who fired into crowds and clubbed people almost at will. Parsons's influence in labor circles increased and in 1879, as a delegate to the national convention of the Socialist Party, he was nominated as the Labor candidate for president of the United States. He respectfully declined the nomination, however, because he had not yet reached the constitutional age of thirty-five years.

The prevailing labor unrest in the 1870s was viewed with disfavor by industrialists and wealthy capitalists, who directed the police to use violent and brutal means to quell these disturbances. The press was used to denounce and discredit labor leaders by labeling them Socialists, Communists, and Anarchists who threatened to destroy the American way of life. In 1880 the Parsonses decided to end their participation in the Labor Party and turned their attention instead to reducing the working day to eight hours. This action was based on the conviction that wage workers would remain disfranchised as long as they were forced to labor for long hours at low wages. On October 1, 1884 the International Working People's Association founded the *Alarm*, a weekly newspaper, and Albert served as its editor until it was seized on May 5, 1886 after the Haymarket Massacre. Lucía helped edit and was a contributor to the *Alarm*.

Momentum for an eight-hour day grew. In 1885, during a convention in Chicago, a resolution was passed that established May 1, 1886 as a day to demand the eight-hour day and to strike if the demand was not met. The hours of labor at this time ranged from twelve to sixteen hours. As the movement spread among the trade and labor unions, there emerged eight-hour clubs, picnics, and parades. Lucy Parsons described the atmosphere that prevailed in Chicago during the strike: "From May 1 to May 3 the strike was spreading like wildfire. The bosses were hostile, the police were brutal to the last degree! On May 3 the Mac-Cormack [sic] Reaper Works Employees were holding a meeting at noon to talk of the strike when two patrol wagons, loaded with police, dashed down upon them and began clubbing and shooting those un-armed workers" (Parsons 1935, p. 6). The incident at the MacCormick Works left at least five persons dead and many more injured, but it was not an isolated act. Two days prior to this, on May 1, a peaceful assem-bly of workers had been dispersed by a large body of police who beat and shot at them on the orders of Police Captain Bonfield. After the May 3 incident, August Spies, editor of the *Arbeiter Zeitung*, was out-raged by the police action and immediately issued a handbill calling for a meeting the following day at the Haymarket to protest these actions.

The Haymarket meeting was peaceful by all accounts and attended by Mayor Harrison, who later testified as to its peacefulness. (For a discussion of the Haymarket affair, see David 1936; Parsons 1935; and Foner 1955, 1965, pp. 105–14, and 1969). As the assembly ended, however, some 200 or 300 police entered with clubs and pistols and commenced to shoot into the crowd and club men, women, and chil-dren. The order to disperse the crowd was given once again by Captain Bonfield, who apparently could not resist the opportunity to maim more people (David 1936, p. 284–85). As the police rushed the crowd, some-one threw a bomb into their ranks and killed several police. While the identity of the persons who threw the bomb was never ascertained, the incident was used as a pretext to persecute the leaders of the strike and make examples of them (Parsons 1935, p. 6).

Those arrested were August Spies, Samuel Fielden, Louis Lingg, Adolph Fischer, George Engel, Parsons, Michael Schwab, and Oscar Neebe, known as the Haymarket martyrs. The defendants were quickly tried and convicted of conspiring to commit murder. All were con-demned to death except Neebe, who was sentenced to fifteen years' imprisonment (Foner 1955, p. 109). (Fielding, Schwab, and Neebe were pardoned by Governor John P. AltGeld on June 26, 1893). During its course it became clear that the trial was not one for murder but for anarchy. In its closing arguments to the jury, the prosecution summed up its case by noting, "Anarchy is on trial. Hang these eight men and save our institutions. These are the leaders; make examples of them" (Parsons 1903, p. 239).

Albert Parsons became a principal figure in the trial, although he was not present when the bomb went off. The evidence against him was that he had brought about the tragedy through his continued "agitation" in articles appearing in the *Alarm* and his famous Haymarket speech of May 4. In fact, only one of the articles quoted in the trial was written by Parsons, and that a full year and a half before the Haymarket. During the trial Parsons redelivered his May 4 speech to a spellbound jury. It was undoubtedly the finest and most eloquent speech of his life.

After the conviction of the Haymarket martyrs, Lucy led the legal battle to reverse the decision, which lasted a year and a half and went all the way to the United States Supreme Court. But the appeal failed, and as the scheduled day of execution approached (November 11, 1887), an all-out effort was launched for signatures to petition the governor for commutation. On November 8, the papers reported that Lingg had accidentally blown his head off with bombs intended to blow up the police and the jail, but according to Lucy, he was murdered (Parsons 1935). Most probably, however, he killed himself (David 1936, p. 455). As a result of his death, the police ordered the tables set up to obtain signatures removed and persons passing out petitions arrested.

On November 11, Lucía took her two small children to the jail so that they might say a final good-bye to their father. She recalled, "I was not admitted, then I pleaded with the police to take them to receive their father's blessing. While I was pleading, a patrol wagon drove up, placed us in it and locked us in the station while the hellish deed was done!" (Parsons 1935, p. 39). Mrs. Parsons and her children were locked in one cell and her good friend, Lizzie Swank-Holmes, in another (Parsons 1903, p. 251). The women and the frightened, crying children were then stripped and searched. Perhaps through some premonition of the eventual outcome, Parsons had bid farewell to his wife and children in a letter written on August 12, 1886, after the verdict was rendered:

> Well, my poor, dear wife, I personally, feel sorry for you and the helpless little babes of our loins.
> You I bequeath to the people, a woman of the people. I have one request to make of you: Commit no rash act to yourself when I am gone, but take up the great cause of Socialism where I am compelled to lay it down.
> My children—well, their father had better die in the endeavor to secure their liberty and happiness than live contented in a society which condemns nine-tenths of its children to a life of wage-slavery

and poverty. Bless them; I love them unspeakably, my poor helpless little ones.

Ah, wife, living or dead, we are as one. For you my affection is everlasting. For the people—humanity. I cry out again and again in the doomed victim's cell: Liberty—Justice—Equality. [Ibid., p. 235]

While Lucía was clearly an exceptional woman, there has been considerable reluctance to give her due recognition as a Chicana. Some have speculated that her ancestry was not really Mexican and Indian but black, despite the fact that her maiden name was González and Albert himself described her as a "charming young Spanish-Indian maiden."

In a biography of Lucy, Carolyn Ashbaugh (1976, p. 6) asserts that she was black and most probably of slave origins. Acknowledging that "little is known of Lucy's origins" (p. 14), Ashbaugh maintains nonetheless that Parsons claimed she was Indian and Spanish in order to counter charges of miscegenation. Ashbaugh then proceeds to delve into Lucía's psyche, suggesting that her Mexican identity was but an excuse in self-denial: "Lucy Parsons internalized the racism of white society to the extent that she denied her own black ancestry. . . . Her denial of her blackness, and therefore of her oppression as a black woman, made it exceedingly difficult for her to analyze her social position in relation to anything but her class status" (p. 66). That Lucy's death certificate lists Pedro Díaz and Marie Gonzáles as her parents is likewise dismissed: "Lucy identified herself as Native American and Chicana in an effort to cover up her black heritage" (p. 268). Yet in describing Lucía's physical appearance Ashbaugh takes note of "the high cheekbones of her Indian ancestors" (p. 15).

While Lucía's true origins are indeterminable and most probably racially mixed, it appears highly improbable that a person wishing to pass as white in nineteenth-century Texas would assume a Mexican-Indian identity. Why Ashbaugh should hold steadfastly to the view that Lucy Gonzáles was black despite the implausibility and internal contradictions of the argument is intriguing indeed. Is it that the liaison between an ex-Confederate soldier turned abolitionist and a black slave girl makes for a more seductive and enticing tale? Or is this characterization simply consistent with that of other feminist "herstorians" who have generally proven insensitive to Chicanas?

There has been reluctance not only to acknowledge Lucía's Chicano heritage but to recognize her as an eminent woman. The fact that she and Albert shared an unusual relationship working in concert until his death has all too often obscured both her brilliance and her independent identity. Lucía had championed socialism and human rights and assumed a leadership position in the emerging labor movement long before the Haymarket. Prior to Albert's death and for approximately fifty-five years afterward she wrote articles, led numerous protests and marches, made stirring speeches, and was said to be considered as "more dangerous than a thousand rioters" by the Chicago police.

One of Lucía's finest qualities was her ability as a public speaker, as she was extremely articulate and perhaps even surpassed Albert as an orator. Her public appearances were enhanced not only by her resonant and melodic voice but by her good looks and tall, dignified appearance. According to an eyewitness account given by Ralph Chaplin (1948, p. 168), "Mrs. Parsons was, as a rule, both frightening and beautiful in her intense earnestness." By all accounts Lucy was extremely beautiful, with golden skin and a vibrant and radiant personality that enabled her to hold her audiences captive as she lashed out against the abuses of capitalism and denounced atrocities perpetrated on workers. She was in addition an excellent and prolific writer who published numerous articles in radical labor journals such as the *Socialist*, the *Alarm*, the *Denver Labor Enquirer*, and the *Labor Defender*. When the first issue of the *Alarm* went to press in 1884, Lucy's article "To Tramps" was on the front page. The article was a call to arms, so to speak, to the poor, downtrodden, and homeless. Since many had died of hunger and exposure or had committed suicide during the previous harsh winter in Chicago, it urged them not to despair and exhorted them to "avail yourselves of those little methods of warfare which Science has placed in the hands of the poor man, and you will become a power in this or any other land. . . . *Learn the use of explosives!*" (Parsons 1884). "To Tramps" was later distributed as a leaflet by the International Working People's Association.

Though the article was quoted out of context by detractors who sought to exploit its radical tone, it clearly refuted the view suggested by some in the news media that she was a simple "woman of color." Lucía in fact was probably much more militant than her husband (Ashbaugh 1976, p. 39). In 1880 there had been a major split within the ranks of the Socialist Labor Party with respect to whether or not workers should arm themselves for the purpose of self-defense against attacks by management and the police (Foner 1955, p. 37). Lucy Parsons strongly supported the Chicago section, which advocated arming workers. She had taken this position after extensive reading of Socialist and

Anarchist thought. She had a keen mind, and her writing reveals a sophisticated political philosophy and deep awareness of the workings of capitalistic society. In the aftermath of the Haymarket she wrote,

"A reign of terror has been inaugurated which would put to shame the most zealous Russian blood-hound. The organized banditti and conscienceless brigands of capital have suspended the only papers which would give the side of those whom they had crammed into prison cells. They have invaded the homes of every one who has ever been known to have raised a voice or sympathized with those who have had aught to say against the present system of robbery and oppression. . . . This organized banditti have arrested me four times; they have subjected me to indignities that should bring the tinge of shame to the calloused cheek of a hardened barbarian.

But evidently becoming convinced that I had nothing to "give away," they have ceased to drag me to the station, for the time at least. But my comrades need have no concern lest these ruffians should, by their brutal treatment of me, drive me to distraction. They simply challenge my contempt. [Parsons 1903, pp. 114–15]

Lucía launched a massive campaign to save the Haymarket martyrs, speaking throughout the country in an effort to gather financial and moral support for the appeal. Although exhausted from the trial and from working long hours as a dressmaker in order to support her family, she rose to the occasion and completed a successful seven-week tour. But her defense of the martyrs was motivated by much more than the grief of a wife whose husband faced execution. Rather, it was but an extension of a radical career, and she was to pursue many other causes with equal fervor. Lucy believed in the sanctity of causes and issues, not in individuals. She and Albert were both prepared to give their lives in defense of their ideals.

Despite the fact that she was unsuccessful in her attempt to save the Haymarket martyrs, the campaign gave impetus to a broader movement to defend political prisoners. She helped found the International Labor Defense (ILD), developed her own branch of the organization, and served as guest of honor at its second annual convention in 1927, held on the fortieth anniversary of the Haymarket executions. The ILD provided legal defense for oppressed workers and political dissidents and published the *Labor Defender*. By 1938 its membership had swelled to over 300,000 and had defended many political prisoners, including the McNamara brothers, Tom Mooney and Warren K. Billings, Sacco and Vanzetti, Angelo Herndon, and the Scottsboro Boys.

Lucía was also one of the founders of the International Workers of

the World (IWW) and a principal speaker at its opening convention in
1905, where she was the first labor leader in the United States to advo-
cate a general strike of workers as a guerrilla tactic in labor's struggle
against capitalism (Foner 1965, p. 140). As a representative of IWW she
traveled extensively to mining camps, lumber camps, and union halls
throughout the country. In 1913, as unemployment worsened and
breadlines grew, the IWW agitated for improved conditions, focusing
its organizational efforts on the West Coast. On December 26, 1913,
1,000 unemployed workers, including Mexicans, held a demonstration
in the Los Angeles Plaza to protest starvation amidst affluence (ibid., p.
437). The police broke up the peaceful assembly with clubs, killing one
worker and injuring many others. Several weeks later Lucy was at the
head of a demonstration of unemployed persons in San Francisco demanding $3 for an eight-hour day and was arrested after the demon-
strators clashed with police (ibid.). In addition, she led a number of
hunger strikes in Chicago, one of the most notable of which was a massive march of more than 1,500 workers on Hull House in January 1915.
Needless to say, she was once again arrested.

Throughout a long and distinguished career, Lucy fought not only
for the rights of workers and protection of the poor but for the liberation of women. In 1879 she became active in the Chicago Working
Women's Union, an organization of housewives and other wageless
women who called for a suffrage plank in the Socialist Labor platform
and demanded equal pay for equal work. There was great resistance at
this time to admitting women into labor unions, and they were frequently forced to serve as scabs in order to obtain employment. In 1882
the Knights of Labor finally voted to admit them, and by 1886 there
were about 50,000 women members in this organization (Foner 1955,
p. 61). On April 25, 1885 Lucía and Lizzy Swank-Holmes led a march
on the new Board of Trade building in Chicago. Both women had
worked as seamtresses and sought to organize sewing women in the
city. Required to work sixteen hours a day for very low wages under
deplorable conditions in basement sweatshops, the sewing women were
among the most exploited workers in the city. On the eve of the Haymarket (May 3, 1886) Lucy and Lizzy had led a march of several hundred women calling for an eight-hour day (Foner 1969, pp. 47–48).

Despite her concern for women's issues, they appeared secondary
to the class struggle (for a discussion of her views on women's issues,
see Ashbaugh 1976, pp. 199–206). For Lucía women's oppression resulted from capitalism, and their slavery to men was a function of their
economic dependence. She argued, "The economic is the first issue to

be settled, . . . it is woman's economical dependence which makes her enslavement to man possible" (Parsons 1895, p. 3). At the same time, she opposed the "free love" advocates within the Anarchist movement, staunchly defending the nuclear family, monogamy, and "the virtue of womanhood" (Ashbaugh 1976, pp. 201–3). Lucía supported a woman's right to divorce, contraception and birth control, freedom from rape, and economic equality.

Lucy González' dedication to women's rights and the labor struggle was unmatched and continued into old age. Even as death approached she was relentless, remaining active in the ILD and writing the story of the Haymarket for the *Labor Defender* in 1935. On March 7, 1942 she died at the age of ninety, virtually blind, in a fire that destroyed her home. The importance of Lucía González Parsons to contemporary Chicanas cannot be overstated. With a lifetime that spans from just after the American takeover until well into the twentieth century, she is a transitional figure linking the nineteenth century woman and the contemporary Chicana. She was the first of a long list of Chicanas such as María Hernández, Luisa Moreno, Emma Tenayuca, and Dolores Huerta, who have struggled to end the exploitation of labor in the United States and to obtain civil rights for Chicanos and other oppressed people.

Four

The Woman in the Family

The preceding chapters sought to uncover the roots of the Chicana in Mexico and the American Southwest. Though our attention now turns to the contemporary Chicana, we will continue to highlight relevant historical information, linking wherever possible her contemporary situation with the past. This chapter is concerned with the woman's role within an institution that is said to have a critical impact on the lives of Chicanos—the family. We hope to show that a number of characteristics of the Chicano family had their counterparts in Aztec society. We will also attempt to enhance our understanding of the Chicano family by analyzing and evaluating it relative to family systems in other societies past and present. A comparative perspective should provide a more meaningful assessment of *la mujer y la familia*.

The Family, Its Structure and Function

Although the universality of the family has been widely debated, it is a basic institution, found in virtually every human society past and present, which performs functions that appear critical to the survival and maintenance of society.[1] The family is charged with the responsibility of perpetuating the species beyond a single generation through reproduction and through socialization of the new generation. The two most basic functions of the family thus are procreation and socialization, the transmission of the culture and values of the group. Other functions performed by the family are the determination of the legitimacy of children, the establishment of rules of descent, sexual gratification for adults, emotional gratification for family members, and in some societies the production and consumption of economic goods and services. The reproductive, economic, and socializing functions are especially important. Society would not persist beyond a single generation without the first, while the second is necessary for the maintenance of life and the third for the transmission of culture (Murdock 1965, p. 10).

Despite its virtual universality, the family has demonstrated considerable variation across societies. One important point of variation is the multiplicity of functions it carries out. Family systems run the gamut from those that perform limited functions and are very dependent on the larger society to those that are multifunctional and relatively self-sufficient. The Israeli kibbutz illustrates the first type of family and the traditional Chinese family the second.[2]

While the modern family in China bears little resemblance to its ancient predecessor,[3] the traditional Chinese family is generally considered to be the prototype of the extended family. The ancient Chinese family was patriarchal, family centered, and male dominated. The patriarch as head of the household was the ultimate authority, exercising almost total control over his wife, children, and all descendants of his children and their spouses. The family emphasized: (1) the father-son relationship, (2) family pride, (3) the large family, (4) the cult of ancestor worship, and (5) joint ownership of property (Lee 1953, pp. 272–73).

It is important to note that this pattern was an ideal, maintained only by the wealthy members of the gentry-scholar class, though emulated by other classes (ibid., p. 272). While peasants identified with and imitated this pattern, they could seldom maintain large households. The ideal was that six generations would live under one roof, and property would be divided only after nine generations; but in practice seldom did more than three or four generations live together, and property was usually divided after the death of the patriarch. The average household in ancient China does not appear to have been much larger than the average American household today. Ping-ti Ho (1965, p. 18) argues that a respectable census in the year 2 A.D. reported that the average household size was 4.87, and this figure has remained relatively stable to the present.

The family in the Israeli kibbutz provides a sharp contrast with the

Chinese family. Although there are differences among kibbutzim, they are generally characterized by collective ownership of property, pooling of income, communal living arrangements, and collective child rearing (Spiro 1968, p. 69). The founders of the kibbutz concept in the early 1800s were Russian Jews who sought to revolutionize the family (Leslie 1973, p. 140). Since the family was a source of allegiance competing with the radical ideology that was required for survival in an adverse or hostile environment, they attempted to minimize its influence (Talmon 1965, pp. 264–65). Hence the family was to be stripped of most of its functions.[4] Women were relieved of the traditional domestic role and the responsibility of child rearing. Children were raised in communal nurseries from infancy, and much of the responsibility for their care and nurturance was assumed by the collective. Kinship lineage was also deemphasized, and a woman was allowed to maintain her maiden name. The family retained only its most basic functions: procreation, emotional gratification, and sexual gratification for adults.

Though child rearing was done communally, children were not lacking intimate, emotional contact. Not only did nurses (metapelet) show warmth and affection toward them, but since the parental role was devoid of power and authority, the parent-child relationship was warm and emotionally gratifying. The attachment between children and their parents was strong (Spiro 1968, p. 74), and parents still played the most influential role in the child's emotional development (Spiro 1958, p. 48).

The Aztec Family

A number of characteristics of the contemporary Chicano family—such as the emphasis on familism and the importance given to extended relatives, the expectation that the individual subordinate his needs to those of the collective, the concept of respect and obedience to elders, as well as cultural norms of feminine virtue—had their counterparts in Aztec society. In both pre-Columbian Mexico and contemporary Chicano culture the woman is to be the hearth of the home; to be chaste, modest, honorable, clean, and, most importantly, to minister to the needs of her husband and children.

While there are numerous secondary sources concerned with the workings of Aztec society, perhaps the richest source of information on the Aztec family and women's roles therein are contained in the Aztec codices, for they present the Indian's own view of their society. They contain a wealth of information on societal norms, prescriptions, and values, many of them expressed as *consejos* (advice) or exhortations recited by elders, especially parents, to youth. Yet the codices are not without limitations. They are in a sense written from the perspective of the native nobility, or *pipiltin*, reflecting an alliance between native elites and the Spaniards which followed the conquest (Blanco 1977, p. 49). The common people, or *macehualtin*, adhered to an oral tradition, and their history was not so readily preserved. The codices also reveal the values and biases of the Spanish clergy, who typically acted as chroniclers and viewed Indian customs and practices from a missionary Christian perspective. Finally, they are more a codification of cultural ideals and values than a description of the real world, although one can infer a great deal about actual conduct from them. These admonitions notwithstanding, the codices are still an invaluable source of information on the daily life of the Aztecs of all social strata and provide considerable insight into the functioning of a complex and rigidly stratified society.

An examination of the codices suggests that parents held the following to be among the most important virtues for their daughters (Hellbom 1967, p. 247):

tenacidad de aguantar las dificultades de la vida
  [tenacity in enduring the difficulties of life]
decencia y honestidad [decency and honesty]
devoción y piedad [devotion and piety]
conocimientos y habilidad en los oficios mujeriles
  [knowledge and mastery of feminine duties]
diligencia [diligence]
castidad [chastity]
obediencia [obedience]
modestia [modesty]

Daughters of the nobility were educated in national history, painting, music, and decorative arts, but the schools observed a rigid separation of the sexes (Bonilla García 1959, p. 261) and the object of their education was preparation in the domestic arts.

The Aztec family was not an extended system like the traditional Chinese family, yet there was great emphasis on familism. One was expected to obey and respect the family and, most importantly, not to dishonor it. The death of a dishonored daughter was preferred by the father, since she dishonored not only herself and family but her ancestors (Hellbom 1967, p. 247). A woman could dishonor her family and ancestors not only by committing adultery but by relatively trivial transgressions such as being immodest in conduct or dress. The emphasis placed on a woman's demeanor was so great that it was a sign of bad manners for her to speak too loudly or too softly or walk too rapidly or too slowly: "No se debia andar despacio, que era señal de pompa, ni de prisa, que indicaba desasosiego; . . . y la cabeza debía ir ni muy erguida ni demasiado baja, sin mirar a un lado y a otro ni volviendo la cabeza; ni enojada, sino con cara serena."[5]

A daughter's obedience to her parents dictated that she accept the husband they selected for her, although in truth she was asked to consent to the match before it was finalized. The process of mate selection was one in which the families of both parties were actively involved, but in which the bride and the groom had little say (ibid., p. 261). Relatives of the bride and groom played an especially important part in the wedding ritual itself.

Marriages were aways initiated by the man's family. When a young man was deemed ready for marriage, his older relatives gathered and selected the girl considered best for him. Several old women, acting as matchmakers, went the next day to the girl's home and asked for her hand on behalf of the young man's family. The ensuing ritual was complex, continuing on for several days and involving the rhetorical flowery phrases by both parties. According to custom, her relatives were to assume a reticent air and to be implored. They protested that the girl was not yet ready for marriage or worthy of the young man. After several days his relatives gave up, but they promised to return again for an answer. The following morning they returned, continuing the ritual until the tables were turned, so that her relatives were now imploring the groom's representatives to return again. Finally, on the fourth day the bride's family showed disbelief in all the interest and fanfare displayed to honor a girl that was unworthy. They were puzzled at how the young man could delude himself, but in view of all the interest expressed, they would inform the girl of his intentions and bring her relatives together so that his representatives might have a definitive answer on the following day. After much discussion her relatives would accede to the match, but not before taking the opportunity to point out the girl's many faults: "Está bien; pues conclúyese que el mozo será muy contento . . . de casarse con ella aunque sufra por esto pobreza y trabajo, pues que parece que está aficionado a esta muchacha, aunque no sabe aun hacer nada, ni es experta en hacer su oficio mujeril."[6]

The wedding day was set after consultation with the soothsayers so that a propitious date would be selected. Elaborate plans and preparations for the feast were made for three days prior to the wedding. On the wedding day guests arrived early and spent the morning eating and drinking. The drinks consisted of a wine made of corn (*atulli*), flour of cacao diluted in water, and several herbal extracts capable of inducing inebriation. Drunkenness was permitted only on such special occasions.

The prenuptial ceremony continued into the afternoon with the grooming and beautification of the bride, which included bathing her and washing her hair and adorning her with colored feathers placed on her legs and arms and daisies on her face. Once these preparations were complete, the bride was placed near the paternal home, and the groom's relatives filed before her, reminding her of her wifely duties: "Ya habéis dejado de ser moza y comenzáis a ser vieja, ahora dejad ya las mocedades y niñerías . . . Habéis de levantaros de noche, barrer la casa, poner fuego antes que amanezca, os habéis de levantar cada día. Mira hija, que no avergoncéis ni deshonréis a los que somos vuestros padres y vuestras madres; vuestros abuelos, que ya son difuntos, no os han de venir a decir lo que os cumple porque son ya muertos; nosotros lo decimos en su nombre."[7] She responded, moved by emotion and in tears, by expressing her appreciation of their precious words of advice and telling them that they had acted like true parents in speaking to her and counseling her.

The groom's relatives now went to the bride's house and announced that they wished to take her. Her relatives placed a cotton blanket on the floor on which the bride knelt; taking it by the corners, they lifted her and transported her to her new home. When they arrived at the house, they placed the bride and groom near the hearth, with the woman to his left, and they received gifts from their respective mothers-in-law. The officiating matchmakers then joined the cotton cloth which the man wore with the woman's dress in a knot to symbolize their union in marriage.

The ceremony completed, the matchmakers led them to their marital quarters, threw them on the bed, and closed the door, leaving them alone for the first time. For four days the matchmakers would wait outside the door while the groom's and the bride's relatives socialized, eating and drinking. At the conclusion of this period, the matchmakers took the mat on which the couple had slept, shook it out ceremoniously in the patio and returned it to its original location. It was now time to congratulate the newlyweds and for the parents and in-laws to give them their final exortations. Before departing, the old female relatives of the groom would also speak to the bride, reminding her of her domestic obligations:

Hija mía, vuestras madres que aquí estamos, y vuestros padres os quieren consolar; esforzaos hija, y no os aflijáis por lar carga del casamiento que tomáis a cuestas. . . . Véis aquí cinco mantas que os da vuestro marido, para que con ellas tratéis en el mercado, y con ellas compréis el *chilli*, la sal el *ocote* y la leña con que habéis guisar la comida. Esta es la costumbre que dejaron los viejos y viejas; trabajad hija y haced vuestro oficio mujeril sola; ninguno os ha de ayudar; ya nos vamos, sed adventurada y próspera como deseamos.[8]

The exhortations completed, the couple was finally left alone to live as husband and wife, but the influence of the family was never ending.

Fidelity in marriage was the norm for both husband and wife, and transgressions brought not only shame to the family and to one's ancestors but the punishment of death. This penalty, moreover, was applied uniformly, with no exception even for rulers or their children (Zorita 1963, p. 130). A jealous husband might beat his wife if he suspected adultery, but this was contrary to Aztec law, which specified that the punishment was to be administered officially and uniformly by the state, not by individuals. If a husband beat his wife unjustly, she could complain to authorities, since the law permitted divorce in such cases (Bonilla García 1959; p. 265). Divorce could also be obtained if a woman proved that her husband did not provide for her nourishment. The man, on the other hand, had grounds for dissolution of the marriage if the woman was sterile, did not perform her domestic duties, or abandoned the household (ibid.).

Yet infidelity and divorce were probably rare occurrences. A daughter was taught from early childhood to walk a straight and narrow path and to be faithful to her husband. Her mother exorted her to "mira que no des tu cuerpo a algún hombre . . . mira que en ninguna manera te conozca más que un varón. . . . Cuando fuere Dios servido de que tomes marido . . . no te atrevas a él; mira que en ningún tiempo ni en ningún lugar le hagas traición que se llama adulterio."[9]

Although fidelity was expected and monogamy was the prevalent pattern in Aztec society, polygyny was permitted. In practice it was a pattern adopted only by rich and powerful families, since it created an added financial burden (Bonilla García 1959; p. 264). Polygyny appears to have been motivated more by practical considerations than sensual ones. It provided the man with more hands to do work, giving him additional time for play and leisure. Playing and gambling were great passions for Aztec men, who seemed especially fond of betting on a ball game which they played. They also demonstrated great interest in a dice game called *patoliztli* (ibid.).

Among noble families it was not uncommon for a man to have several secondary wives and concubines, but a distinction was made between the principal wife, who partook in the elaborate marriage ceremony, and secondary wives. While only the children of the principal marriage were legitimate, the children of secondary unions among noble families might be given a role in the affairs of the state (ibid., p. 265).

The socialization of children was an enterprise undertaken with considerable zeal and vigilance by nobles and commoners alike. Mothers were expected to nurse their own children or to obtain a good wet nurse, in the event that they were unable to nurse them. Nursing continued for about four years, and it was not unusual for nursing mothers to refrain from sexual relations during this time in order to avert pregnancy (Las Casas 1974, p. 154).

The children of the nobility were reared under great discipline in order to develop qualities that were deemed desirable for those of their station. Male children were taken to the temple at the age of five so that they could begin to serve the gods and receive instruction in religious matters. Here they were raised and indoctrinated in preparation for their adult roles. Marriage marked the transition into adulthood, and it was not until then that one left the temple and the group of boys (*mancebos*) with whom he was raised. When it was time for a young man to marry, a member of his family spoke to his age cohort and his teachers: "Aquí estáis presente señores y maestros de los mancebos. No recibáis pena porque vuestro hermano N. nuestro hijo se quiere apartar de vuestra compañía, ya quiere tomar mujer; aquí está, esta hacha es señal de cómo se quiere apartar ya de vuestra companía."[10] The ax thus symbolized the severing of ties to youth and entrance into adult society.

Daughters of noble families were reared with even greater concern for propriety, discipline, and solicitude (Zorita 1963, p. 136). They were raised in palaces and were always in the company of older women who guarded them and instructed them. From the age of four they were taught to be dignified in speech, appearance, and bearing and to develop a profound love for reclusion (Las Casas 1974, p. 165). They were allowed to go out in public only on special occasions, and then accompanied by many old women and with their eyes fixed on the ground. Men never ate at their table, and the girls were expected to eat in silence. Although they lived apart from the men in separate quarters, they were not permitted to go into the gardens or grounds without a chaperone. Those who transgressed and ventured forth alone were punished severely by having their feet pricked with a spine until they bled (ibid.,

p. 155). The expectation that young women were not to be seen by men or to have any contact with them was rigidly observed. It is said that the son of a noble family once climbed the wall where the daughters of the king of Texcoco were quartered to see and speak with one of them. Although the boy escaped without penalty, the king ordered his daughter executed by drowning so that he would not be judged unjust and cowardly by his subjects. This same king had another daughter executed for committing adultery even though her husband forgave her and pleaded for her life[11] (ibid., p. 156).

In addition to being chaste, modest, and dignified, noble young girls were expected to be diligent and industrious. At the age of five they were taught to embroider, sew, and weave. Nurses were instructed to supervise them carefully so that they would work from early in the morning until late in the day. Laziness and idleness were seen as causes of vice and decadence. Cleanliness was another virtuous trademark. The girls were expected to bathe two or three times per day.

Although the *macehualtin* occupied the lowest positions in society, they demonstrated no less care in the rearing and instruction of children (Zorita 1963, p. 138). *Masehual* children too were cautioned against vice and instructed in religion. They were taken to the temples by parents and placed in the service of the gods. While the sons of nobles were raised in temples, the sons of commoners were brought up in the Houses of Youth maintained in each barrio (ibid.). An elder was in charge of each house and was responsible for their instruction. The boys brought wood for fuel in order to keep the fires burning perpetually before the gods, repaired the temples, labored in public works projects, and helped in the construction of the houses of the nobility. They were encouraged to assume a trade consistent with their abilities and predilections, but most often they entered the same trade as their fathers. Parents were also concerned with moral instruction, and they were quick to punish with great diligence and rigor when their children were mischievous or ill bred. The punishment for violations of parental wishes was severe. Sometimes children were simply admonished verbally, but other times they were beaten with a stick throughout the body and, when necessary, hung by the feet while smoke was put up their nostrils (Las Casas 1974, p. 157). Girls were similarly punished by their mothers when they disobeyed. If children ran away from home, parents looked for them and brought them back, but when this was done repeatedly they were judged incorrigible and given up as rogues. Many ended up on the gallows or as slaves. There was also great concern among parents with teaching children to be truthful. The punishment for lying was to cut or prick a lip with a maguey spine (Zorita 1963, p. 138).

The daughters of the *macehualtin* were taught and carefully guarded by their mothers, and when they married they were admonished to continue on a virtuous path and avoid moral pitfalls. Each parent told the daughter how best to honor and serve her husband, but since the mother was directly responsible for moral instruction, her exhortations were longer and more intense. The mother would say, "Hija mía muy amada, ya vees cómo te vas para tu marido . . . ya sabes que es costumbre que las mujeres vayan y sigan a sus maridos y estén con ellos y vivan en sus casas. . . . Ten, hija mía, aviso de no ser defectuosa, ni mal criada; mas mira que de tal manera vivas que seas ejemplo a las mujeres otras."[12] The girl was also told that if she worked hard and took care of her husband, she would make her parents happy and proud, but if she did not, she would cause them much pain and dishonor them.

While women of both noble and common origins were protected and relegated to the domestic sphere, in reality the common woman appears to have been granted considerably more independence and freedom of movement. She attended parties and ceremonies and worked both inside and outside the home (Blanco 1977, p. 62). *Macehuales* provided most of the labor for the society, producing almost all necessary goods and services required for basic sustenance. The exploitation of this labor enabled the *pipiltin*, as a leisure class, to enjoy a life of luxury and extravagance. The marketplace served not only as a center of commerce but as a gathering place for prostitutes, hermaphrodites, and procurers, and women were warned of the dangers contained therein. But the common woman could not escape the marketplace, for it was here that she purchased necessary goods for her family and sold the goods she produced (ibid., pp. 64–65). The common woman was thus much more than wife, mother, and propagator of the race; she also contributed to the economic production of the society. The textiles she produced astonished the Spaniards both in the quantity produced and the quality of workmanship (ibid., p. 62).

Marriages among the *macehual* were sometimes less formal and perhaps without the benefit of religious sanction. Yet such informally established unions could be as durable as formal marriages (ibid., p. 63). Divorce was permitted but generally frowned on.

Despite differences between noble and common women, basic expectations of feminine virtue transcended class lines. Three expectations of all women were that they (1) serve and worship the gods, (2) maintain themselves and preserve their personal dignity, and (3) love, revere, and serve their husbands (Las Casas 1974, p. 160).

The Chicano Family in Comparative Perspective

Now that we have presented an overview of the Aztec family, our attention turns to an analysis of the Chicano family in a comparative cross-cultural perspective. The multifunctional Chinese family and the limited-function Israeli kibbutz family provide a starting point for comparing and evaluating the structure and function of the Chicano family. They also enable us to compare the Chicano family and the dominant American family. While there is considerable ethnic, class, and regional diversity among families in the United States, we can characterize the modal family type by focusing on its more general and basic features. Let us characterize the modal American family and then contrast it with the Chicano family.

The modal American family does not fall into either the extreme multifunctional type or the unifunctional type but is similar to the kibbutz in having limited functions. The traditional Chinese family was relatively self-sufficient, multifunctional, large, and stable; the American family is dependent, has limited functions, is small and fairly unstable. This is not surprising, since the extended family seems to flourish in stable agricultural societies in which wealth and social position are determined largely by one's relation to the land, whereas the nuclear family (husband, wife, and offspring) predominates in more unstable urban-industrial societies and in hunting and gathering tribes (Nimkoff and Middleton 1960, pp. 216–17). But the American family of course retains two universal functions—sexual gratification for adult members and reproduction. Despite a rising divorce rate and greater tolerance of sex outside of marriage and illegitimacy, marriage remains an important sexual outlet for most adults, and births are expected to be sanctioned by marital union. Many of the economic and socialization functions of the family, however, have been taken on by other institutions. The contemporary American family is certainly not a unit of economic production, although it is a unit of consumption and the primary mechanism for distributing goods and services. The family also provides emotional gratification for its members and socializes children. It is probably still the single most important influence on the intellectual and moral development of the child, since its impact during the critical first five years of life is substantial, but this influence appears to be declining. The socialization function is increasingly assumed by other institutions and agencies. With the liberation of women and their greater involvement in the labor force, much of the early socialization of children is being assumed by day-care centers, nursery schools, and baby sitters. The impact of the school is felt earlier and is prolonged over a longer period of time. The school introduces another competing source of allegiance. The decline in the family has been accompanied by an increase in the influence of peers as agents of socialization and sources of emotional gratification.

The Chicano family exists within a complex urban-industrial society and is subject to many of the same pressures and sources of influence as the Anglo-American family. Nonetheless, it has certain distinguishing characteristics, some of which have remained intact since pre-Columbian days. Chicano culture places more emphasis on *la familia*, which includes the immediate family and extended relatives, than does Anglo culture (see Sotomayor 1972, p. 321; and Temple-Trujillo 1974, p. 18). This is not to suggest that Chicanos maintain an extended system like the traditional Chinese family, since most live in urban areas and there is not much wealth or land to distribute or hoard; rather, a positive value is placed on familism. Anglos are more individualistic, so that even the family itself idealizes the development and accomplishments of the individual, whereas Chicanos are more oriented toward the group and seek to enhance its welfare. As in Aztec society, the needs of the collective frequently take precedence over those of the individual (Grebler, Moore, and Guzman 1970, p. 351), and achievement and success are measured according to the contribution made to the family. The emphasis on familism is such that it includes not only the immediate family and extended relatives but fictive relations (Alvirez and Bean 1976, p. 277; and Sotomayor 1972, p. 321). *Compadrazgo* is a system whereby good friends are symbolically initiated into the family as they become godparents for one's children.[13] To be a *compadre* or *comadre* is a great honor, for it indicates that one is "family" even though a consanguine relation is not present. In time of need one can count on family and *compadres* as well.[14]

From the preceding it seems reasonable to conclude that Chicanos generally derive more emotional gratification from the family than Anglos (Sotomayor 1972, p. 321; and Temple Trujillo 1974, p. 18). Available evidence indicates that for Chicanos the family is by far the single most important unit in life (Murillo 1971, p. 102). It is the basic source of emotional gratification and support. The Chicano family also appears to have retained more control over socialization than its Anglo counterpart. Its influence is undoubtedly declining with increasing urbanization, industrialization, and acculturation, but *la familia* appears to have retained most of its basic functions.

In addition to socialization and emotional gratification, the Chicano family fulfills the functions of procreation and sexual gratification for adults. The rate of fertility for Chicanos is considerably higher than the rate for the society as a whole (Bradshaw and Bean 1972, p. 143; and U.S. Bureau of the Census 1971, p. 1). Marriage is also a major source of sexual gratification. In fact for women it is the only legitimate and publicly recognized outlet. Although the Chicano family is not engaged in economic production, its economic function appears greater. Chicano culture emphasizes cooperation and mutual aid. It is not uncommon for Chicanos to pool their resources to help members of the immediate family or other relatives; older siblings will work so younger ones can complete school, or resources may be combined to purchase large, expensive items such as a car or a house (Alvirez and Bean 1976, p. 277). Public agencies sometimes find it difficult to understand why impoverished families share badly needed goods or money with less fortunate friends or relatives (Murillo 1971, p. 103).

In summary, Chicanos are familistic. Though the Chicano family is not an extended system in the same sense as the traditional Chinese family, it retains certain basic features of the extended system. Several generations may live under one roof (Goodman and Beman 1971, p. 111), and whether living together or not, relatives provide help and comfort to one another. There is also respect for elders, and aging parents are more likely to be cared for in the home than in an institution. The culture tends to be male oriented, with the head of the household accorded respect and deference. The Chicano family is undergoing change and modification, but it retains much of its vitality.

The Social Science Myth of the Mexican-American Family

There is a marked disparity between the warm, nurturing, and supportive unit described above and social science depictions of the Mexican-American family (see Mirandé 1977). Despite the paucity of systematic research, social science literature is filled with generalizations about the Chicano family. A pejorative and pathological picture is consistently painted. Analyses based neither on empirical research nor on close contact and familiarity with the nuances of the culture have perpetuated preconceived notions and erroneous stereotypes. Such studies, according to Miguel Montiel (1970), lack theoretical and methodological sophistication and uncritically accept the concept of *machismo* as a catch-all that explains all the pathologies found in the Mexican and the Mexican-American family. These studies make a number of questionable assumptions. First, they are infused with psychoanalytic concepts and paradigms that attempt to establish a modal Mexican personality type which is characterized by a pervasive feeling of inferiority and a rejection of authority. Second, the dynamics of Mexican family life are explained through reference to the all-encompassing concept of *machismo*. Finally, it is assumed that the Mexican family and the Mexican-American family are isomorphic. Despite the obvious hazards in extrapolating psychoanalytically based Mexican national character studies to the United States, these explorations "have been accepted as the 'true' description of the Mexican character, the Mexican male, and ultimately the Mexican and Mexican American family" (ibid., p. 58).

Formulations of the Mexican-American family have been influenced substantially by Mexican family studies. One of the best known of these studies is Maria Bermúdez's *La vida familiar del Mexicano* (1955). Building on the work of Samuel Ramos, she argues that Mexicans are locked into rigid conceptions of masculinity and femininity which make it difficult for men to be "candid and humane" and for women to be "dignified and independent" (p. 101). This basic deficiency in the Mexican produces family disunity and impedes development in many areas. Among other things, it obstructs philosophical, scientific, and industrial progress (p. 102). Díaz-Guerrero, a noted Mexican psychiatrist, similarly postulates that the father is the absolute and supreme ruler of the family, while the mother is a quiet, persistently self-sacrificing figure (1975, p. 3). Though his research is based on only eleven structured questions, he concludes that the male and the female are unable to fulfill these extreme, rigid role expectations and consequently tend toward neurosis (p. 10). The pejorative and deficient model of Mexican family life is again found in G. M. Gilbert's study (1959) of mental health in a Mexican village. On the basis of interviews with nine older adult males, he concludes that there is "a pronounced tendency to either severely constricted affect or to morbid-depressed-hypochon-driacal types of responses among the older males . . . this may be indicative of increasing impotence and 'castration anxiety' as the males fail in the lifelong struggle to live up to the demands of *machismo*" (p. 212). Despite the psychoanalytic jargon and pseudo-scientific qualifiers of these studies, they inevitably conclude that *machismo* produces maladaptive, pathological responses. In the hands of these researchers, social science becomes a tool for legitimating deeply ingrained though unfounded assumptions about Mexican culture. Significantly, some of the perpetrators of this pathological model are themselves Mexican, but their work is infused nonetheless with European and North American thought and paradigms. They have adopted a simple psychoanalytic model which sees *machismo* as a malady and Mexican cultural traits as symptomatic of illness or disease. Ramos, for example, relied heavily on Alfred Adler's theory of "masculine protest" to explain the persistent feeling of inferiority which is said to permeate the Mexican character (Montiel 1970, p. 57).

These paradigms in turn have been applied by American social scientists to Chicanos. Thus researcher after researcher, without the benefit of empirical evidence, continues to depict a *macho*-dominated, authoritarian Mexican-American family. Stereotypically, the man is the lord and master of the household, with the woman relegated to an insignificant, subordinate position (Humphrey 1944, p. 622; and Jones 1948, p. 451). Women who do not accept their subordinate status are apt to arouse the ire of the *macho*. "Physical punishment of a wife by her husband is accepted as customary" (Hayden 1966, p. 20), according to this view. The male is free to come and go as he pleases and to demand complete respect, deference, and obedience. He indulges in *parrandas* (binges), drinks, fights, and can even establish a second household (*casa chica*) with impunity (Montiel 1970, pp. 60–61). The man, in short, can pursue the same pattern of social life after marriage that he did as a bachelor; "the woman's position, on the other hand, is completely tied in with her marital status, and her behavior rigidly circumscribed by it" (Peñalosa 1968, p. 683). Life for the male is also characterized by an incessant preoccupation with sex. Women are divided into one of two categories. The good, one's mother, wife, and daughters, are saintly, virginal figures to be protected, idealized, revered, and held on a pedestal so that they are kept out of the reach of male predators. They are virtuous creatures who do not enjoy sex. Sexual enjoyment is to be had with bad women: less respectable females that one can take as mistresses, girl friends, or playmates (ibid.).

The rigidity of the family is assumed by these social scientists to have negative effects on the personality development of children. The authoritarian household does not engender achievement, independence, self-reliance, or self-worth, values which are highly esteemed in American society. Celia Heller (1966, pp. 34–35) observes, "The kind of socialization that Mexican American children generally receive at home is not conducive to the development of the capacities needed for advancement . . . by stressing values that hinder mobility—family ties, honor, masculinity, and living in the present—and by neglecting the values that are conducive to it—achievement, independence, and deferred gratification." The authoritarian Mexican-American family constellation thus produces dependence and subordination and reinforces a present-time orientation which impedes advancement. Chicanos live in a perpetual "mañana land." It happens, then, that while Anglo culture stresses achievement and control of the environment, Chicano culture stresses fatalism and resignation (Samora and Lamanna 1967, p. 135). Alvin Rudoff's categorical condemnation of the Chicano family and culture illustrates this classic pathological view. "The family constellation is an unstable one as the father is seen as withdrawn and the mother as a self-sacrificing and saintly figure. The Mexican-American has little concern for the future, perceives himself as predestined to be poor and subordinate, is still influenced by magic, is gang-minded, distrusts women, sees authority as arbitrary, tends to be passive and dependent, and is alienated from the Anglo culture" (1971, pp. 236–37).

The Chicano Family: Values and Characteristics

Social scientists unfamiliar with Chicano culture have thus created a stereotypical caricature of family life. In this section we attempt to present a more realistic and sympathetic interpretation of the Chicano family. Not wishing to perpetuate additional stereotypes, however, we would like to caution that the family system depicted is an ideal type that may not correspond to any real family. There is no one Chicano family but a number of family types that may vary according to region, duration of residence in the United States, education, social class, age, and urban-rural place of residence. Given this internal diversity, it is useful to extrapolate key features that tend to characterize Chicano families across various settings. The characteristics we attribute to the Chicano family are not true of all families, but they are more likely to characterize the Chicano than the Anglo family.

That the Mexican-American family has been depicted as a tangle of pathology is ironic, for few institutions have proved more stable or resilient. Detractors of the Chicano family claim that the clannish and parochial orientation of Chicanos may have an adverse effect on their advancement. It has been suggested that their strong familistic orientation may very well serve as an impediment to achievement and mobility in an urban-industrial society and that nepostistic values may be incongruous with the rational business ethos which prevails in the United States (Grebler et al. 1970, p. 351; and Moore 1976, p. 130).

Successful family business ventures are certainly not uncommon in the barrio, however, and they serve to counter this critique. Familism can facilitate and enhance achievement by providing needed aid and support. Despite their differing views, detractors and supporters of the Chicano family agree that it is an important social institution which provides needed warmth and support in an otherwise hostile, unrewarding environment.

An important feature of Chicano culture is its emphasis on respect. Respect derives from two sources: a long-standing deference to elders and a predisposition to see the male as superior. Respect toward men and elders is pervasive in fact, it is sometimes said that the older order the younger and the men, the women. As the ultimate authority in the family, the husband-father is accorded the most deference and respect, but other adults are also respected, commensurate with their age and sex. Grandparents (*abuelitos*) play an important part. They are more likely to be seen as warm and affectionate than as authority figures. "Grandparents appear to be highly influential, as distinguished from being powerful" (Goodman and Beman 1971, p. 111). Like parents in the kibbutz, they are free of the responsibilities of parenthood, and their relationships with grandchildren tend to be warm and affectionate.

The respect the man is accorded also includes granting him special privileges, acknowledging his authority, and seeing his *machismo* in a positive light. Men are usually allowed more freedom and privileges than women. The man derives much of his sense of self-worth outside the home in his job, from his friends, *compadres*, etc. As the ultimate authority in the family, the father is responsible to the outside world for the behavior of family members. "An important part of his concept of *machismo* or maleness, however, is that of using his authority within the family in a just and fair manner. Should he misuse his authority, he will lose respect" (Murillo 1971, p. 103) not only within the family but in the community at large. In times of conflict or disputes, the father is to be the ultimate arbitrator and authority.

Despite the importance and respect granted the father, he is frequently perceived as aloof or distant by other family members, especially children. The father tends to be warm and affectionate when the children are little. But as they enter puberty, relations between children and the father become more discontinuous (Rubel 1966, p. 66).

The wife-mother role provides a sharp contrast to the male role. "The female is clearly valued less, despite the various circumstances in which she is placed on a pedestal by males" (Peñalosa 1968, p. 683).

Separation of male and female roles for contemporary Chicanos is almost as rigid as it was in the ancient society of their Aztec forebears. Almost total devotion to the family is expected from the female (Murillo 1971, p. 104). She should be warm, nurturing, and minister to the needs of her husband and children. Despite their lowly status as women, ministering mothers are respected, revered, and recognized as important figures. For children, their importance to the family takes precedence over that of the father. A study of Chicano children suggests that the father may be seen as a somewhat distant authority and is likely to be slighted, by boys in particular. "Few say they go to him with questions, either for information or for permission to do something" (Goodman and Beman 1971, p. 112). Significantly, few want to be "like father" when they grow up or to have a job like his. This remoteness may result from his frequent absence from home. He may leave home early before the children are awake and not return until late in the evening (ibid.). Mothers and grandmothers, on the other hand, play a critical part in the lives of children. They perform many domestic tasks and are also responsible for setting parameters on the children's behavior. They determine when one gets up or goes to bed and when one comes in from playing. "She scolds, she sometimes slaps or spanks for disobeying small rules, and she stops sibling squabbles" (ibid.). Thus while the woman may not have the prestige or status of the man, she appears to have great influence in the home.

The influence of the mother filters into relationships with her children which are characterized by warmth and affection. Whereas the father-son relationship is somewhat distant, the mother's relation with her daughter is more intimate. This close bond begins in childhood and is maintained even after the daughter reaches adulthood. Early participation in the domestic realm produces identification with the mother and her maternal role. "Little girls learn early to assume responsibilities and tasks, especially those that are particularly maternal in character, such as taking care of smaller siblings" (Peñalosa 1968, p. 687). In addition, "The confinement of females within the home gives rise to a closely knit group of a mother and her daughters, a relationship which perdures throughout the lifetime of the individuals" (Rubel 1966, p. 100). The same close environment gives rise to enduring relationships between sisters.

Although the mother-son relationship does not appear to be as strong as the mother-daughter relationship, it is nonetheless a close bond. During childhood she is more likely to be pampering and indulgent with her son than with a daughter. Boys are less restricted, and there is more tolerance of them (Peñalosa 1968, p. 687). During adolescence especially, mothers are permissive with their sons, and their behavior is less regulated than the behavior of daughters. These socialization practices are indicative of a dualistic conception of appropriate behavior for males and females. The boy is a fledging *macho* who must be allowed to venture out of the home so he may test his wings and establish a masculine identity. Peers contribute significantly to the process of socialization into manhood. He begins to hang out with other boys, or *la palomilla*, and peer relations may begin to rival family ties in importance. These associations are prominent for the man and are retained even after marriage.

Adolescent girls are much more restricted and sheltered than adolescent boys. Throughout her life, a female is prepared for marriage and motherhood.

> The girl has been brought up in such a manner that she represents herself as a paragon of virtue, a woman fit to mother the children of a respectable male of *la raza*. Early in her life she was made aware that she represented her household group fully as much as she represented herself, an individual. In all instances her claims to enjoyment were made secondary to the claim of propriety. In other words, hers was a road carefully planned from girlhood to womanhood within the tight restraint of family discipline. [Rubel 1966, p. 77]

Premarital chastity is the zenith of feminine virtue. The norm of premarital virginity prevails, although its enforcement may prove more difficult today than in the past. Thus the behavior and character of the contemporary Chicana, like that of her ancient forebears, is circumscribed by role expectations which limit her activities to the domestic sphere. The exhortation an Aztec mother gave her daughter when the latter became of marrying age spelling out her wifely, submissive role might well be invoked today: "Cuando fuere Dios servido de que tomes marido . . . mira que no le menosprecies . . . no te atrevas a él; . . . te ve Dios que está en todo lugar, enojarse ha contra ti, y se vengará como él quisiere o te tullirás por su mandato, o cegarás, o se te podrirá el cuerpo, o vendrás a la última pobreza porque te atreviste y arrojaste a obrar contra tu marido, que por ventura te dará la muerte, o te pondrá debajo de sus pies enviándote al infierno."[15]

A persistent view espoused by Chicanos is that *la familia* is the basic source of emotional and physical support for the individual. This view is at variance with the cold, rigid, authoritarian family depicted by social scientists. Though the father may be somewhat aloof as the child enters adolescence, the mother in the family is typically warm and nurturant. The child develops close emotional bonds not only with members of the immediate family but with grandparents, aunts and uncles, cousins, and family friends. A study of young children, aged seven to thirteen, in the Houston barrio concluded that "in the child's-eye-view [sic] the central feature is home, and the people at home" (Goodman and Beman 1971, p. 111). One of the questions the children were asked was simply, "Whom do you love?" Significantly, none of the barrio children included anyone but relatives in their list of persons loved, whereas Anglo and black children included many non-family members, and friends played a prominent part in their listing (ibid., p. 112).

Machismo and Hembrismo: A Reevaluation of the Woman's Role in the Family

Now that we have presented the mythical social science view of the family and contrasted it with the family as seen and experienced by Chicanos themselves, we can begin to reexamine and reevaluate the bases of the social science mythology and concurrently the woman's role within the family. The social science myth of the family is not unlike most myths in that it has some grounding in reality. Myths, after all, are mechanisms employed by people to structure and order a complex world. Social scientists have taken the fact of male dominance in Chicano culture and amplified and distorted it so that it has become a deterministic, uncontrollable, pathological force. Rather than simply recognizing *machismo* as an important cultural trait and isolating its effects on other elements in the culture, they have instead turned this phenomenon into a sickness or disease that "explains" all that is wrong with Mexican-Americans. Other key elements in Chicano culture have been stereotyped and distorted to meet the ends and needs of social scientists. Concepts thus reified no longer enhance our understanding of Chicano culture.

Myths are not random, however; they are selective and frequently fulfill vital functions for the group that generates them. It is no accident that social science depictions of the Chicano, whether they involve the family or some other area, are almost inevitably pejorative and/or pathological, for they reinforce and legitimate the lowly status of Chicanos. The lack of achievement and the disadvantaged position of Chicanos are more readily attributed to some deficiency in their culture or family life than to their status as an oppressed internal colony. The myth of the Mexican-American family, then, is a useful myth in blaming the problems and oppression of Chicanos on themselves and their culture rather than on prejudice, discrimination, colonization, or the dominant Anglo culture.

The stereotypical view of *machismo* has its complementary opposite in *hembrismo*. The *macho* is depicted as powerful, assertive, and dominant; the *hembra* as weak, docile, and submissive. Anyone who has grown up in a Chicano family would scoff at the notion that the woman is weak, quiet, or submissive. If there is a persistent image of the woman in Chicano culture, it is that she is a strong and enduring figure. The family is undoubtedly the most important institution for Chicanos, and the woman in turn is the backbone of the culture. Although the woman is largely relegated to the home, her domestic role is not passive. She is charged with essential familial functions: reproduction of the species, transmission of cultural values and beliefs to the next generation, and provision of needed warmth, support, and affection for family members who must survive in a hostile environment.

We can now recast the woman's role in the family and in the culture. Whereas the female is viewed as passive, docile, and confined to the home, it is from within the confines of the home that her traditional activity has emanated. The *macho* is typically considered to resist oppression and colonization actively, but the woman in fact has resisted this force actively and equally via her own role. As the center of the family and mainstay of the culture and tradition, the Chicana has helped counter the insidious and pervasive encroachment of colonial institutions. The Chicano family has proved remarkably resilient and impervious to external forces, and the preservation of cultural values and language are a tribute to her at its center. But myths die hard in both Chicano culture and social science. The inherited rigidity of separation of roles according to gender originally implied a separate but relatively equal status for males and females in Aztec society. The female ideally found joy in her feminine role. Today, stereotypical accounts of her ascribe an enduring attitude to her that makes her role appear unequal to the male's. Social scientists insist on adhering to a timeworn notion of her submissiveness and subordination and are reluctant to discard it even in the face of evidence to the contrary. Two researchers were struck by their unexpected finding that the prevailing pattern of decision making and action taking among husbands and wives in Chicano migrant farm families was egalitarian (Hawkes and Taylor 1975, p. 807). After unsuccessful attempts to account for these serendipitous results by considering such factors as differential levels of acculturation and urbanization, the authors reluctantly suggest that "many of the traditional stereotypes of groups such as ethnic minorities noted in the literature and in public assumptions need more adequate verification. It is possible that more sophisticated methods of research may negate many of our previous assumptions" (ibid., p. 811). Other recent investigations similarly challenge the traditional social science view of the Chicana as a passive and submissive member of the family. An in-depth analysis by Leonarda Ybarra of 100 married couples in Fresno, California, representing a broad cross section of the Chicano population, revealed that while the families demonstrated a wide range of conjugal role patterns, most couples shared in decision making. There was, moreover, no relationship between level of acculturation, education, or income and the type of role relationship exhibited. After an extensive review of literature on conjugal role relationships, Maxine Baca Zinn (1976, p. 26) concluded that although the Chicano family is ostensibly patriarchal, it is in fact mother centered. This pattern may appear contradictory but is not, since "both sexes have responsibility in their own spheres" (p. 27). Men have power and authority relative to outside institutions, and women are responsible for the daily affairs of the family. Just as the world was divided into masculine and feminine realms in Aztec society, so there is a complex division of labor between men and women in Chicano culture, with each granted power and authority within their respective spheres.

Five

Work, Education, and the Chicana

From the preceding chapters it has become evident that works on the Chicana are shrouded in myths. One of the most persistent of these is that she is a meek and subordinate creature who never ventures beyond the safety and confines of the home. Values both within the Chicano community and in the society at large have idealized her domestic and maternal roles. While the Chicana has been critical in maintaining the strength and integrity of the family, she has also made important contributions outside of the home. Our discussion of the cultural heritage of the Chicana has pointed to numerous examples of women with extraordinary achievements. Yet in a sense these women are outstanding or unusual; they are deviations from the cultural norm. This chapter is therefore concerned not with the achievements of exemplars but, rather, with the labor force participation of ordinary women. The chapter presents an overview of the socioeconomic status of the contemporary Chicana and evaluates the implications of that status.

The colonization of Chicanos means that they are culturally, politically, and economically oppressed as a group, not as individuals. The oppression therefore cuts across native and Mexican birth, urban-rural residence, geographic areas, economic groups, and sexes. The collective condition of Chicanos, however, should not obscure internal differences in the experience of members of this group, nor should it obscure the specific oppression and exploitation of Mexican-American women. The condition of Chicanas has important implications not only for them but for Chicanos as a people, for they constitute a majority of the Chicano population. By almost any available standard, Chicanas are economically exploited not only relative to Anglo men and women but also relative to Chicanos.

Labor Force Participation, Income, and Education of Chicanas

A number of factors make the acquisition of reliable statistics on the labor force participation of Chicanas a difficult task. Until very recently government agencies have either completely neglected Chicanos or grouped them within broad categories such as Hispanic American, Spanish surnamed, or Spanish speaking. These categories include groups with vastly different experiences and economic conditions, such as Puerto Ricans, Cubans, and other Central and South American peoples. The Bureau of the Census has recently modified its method of classification to include a breakdown of persons of Mexican origin within the category of Spanish origin, but the Department of Labor continues to classify all Hispanic Americans as "white," arguing that about 96 percent of the Hispanic-origin population is white (U.S. Department of Labor 1977, p. 20). These euphemistic labels obscure huge internal differences among persons of Spanish origin. The median age of Cubans, for example, is higher, and they are better educated, have higher incomes, and are more likely to occupy professional and more prestigious positions than persons of Mexican or Puerto Rican origin. Compounding the problem is the lack of sensitivity of these agencies to the specific condition of the Chicana.

According to Department of Labor statistics, the unemployment rate for 1976 was 7.0 percent for white, 13.8 percent for black, and 11.5 percent for Hispanic-origin workers (ibid., p. 20). The downward trend in the labor force participation of Hispanic-American workers is seen by the Labor Department as resulting from differential labor force participation of adult women in each group: "In recent years, . . . the rise in overall female labor force participation has been confined to white women, while the participation rate for black women has shown little upward movement since the early 1960's. Hispanic-origin women— particularly those of Mexican and Puerto Rican origin—are somewhat more likely to adhere to the traditional homemaking role than are other American women and therefore have a lower labor participation rate" (ibid.). Yet Labor's own figures show that the rate of labor force participation of Hispanic women is roughly comparable to that of white women, although lower than the participation of black women. Specifically, 44.4 percent of Hispanic-origin women were in the work force in 1976, compared with 46.2 percent of white women and 52.4 percent of black women (ibid., p. 149). The labor force participation of Hispanic men, on the other hand, is greater than that of white or black male workers. The percentage in the labor force was 84.1 for Hispanic men, 80.3 percent for white men, and 75.1 percent for black men. Hispanic-origin persons thus have both high rates of employment and unemployment. This appears incongruous at first glance, but it is not, since all persons who are not in the labor force are not officially counted as unemployed. To be unemployed, according to the Labor Department definition, one needs to be out of work and actively seeking employment.[1] This definition has important implications in that it excludes persons who for one reason or another have given up hope of finding work and is therefore a very conservative estimate of the true rate of unemployment in the country. The index is especially apt to underestimate the level of unemployment among the poor, the aged, youth, racial and ethnic minorities, those in transient occupations, and persons with little formal education and few marketable skills. Ironically, then, it is the very persons who are least employable who are also least likely to be counted as unemployed. While statistics on the unofficial or real rate of unemployment of Chicanas are not available, there is little doubt that their unemployment level is grossly underestimated by official statistics. Many Chicanas do not actively seek employment because they are either lacking formal skills or training, are in transient occupations such as farm labor or domestic service, lack English language skills, are in the United States illegally, or have been subjected to prejudice and discrimination and have given up hope of finding employment.

A breakdown of Labor Department statistics by sex shows that the unemployment rate for Hispanic-origin women twenty years and older is about the same as the rate for black men and women, slightly higher than the rate for Hispanic-origin men, and substantially greater than the rate for white men and women. The percentage unemployed was 11.5 for Hispanic women, 11.2 for black men, 1.6 for black women, 9.3 for Hispanic men, 5.4 for white men, and 6.8 for white women (ibid., p. 149).

But what about the specific rate of unemployment and labor force participation of Chicanas? Is it possible that the low rate of labor force participation attributed by the Labor Department to women of Mexican

and Puerto Rican origin is offset by relatively high labor force participation on the part of Cuban and Central and South American women?

Table 1 presents Census Bureau data on the "Employment Status
and Major Occupation Group of the Total Spanish Origin Population
16 Years Old and Over by Sex and Type of Spanish Origin" as of March
1976. The table enables us to obtain the labor force participation of
Hispanic-origin women by dividing the number of women in the civilian
labor force by the total number of women sixteen years old and over.
These computations reveal that the labor force participation of Chicanas is actually greater than the average participation of Hispanic-
origin women and only slightly lower than the participation rate of
other women in the United States. The rate of labor force participation
was 44 percent for women of Mexican-origin, 42 percent for all
Hispanic-origin women, and 47 percent for all women in the population.
The highest rate of labor force participation within the Hispanic groups
was found among women of Cuban origin (48 percent) and the lowest
among those of Puerto Rican origin (31 percent). These figures effectively counter the myths perpetrated by the Labor Department and
others who feel that Chicanas "adhere to the traditional homemaking
role" and "therefore have a lower labor participation rate."

Table 1 also shows that the unemployment rate of Chicanas is very
high. Their rate of unemployment (14%) was somewhat higher than
the rate for all Hispanic women (12.5%), considerably higher than the
rate for Chicano men (10.5%), and much higher than the rate for the
total United States male (7.8%) and female (8.5%) population. These
data suggest that in the case of Chicanos ethnic background is more significant than gender in determining unemployment. That is, differences
in rates of unemployment between Chicanas and other women and between Chicanos and other men are much greater than the differences
between other men and women. It should be noted that the unemployment rate for Anglo men and women is even lower than the same rate
for all men and women, since black and Hispanic-origin persons are included in the computation of the rate for the total United States
population.

A glance at the occupational distribution in table 1 reveals over 90
percent of all Chicanas in the civilian work force are in menial, low-
paying jobs. The highest percentage (about 30%) are in clerical work,
22 percent are operatives, and 26 percent are service workers, while
only 6 percent are in professional and 3 percent in managerial and administrative positions. Given the low prestige of positions occupied by
Chicanas, it is not surprising that their earned income is on the average

much less than that of either Chicano men or men and women in the population at large. About 39 percent of Chicano men with income had incomes under $5,000 in 1975, whereas 75 percent of Chicano women had incomes below this level (U.S. Bureau of the Census 1977, p. 6). Table 2 indicates that the median income for women of Mexican origin with income was only $2,750 and the mean was $3,414, whereas the median for men of Mexican origin was $6,450, with a mean of $7,355. The low economic position of Chicanas becomes even more evident when one considers that fewer than 0.1 percent of Chicanas with incomes earned $25,000 or more, and only 0.6 percent earned between $15,000 and $24,999. In fact only about 4 percent of Chicanas with income had incomes in excess of $10,000.

The average income earned by Chicanas is less than the average income of all females in the population and all males in the population. The mean income for all females with income was $4,513 (median = $3,385), and for all males with income it was $10,429 (median =

Table 1   **Employment Status and Major Occupation Group of the Total and Spanish-Origin Population 16 Years Old and Over, by Sex and Type of Spanish Origin, for the United States: March 1976**

| | Both Sexes | | | | |
| | Total popula-tion | Spanish Origin | | | |
Employment Status and Occupation		Mexican	Puerto Rican	Cuban	Other
Person 16 years old and over (1,000's)	154,094	3,906	1,015	522	1,237
In civilian labor force (1,000's)	93,063	2,393	473	320	750
% unemployed	8.1	11.8	14.0	11.6	8.4
1,000's employed	85,533	2,110	406	282	686
Occupation (%):					
Professional, technical, and kindred workers	15.7	5.7	6.9	12.5	12.4
Managers and administrators, except farm	10.8	4.7	3.9	4.6	8.3
Sales workers	6.3	3.0	4.0	5.2	4.8
Clerical and kindred workers	18.0	13.9	14.8	16.9	21.1
Craft and kindred workers	12.8	13.4	10.5	11.2	14.1
Operatives, including transport	15.1	26.7	30.1	30.5	20.6
Laborers, excluding farm	4.7	9.8	6.1	4.9	3.5
Farmers and farm managers	1.6	0.4	...	...	0.1
Farm laborers and supervisors	1.3	5.9	1.7	...	0.4
Service workers	13.9	16.4	21.9	14.2	14.7

SOURCE   U.S. Bureau of the Census 1977, p. 27.

NOTE   "Other" category includes Central or South American and other Spanish origin.

$8,853) (U.S. Bureau of the Census 1977, p. 28). The overall income of Chicano families is also well below the national average. The median income for families of Mexican origin was $9,500 in 1975, compared with a median income for all families in the United States of $13,719 (ibid., p. 9). Once again, it is important to note that the median income for white families is higher than the median income for all families in the population.

Not only are Chicanas economically oppressed, but as would be expected, their educational attainment is minimal. Figure 4 graphically demonstrates the low educational level of persons of Mexican origin relative to persons of other Spanish origin and persons in the population at large. Some 24 percent of persons of Mexican origin twenty-five years old and over had completed fewer than five years of school in March 1976, whereas 18.7 percent of the Puerto Rican, 9.5 percent of the Cuban, 7 percent of the other Spanish, and only 3.8 percent of the total population had received less than five years of schooling. Persons

| | Male | | | | | Female | | | |
| Total popula-tion | Spanish Origin | | | | Total popula-tion | Spanish Origin | | | |
	Mexican	Puerto Rican	Cuban	Other		Mexican	Puerto Rican	Cuban	Other
73,260	1,912	453	237	549	80,834	1,995	561	286	688
55,246	1,517	301	183	419	37,817	876	171	137	331
7.8	10.5	14.3	12.0	8.4	8.5	14.0	14.0	10.9	8.8
50,924	1,358	259	160	384	34,609	753	148	122	303
15.4	5.5	6.1	13.4	13.8	16.2	6.0	8.1	11.4	10.9
14.2	5.6	5.9	5.1	12.0	5.7	3.2	0.5	4.0	3.6
6.1	2.1	3.8	5.3	4.7	6.6	4.8	4.5	4.9	5.0
6.3	4.9	6.3	10.3	10.2	35.1	30.1	29.7	25.4	35.0
20.5	19.1	15.0	18.0	23.7	1.4	3.0	2.7	2.1	1.7
17.0	29.0	27.6	21.6	18.5	12.0	22.3	34.5	42.4	23.4
7.1	14.3	8.5	7.6	5.5	1.1	1.7	1.8	1.4	0.7
2.6	0.6	...	...	0.3	0.2	0.1	...	...	...
1.6	7.8	2.7	...	0.5	0.7	2.5	...	...	0.3
9.0	10.9	24.0	18.6	11.5	21.0	26.3	18.2	8.3	19.1

Table 2　　**Income in 1975 of Persons of Spanish and Mexican Origin 14 Years Old and Over by Age and Sex, for the United States: March 1976**

Type of Spanish Origin, Sex, and Age	Number of Persons (1,000's)	Number of Persons with Income (1,000's)	$1–$999 or Less	$1,000–$1,999	$2,000–$2,999	$3,000–$3,999
Spanish origin, male:						
14 and over	3,415	2,935	8.4	7.2	7.3	6.8
14–24	1,214	769	26.1	14.3	10.4	7.0
25–44	1,323	1,307	1.9	2.2	3.4	5.0
45–64	698	689	2.8	6.3	5.6	5.9
65+	181	179	0.9	16.4	27.7	22.5
Spanish origin, female:						
14 and over	3,777	2,380	17.2	17.3	12.6	12.8
14–24	1,222	645	31.9	19.7	13.1	10.8
25–44	1,568	1,030	12.5	10.7	9.2	14.3
45–64	746	499	10.6	17.0	14.6	13.1
65+	240	206	11.0	44.5	23.2	11.0
Mexican origin, male:						
14 and over	2,067	1,817	8.8	7.9	7.4	7.9
14–24	756	522	25.7	14.6	9.7	8.5
25–44	798	789	1.9	2.6	3.6	6.4
45–64	411	405	2.1	7.2	6.2	5.9
65+	102	102	1.4	16.7	29.4	24.3
Mexican origin, female:						
14 and over	2,147	1,326	20.5	19.5	12.9	12.9
14–24	757	415	33.4	21.1	31.6	10.9
25–44	872	561	15.2	13.2	10.3	14.3
45–64	390	236	14.8	20.9	12.1	12.9
65+	128	114	11.5	41.6	25.8	12.6

SOURCE　　U.S. Bureau of the Census 1977, p. 29.

of Mexican origin are also far less likely to have completed high school: only 32.5 percent of Mexican origin persons had completed four years of secondary school or more; the corresponding figure is 51.5 percent for Cubans, 60.3 percent for other Spanish, and 64.1 percent for all persons in the population.

Table 3 contains a more refined analysis of years of school completed by persons of Mexican origin in the same period. When we look at persons twenty-five and over (who are likely to have completed their education), we find that the median years of school completed by men (9.0) and women (8.6) and the proportion of high school graduates in

$4,000–$4,999	$5,000–$6,999	$7,000–$7,999	$8,000–$9,999	$10,000–$14,999	$15,000–$24,999	$25,000+	Median Income of Persons with Income	Mean Income of Persons with Income
6.9	15.2	7.9	12.5	18.0	8.3	1.5	$6,777	$7,680
7.2	13.6	6.0	8.1	6.0	1.0	0.1	2,910	3,959
5.6	17.3	10.5	15.4	24.6	12.1	1.8	8,530	9,436
8.2	15.0	6.5	13.3	22.4	11.0	2.9	7,940	9,292
9.8	7.5	2.2	7.4	3.4	1.4	0.9	3,215	4,630
10.7	14.5	4.3	5.5	4.2	0.6	...	3,202	3,798
8.6	9.2	2.4	3.1	1.1	...	...	1,922	2,613
13.7	18.5	5.8	7.6	6.7	1.1	0.1	4,244	4,652
10.1	17.9	5.5	5.8	4.4	1.0	...	3,506	4,159
4.3	3.2	0.3	1.6	0.8	...	...	1,897	2,359
7.0	14.9	7.2	12.0	17.7	8.2	1.2	6,450	7,355
7.6	13.4	6.1	6.5	6.6	1.2	0.1	2,999	3,955
5.9	17.2	9.0	15.9	23.9	12.6	1.1	8,456	9,087
7.6	14.2	6.3	13.1	24.0	10.8	2.6	8,057	9,115
9.9	7.7	2.3	4.8	1.6	0.8	0.9	3,112	4,354
9.4	12.8	3.5	4.9	3.1	0.5	0.1	2,750	3,414
9.2	7.4	1.6	2.4	0.6	...	...	1,790	2,387
10.6	17.4	5.2	7.2	5.5	1.0	0.1	3,800	4,310
9.4	16.8	4.4	4.9	3.4	0.3	...	3,139	3,627
3.6	2.1	...	2.9	...	...	...	1,927	2,308

each group (34.6 percent men and 30.5 percent women) are about the same. The table also suggests that despite the push for women's equality in the society at large, the educational attainment of Mexican women relative to Mexican men has remained fairly constant over the years. If we look at the educational attainment of persons of sixty-five years and over, who are representative of earlier generations, we find that the median number of school years completed by men was 2.9 and the percentage who had graduated from high school was 5.0; for women in this age group, the figures were 2.2 and 3.9, respectively. A comparison of the educational attainment of persons sixty-five and

Table 3   Years of School Completed by Persons of Mexican
Origin 14 Years Old and Over by Age and Sex for
the United States: March 1976

Sex and Age	Total (1,000's)	Years of School Completed		
		Elementary School		
		0–4	5–7	8
Both sexes:				
Total, 14 and over	4,215	16.7	17.4	10.9
14–19	876	1.3	16.5	22.6
20–24	637	6.4	10.5	6.3
25+	2,701	24.2	19.3	8.2
25–34	979	8.6	17.0	6.1
25–29	564	6.0	15.4	6.0
30–34	415	12.0	19.2	6.4
35–44	691	19.7	21.5	9.2
45–64	802	34.7	21.2	10.0
65+	230	67.5	16.0	8.0
Male:				
Total, 14 and over	2,067	16.0	17.6	10.8
14–19	437	1.1	18.6	22.4
20–24	319	7.8	9.9	6.4
25+	1,311	23.0	19.2	7.9
25–34	460	8.0	15.2	6.1
25–29	282	5.7	15.5	4.7
30–34	178	12.0	15.0	8.2
35–44	338	18.7	22.2	8.1
45–64	411	33.0	21.7	9.4
65+	102	63.8	16.7	10.1
Female:				
Total, 14 and over	2,147	17.3	17.2	11.1
14–19	439	1.5	14.3	22.8
20–24	318	4.8	11.2	6.3
25+	1,390	25.2	19.4	8.5
25–34	519	9.1	18.5	6.2
25–29	281	6.2	15.3	7.2
30–34	237	12.1	22.4	5.1
35–44	353	20.6	20.8	10.4
45–64	390	36.5	20.7	10.6
65+	128	70.3	15.6	6.3

SOURCE   U.S. Bureau of the Census 1977, pp. 23–24.

Years of School Completed				Median School Years Completed	% High School Graduates	% High School Graduates, 1 or More Years of College
High School		College				
1–3	4	1–3	4 or more			
22.9	21.7	7.4	2.9	9.6	32.1	10.3
45.6	12.2	1.8	0.1	9.6	14.1	1.9
21.9	35.0	17.5	2.5	12.1	54.9	19.9
15.8	21.7	6.9	3.9	8.8	32.5	10.8
19.1	31.4	12.3	5.5	11.9	49.1	17.7
19.0	35.1	13.0	5.7	12.1	53.7	18.6
19.4	26.4	11.3	5.3	10.9	43.0	16.5
17.4	22.5	5.7	4.0	9.0	32.2	9.7
13.6	14.7	3.1	2.7	7.2	20.5	5.8
4.1	2.5	0.4	1.5	2.5	4.4	1.9
22.4	20.7	8.3	4.2	9.7	33.1	12.5
45.6	10.9	1.4	...	9.5	12.3	1.4
20.2	33.0	19.6	3.1	12.2	55.6	22.7
15.2	20.9	7.9	5.9	9.0	34.6	13.7
18.7	29.6	14.8	7.4	12.1	51.9	22.2
20.2	32.0	14.0	7.9	12.1	53.9	21.9
16.2	25.8	16.0	6.8	11.6	48.6	22.8
16.6	22.1	5.7	6.7	9.2	34.5	12.3
13.0	14.8	3.7	4.4	7.4	22.9	8.1
4.4	2.5	0.9	1.6	2.9	5.0	2.5
23.4	22.7	6.6	1.7	9.5	31.0	8.3
45.6	13.4	2.3	0.2	9.7	15.9	2.4
23.7	37.0	15.4	1.8	12.1	54.2	17.2
16.3	22.4	5.9	2.1	8.6	30.5	8.0
19.7	32.9	10.0	3.7	11.5	46.7	13.7
17.8	38.1	11.9	3.4	12.1	53.5	15.3
21.7	26.9	7.7	4.1	10.5	38.7	11.9
18.2	22.9	5.8	1.4	8.8	30.0	7.2
14.3	14.5	2.5	0.9	7.0	18.0	3.4
3.9	2.5	...	1.4	2.2	3.9	1.4

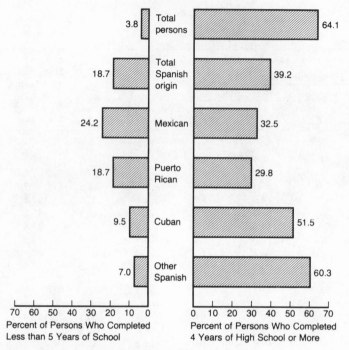

Fig. 4   Percentage of persons of Spanish origin
25 years old and over by years of school completed
and type of Spanish origin, March 1976. Source:
U.S. Bureau of the Census 1977, p. 5. "Other
Spanish" includes Central or South American and
other Spanish origin.

over with those twenty-five to twenty-nine years old, an age group old
enough to have completed their education but young enough to have
benefited from recent improvements in educational opportunities, suggests that the position of women relative to men has not changed
appreciably. Among men the median years of school completed was
12.1 and the percentage of high school graduates was 53.9, whereas
for women the median years of school was also 12.1, and the percentage
of high school graduates was 53.5. Thus, while the educational attainment of persons of Mexican origin has shown a marked absolute increase, the position of Chicanas relative to Chicanos has not changed
dramatically.

Differences in educational attainment between Chicanas and Chicanos and between them and men and women in the population at

large are even more striking. Among persons of Mexican origin twenty-five years of age and over, 5.9 percent of the men and 2.1 percent of the women have completed four years of college or more; in the total population, 18.6 percent of the men and 11.3 percent of the women have completed the same number of years of school. Chicano men are thus about three times more likely than Chicano women to have completed four years of college or more, while Anglo women are almost five and one-half times more likely and Anglo men nine times more likely to have completed four years of college. Interracial differences are much greater than intraracial gender differences. Anglo women, for instance, are almost twice as likely to have completed four years of college as Chicano men (U.S. Bureau of the Census 1977, p. 22).

Returning to table 3, we find a disturbing pattern—namely, that the gap in the college education of Mexican men and women appears to be widening. Among persons sixty-five and over 1.6 percent of the men and 1.4 percent of the women had completed four years of college or more; among those aged twenty-five to twenty-nine, 7.9 percent of the men and 3.4 percent of the women had this much schooling. Thus the benefits in the limited increased access to higher education in recent years have accrued mostly to men. Among Anglos, on the other hand, there has been a clear movement toward equalization of educational opportunities among the sexes. The proportion of those persons in the white population who have completed four years of college or more is 6.1 percent among men aged sixty-five and over and 4.7 percent among women of the same age; for men and women twenty-five to twenty-nine, the percentages are 15.5 and 13.9, respectively (U.S. Bureau of the Census 1976, pp. 10–11).

The low educational attainment of Chicanas has important consequences, for in American society education is said to be the key to success and upward social mobility for the poor and racial and ethnic minorities as well. Yet available data indicate that Chicanas continue to receive low wages regardless of their educational attainment. The median income for Chicanos who have completed eight years of school is $7,758, but for Chicanas who have completed this much schooling it is only $2,937, or only 38 percent of the men's income (U.S. Bureau of the Census 1977, p. 34). The median income for Chicanos who have completed four years of high school is $10,449, and for Chicanas it is $5,285, about 50 percent of male income.[2] The median income of Chicanas with a high school diploma, in fact, is lower than the median income of Chicano men with one to four years of elementary school ($5,489) (ibid.).

The low economic position of Chicanas appears even more alarming when one considers that many are heads of households and have to provide for dependent children. The problem is intensified by differences in the marital status of men and women of Mexican origin. Largely because men tend to marry at a later age, there are proportionately more single men of Mexican origin (34.5%) than single women (26.7%). While the proportion of married men and women is about the same (approximately 61%), Mexican women are more likely to be widowed or divorced (ibid., p. 3). The proportion of widowed men is 1.8% and of divorced men it is 2.8%, as compared to 6.1 percent of the women who are widowed and 5.7% who are divorced.[3] Thus Chicanas are about three times more likely to be widowed and about twice as likely to be divorced. Predictably, the median income of Chicano families with a female head ($4,569) is 50 percent of the income of families with a male head and the wife not in the labor force ($9,174) and about 35 percent of the income of families with a male head with the wife in the labor force ($13,182) (ibid., p. 45). These figures indicate that Chicano family income approaches Anglo family income only when the wife is gainfully employed.

To summarize, data on the labor force participation, educational attainment, and income of Chicanas reveal a consistent picture. The stereotype of the Chicana as a homebody is called into question by figures which show that her rate of labor force participation is almost on a par with other women. Yet Chicanas have a high rate of unemployment, and their educational attainment and income are lower than those of Chicano men or Anglo men and women. The low economic return for the labor force participation of Chicanas is typically blamed on their lack of marketable skills and low education, but the income gap persists even among Chicanas who have acquired more skills and education. While Chicanos have made modest absolute gains in obtaining access to higher education in recent years, the position of Chicanas relative to Chicano males and Anglo men and women has not improved.

The Socioeconomic Oppression of Chicanas

Ethnic minorities and women in American society have been victims of a collective economic oppression that tends to exclude them from the more prestigious, rewarding, and powerful occupations. American society and the economy are controlled, in other words, by Anglo males. The oppression of the Chicana is therefore threefold—as an ethnic minority, as a woman, and through internal oppression within her own culture. Yet her oppression is unique and not simply the additive sum of the effects of these forces. If the effects were additive, one would expect that her position would improve as the collective position of women and of Chicanos improved, but this has not been the case. In recent years Chicano males have made small gains and white women substantial ones. In fact it is fair to say that the primary beneficiaries of the women's liberation movement have been not minority women but Anglo women. Any analysis of the economic and occupational condition of the Chicana must not only take into account her threefold oppression but must also uncover those obstacles that stand in the way of her achievement.

Much of the economic oppression of Chicanas is external, emanating from the colonial oppression of Chicanos as a people. Since the war with Mexico Chicanos have been relegated to menial, unskilled jobs. They have provided the cheap labor in the Southwest that was used to develop agriculture, build railroads, and exploit mineral resources. With the advent of industrialization, they provided the cheap unskilled labor in factories and industry. Chicanas have fared no better, serving as farm laborers, domestic and service workers, and as unskilled laborers in canneries and other industries. Even contemporary Chicanas are limited mostly to service work, menial factory jobs, and low-level clerical and secretarial positions. Their exclusion from professional and managerial positions and from skilled trades has meant that one of the few areas of employment open to Chicanas, other than service work, is secretarial and clerical employment. For many Chicanas secretarial work has, in fact, become highly desirable: "For the Chicana the position of secretary is one which embodies in it all the aspirations of the American Dream. For the Chicana the alternatives are few enough, and filing papers and typing in an office is a far better life than working in a factory" (Nava 1973, p. 21). Channeling Chicanas into secretarial work helps to maintain a sexist occupational structure; yet for many who have dropped out of school and have little or no formal training, few realistic options are available. Secretarial and clerical work is not a panacea or even a legitimate long-run solution for the employment problems of Chicanas, but for some it becomes a desirable short-term solution in an employment market that severely limits their options.

In order to understand the economic exploitation of Chicanas further, it is necessary to provide an outline of the relation of Chicanos as a people to the educational institution, especially in the Southwestern United States; for education in American society is ostensibly the key to social mobility and economic advancement. The drop-out rate of

Chicanos in the Southwest is extremely high, higher than the rate for white or black students. It is estimated that out of every 100 Chicano children who enter first grade, only 60 will graduate from high school, whereas 67 black and 86 white youngsters will graduate (U.S. Commission on Civil Rights 1971, p. 42). Much of the poor holding power of the schools is undoubtedly due to the fact that the public schools do not serve Mexican-American children. There is reason to believe that the schools not only do not serve Chicanos but that in many ways they push them out. The U.S. Commission on Civil Rights, a bipartisan agency established by Congress to investigate allegations of denial of equal protection of the law because of race, color, religion, sex, or national origin, has carried out an extensive five-year study of education in the Southwest. The commission concluded (1974, p. 67) that the schools have failed to provide equal educational opportunity for Mexican Americans: "The findings of this report reflect more than inadequacies regarding the specific conditions and practices examined. They reflect a systematic failure of the educational process, which not only ignores the educational needs of Chicano students but also suppresses their culture and stifles their hopes and ambitions. In a very real sense, the Chicano is the excluded student."

While the various reports of the Commission on Civil Rights are a valuable source of information on the quality of education received by Chicanos in the Southwest, it is unfortunate that they do not focus in on intraracial gender differences in educational opportunity. In addition to language difficulties, inadequate curriculum, and other obstacles shared with Chicanos, the Chicana faces a number of unique problems. All Chicano children are likely to view the Anglo teacher as an alien being with values and actions that deviate from cultural expectations, but the Chicanita also finds that the teacher does not conform to her expectations of feminine behavior. She finds it difficult to identify with the teacher as a woman because the latter does not act like other women she has known. Women are expected to be warm and nurturing, yet the teacher is aloof, cold, and assertive. Those very qualities which the school seeks to engender are typically in conflict with cultural expectations of feminine behavior. The school seeks to develop independence, competitiveness, and self-assertiveness, while Chicano culture emphasizes cooperation, respect, and obedience to elders. These qualities are especially valued in females. Acceptance of the dominant values of the schools thus becomes especially problematic for Chicanitas. To the extent that they conform to these expectations by becoming assertive, competitive, and self-reliant, they deviate from their own cultural expectations. The gap between school achievement intensifies with increasing education, and the high-achieving Chicana becomes estranged not only from the parental culture but from peers as well. Even in college, the norm that boys should be smarter and do better prevails. The woman is still

> the symbol of tradition and of fierce mother love. In public, loyalty represses any open disagreement that she may feel in order not to disrupt the public image of the male authority be it her father, her brother, her boyfriend, or her husband. Success in the classroom involves analytical thought, investigative orientation, and an independent motivation as an individual. . . .
> These two roles work against each other in situations that require the traditional role in relation to men, and at the same time demand independently minded student [sic]. [Nieto-Gómez 1973, p. 49]

Anna Nieto-Gómez (1973, pp. 49–51) has isolated three dominant adaptations to this role conflict: the "companion," the "quiet Chicana," and the "vocal Chicana." The identity of the companion is always defined via a man; she is the wife, girl friend, or sister of some man. She many enhance the status or position of a man by virtue of her attributes, but she has little or no identity of her own: "In the classroom, the companion may play her traditional role by taking notes for 'her man,' while he listens attentively to the lecturer, she types all his term papers first. It is assumed that his beliefs are her beliefs or should be, but never the other way around. . . . Any public disagreement will be considered by his peers as failure to control 'his woman' " (p. 50).

The quiet Chicana assumes the traditional role even more completely than the companion Chicana. Her byword is that it is better to be seen and not heard. Although not necessarily inwardly insecure, the quiet Chicana comes to believe that vocal behavior inside the classroom or out is inappropriate. She may feel unqualified to speak or simply realize that class participation will be defined as aggressive and undesirable.

The vocal Chicana deviates from the traditional role by openly expressing her opinions. She disrupts the status quo and is likely to threaten not only men but other women because she does not act as women should. Her behavior is likely to be seen as unfeminine or masculine, given that aggressiveness and assertiveness are defined as male traits. The vocal Chicana is ostracized by her peers and may even have difficulty attracting boy friends. She learns that women whose behavior goes beyond "moderation" (as defined by men) are not considered attractive or feminine and may even be termed *agabachadas*, or women's libbers, because aggressiveness and vocal behavior are characteristics which are also associated with "liberated" Anglo women. She may also incur the label of frustrated woman because no man controls her actions. If she acquires a boy friend or husband, the expectation is that she will stay in her place (ibid., p. 51).

The overall pattern which emerges is one in which the educated Chicana becomes increasingly alienated from her culture. This alienation stems in part from the general lack of support for the education of women. Education is defined largely as a male prerogative. For men it is valued as a mechanism for improving oneself so that one can have a better job and make more money, but for women it is likely to be seen as unnecessary, superfluous, or even wasteful. While young unmarried women are expected to work to help out the family, ultimately they should marry and have children. Older sisters are frequently forced to drop out of school to help put a younger brother through school. Even if she is extremely bright and highly motivated, a girl's educational and occupational goals are considered less important, because she will eventually have a man to take care of her. The family is more likely to invest limited resources in the educational and occupational training of male children.

Even if a family can afford to send a girl to college, her entrance into a university is viewed with fear and suspicion. Parents may be apprehensive about having their daughters living in a strange and distant place that limits their own influence or authority (ibid., p. 47). Since the college environment is perceived as permissive, fears of sexual promiscuity and unwanted pregnancies may arise. Also, if the daughter has played an important part in the family, they feel her absence. The result is that the Chicana experiences severe conflict between familial obligations and career demands and pressures. She feels guilty about her failure to live up to family obligations, particularly if there is some family crisis (ibid.). Since the Chicana's identity is defined largely within the context of the family, college attendance introduces pressures that are not felt by men. To the extent that she ignores or minimizes familial demands, she is likely to feel guilt, but to the extent that she accedes to them, her school work is likely to suffer.

From the data which have been presented on the employment status of Chicanas, it is clear that there is a huge gap between the cultural expectations that parents have for their daughters and the reality which they eventually encounter. Despite the parental expectation that daughters will find a man to take care of them, most Chicanas will seek full-time employment at some point during their adult life, whether they

marry or not. Those who are single, separated, divorced, or widowed
will have to fend for themselves. Even Chicanas who marry will typically find that their husband's income is not adequate to support the
family and that they must find work to help out. The result is that many
Chicanas will be forced to work out of economic necessity, but they
will work mostly in menial, low-paying jobs (U.S. Department of Labor
1976, p. 1).

The myth that married Chicanas do not work is easily refuted by
data that show that in 1970 about 39 percent of all married Chicanas
worked at some time during the year (ibid., p. 12). This figure is only
slightly lower than the proportion of all Chicanas who are employed.
It is also significant that about 17 percent of all families of Mexican
origin were headed by a woman, and there was a very high likelihood
that such families would be poor. About 58 percent of all families
headed by a Chicana were below the poverty level (U.S. Bureau of the
Census 1977, p. 53).

The difficulties encountered by the university woman are but an
attenuation of problems which Chicanas encounter from the first day
of school. A number of forces operating within Chicano culture and in
the educational institution at large serve to alienate the Chicana from
education and eventually push her out of school. We have already noted
how the values which the school holds conflict with cultural expectations of feminine behavior and the difficulty Chicanitas are likely to
encounter in identifying with Anglo female teachers. Sex-role stereotyping is also very common in schools, so that teachers overtly or
covertly encourage the perpetuation of traditional male and female
roles. When the effects of sex-role stereotyping are coupled with the
effects of racial stereotyping, the results are devastating. It is expected
that Chicano boys will assume masculine occupations, but because
of their limited opportunities it would be "unrealistic" to counsel them
to enter professional and managerial occupations; instead, they are
encouraged to go into skilled trades and crafts. Very early on teachers
and counselors push Mexican-American boys into a vocational curriculum which includes things like auto shop, wood shop, driver education,
metal shop, and other industrial arts. Chicanas, on the other hand, are
encouraged to take homemaking, typing, retailing, and other courses
which prepare them either to be housewives or secretaries and clerks.
The point is simply that there is a hidden or unspoken curriculum that
tracks Chicano students into positions that maintain the status quo.

The problem of sex-race tracking is aggravated by a lack of adequate
vocational counseling for Chicanas. The Commission on Civil Rights

(1974, pp. 73–74) found that in school districts 10 percent or more Chicano, the overall counselor-to-student ratio was 1,123 to 1, and a very small proportion of these counselors (5.4%) were Mexican-American, whereas 28.5 percent of the students were Mexican-American. While the commission does not give a sex breakdown, it is safe to assume that most of the Chicano counselors are men. Throughout her educational career, the Chicana is without adequate vocational and personal guidance. The ethnocentric and myopic counselor typically operates with a double standard when it comes to counseling middle- and lower-income women. She is likely to encourage middle-class Anglo girls to break down traditional barriers and to gear them away from accepted feminine professions like teaching and secretarial work (Nieto-Gómez 1973, p. 45), but she will encourage Chicanas and other low-income women to enter trade school or secretarial school. In fact a popular rationale for such counsel is that more opportunities are present in technical and vocational areas as white middle-class women move into more desirable jobs. The military service is another alternative that is presented for minority women, for in the military they can also learn valuable trades. The net result is that counselors perpetuate the notion that Chicanas are only qualified to assume domestic or service work:

> The Chicana's opportunities are limited to one uniform or another. Cleaning bed pans, doing the laundry, ironing, and housecleaning are not new jobs for the Chicana. What has changed is that she may be able to charge more money per shirt, and there are more people who will hire her in her uniform. These educators do not see a need to increase the opportunities of the poor woman. Unfortunately when institutions begin to open their doors to women, it is not a victory for all women, but for women of a specific economic class. [Ibid., p. 46]

Even university Chicanas are faced with a system that is geared toward meeting the needs of Anglo students and has little or no sensitivity to her unique needs and problems. Not only is the Chicana less actively recruited than her male counterpart, but her needs are less likely to be met than his. As a result, the college drop-out rate among Chicanas is higher. The Chicana has unique needs and concerns as a woman, a Chicana, and a member of a low-income group. "She is a Chicana in higher education where most colleges and universities reflect anglo-saxon, middle-class, male oriented values" (C. Sánchez 1973, p. 28). She is likely to feel neglected not only by the university but by Chicanos as well. Faced with male teachers, administrators and counselors, and a curriculum which is male oriented, the Chicana finds herself badly in need not only of vocational counseling but of personal counseling. Most Chicanas believe that only another Chicana would be able to understand her situation and to provide meaningful advice, but Chicana counselors are few and far between. As Corinne Sánchez has observed (ibid., p. 31), "Chicana students need women that are aware and sensitive to their circumstances. And the need for bilingual/bicultural women who are aware is strongly recommended for Chicana students in order to provide guidance and encouragement. This is especially important in order to motivate young Chicanas into areas that will provide full utilization of her potential." If the college environment is to be relevant to Chicanas and to meet their needs, it is necessary not only that more Chicana counselors be recruited and that a meaningful curriculum be provided but that more *raza* women be employed as teachers and placed in important administrative positions. All too often the positions they assume are token ones.

There is reason to believe that the quality of teacher-student interaction is another extremely important component in the educational process. If education is to be a meaningful experience, it is necessary that students perceive the teacher as receptive to their ideas and that their contributions in class be recognized and rewarded. The Commission on Civil Rights discovered important differences in the quality of teacher interaction with Mexican-American and Anglo students. Specifically, it found that the schools fail to involve Chicano students in classroom activities as much as Anglo students. Teachers more often praised and encouraged Anglo students, built on and encouraged their contributions, and addressed them in a noncritical way. Given the overall lack of attention they receive, it is not surprising that Chicano children participate less in class both as a response to the teacher and on their own. In summary, "the total picture that emerges from this study of classroom interaction is one in which Mexican American students are ignored compared to their Anglo counterparts" (U.S. Commission on Civil Rights 1973, p. 43).

The commission study does not focus on gender differences, but such differences undoubtedly exist. Chicanas are probably even more adversely affected than Chicanos by the differential treatment of Chicano and Anglo students in the classroom. Given the cultural norm that women should be seen and not heard, one would expect Chicanas to be very inhibited in their classroom participation, especially if the contributions which they do make are neither acknowledged nor praised.

Fig. 5   Contemporary Chicanas. Courtesy of Tim
Gergen, Los Padrinos, Colton, California.

Another finding of the commission that is widely recognized is that
the curriculum in the schools of the Southwest does not meet the needs
of Chicano students (U.S. Commission on Civil Rights 1974, p. 4). The
curriculum is geared for the white, middle-class, monolingual English-
speaking child, excluding the language and culture of Mexican-American children. Textbooks are written from the perspective of the dominant group and omit, minimize, or denigrate the contributions of
Mexican-Americans. The commission found that fewer than 2.3 percent
of Chicano students had taken a Chicano studies course and only 1.8
percent a Chicano history course (ibid., p. 71).

If the school curriculum has neglected the contributions of Mexican-
Americans in general, it has completely ignored the contributions of
Mexican-American women. When Chicano history or culture is recognized, it almost always entails the contributions only of men. Chicano
studies and Chicano history courses are no exception. Thus a young
Chicano may know that Miguel Hidalgo was a great leader in the war
of independence from Spain or that César Chávez is an important
contemporary figure, but he is far less likely to have heard of feminine
counterparts such as Doña María Josefa Ortiz de Domínguez and
Dolores Huerta.

The need to make Chicano studies more relevant to women is as apparent at the college level as at the elementary and high school levels.
A number of Chicanas have proposed that Chicana courses become an
integral part of the curriculum. Some have gone one step further, arguing that at least one course on the Chicana be required of Chicano
studies majors. Such a recommendation came out of a workshop on
women at a MECHA[4] conference at California State University, North-
ridge (Nieto-Gómez 1973, p. 59). There is a need not only for courses
that deal with the general state of the Chicana but for those that focus
on more specific areas such as the Chicana in education, the history of
the Chicana, the Chicana and the law, religion and *la mujer*, and the
psychology of the Chicana (ibid., p. 58).

The need for such courses becomes even more apparent when one
recognizes that minority women are not typically incorporated into
women's studies, except perhaps in a token manner. There seems to
be general agreement among Chicanas that women's studies courses are
largely irrelevant to them (Cotera 1972, p. 24; Sosa Riddell 1974, p.
162; and Nieto-Gómez 1974, p. 44). Women's history books and

courses, for example, have been termed "Herstory." According to Nieto-Gómez (1974, p. 44): " 'Herstory,' unfortunately, also tends to exclude the history of the Chicana. Herstorians have ethnocentristically made women's history synonymous with the Indo-European Heritage. More often than not, indigenous women of the Americas are either ignored or tokenistically offered a sentence or two." The attitude of Anglo feminists has been paternalistic and chauvinistic. They have assumed that all the problems faced by Chicanas will be solved if they join ranks with other women. "The Anglo woman's chauvinistic attitude is: 'Look, we are achieving political status and we're going to liberate ourselves and then liberate Chicanas, Blacks and all the women' " (Cotera 1972, p. 24).

Chicana Education and Employment: Prospects for the Future

The data presented here on employment, education, and income paint a bleak picture of the socioeconomic status of the Chicana. Despite the prevalence of traditional norms which hold that a woman's place is in the home and that most women will have a man to take care of them, Chicanas are forced to work out of economic necessity; and because of limited education and training, they assume menial jobs with little economic remuneration. Recent years have witnessed substantial changes in universities and the employment market so that more women are gaining access to higher education and more desirable jobs, but the primary beneficiaries of these changes have been Anglo women. Chicanos as a group have also made modest absolute gains in these areas,[5] yet Chicano men have benefited more from them than Chicano women.

If the socioeconomic position of the Chicana is to improve, significant changes must occur in the society at large and within Chicano culture. Norms which relegate the Chicana to domestic or menial positions must be discarded in favor of those which recognize her true potential and abilities as a productive member of society. There must also be changes in the tracking of Chicanas by teachers and counselors into domestic and clerical occupations, and the school curriculum must be made meaningful so that they are provided with role models of exemplary *mujeres* who have transcended conventional norms of feminine behavior. Chicanas should know that their female forebears were not passive and meek creatures but active agents in determining their own destiny. Cultural norms which relegate the woman to a subordinate position must be modified accordingly. In short, before the Chicana can reach her socioeconomic potential, there is a need to demythicize her not only in the eyes of Anglo society but within Chicano culture.

Despite the bleakness of the data presented here, there is reason for optimism. There are signs which indicate that traditional barriers are breaking down and that stereotypes of the Chicana as dependent and nonproductive are being modified. With more Chicanas attending college and assuming nontraditional roles, new models are emerging for younger Chicanas who also seek to move out of conventional feminine roles. Young educated Chicanas are demonstrating that they can assume positions of responsibility and leadership commensurate with their abilities, without becoming masculinized or rejecting their family and culture. There is growing recognition of a new emerging Chicana who is educated and assertive and who successfully merges occupational and familial roles. As Chicano men become more secure, they are realizing that their women can pursue interests outside the home without theatening their own masculinity or the stability of the family. More and more, the employment of the woman outside the home is seen not as a disruptive force but as a meaningful contribution to the welfare and maintenance of the entire family.

Six

Images
in
Literature

We now turn to an analysis of the Chicana in literature, on the premise that literature is an organic and viable medium through which socio-historical and cultural views have been recorded. American travel accounts of the mid-nineteenth century are used to illustrate stereotypical reactions to *mexicanas* which reflect a cultural clash between Mexican and American attitudes toward women. Romanticized feminine stereotyping occurs in American fiction of the turn of the century and eventually assumes a condescendingly colonial perspective in social Darwinist works by more modern authors.

Internal colonization has historically denied Chicanos literary outlets, so it was not until the second half of this century that Chicano literature made its appearance. Chicano writers present new perspectives on Chicano culture, but a number of their works propagate a negative typecasting of women. It is only when they turn to those women who more immediately surround them—mothers, sisters, and girl friends—that a more accurate view of the role of women in Chicano culture begins to emerge. Despite its shortcomings, Chicano literature is distinguished from American literature in that portrayals of Chicanos occur within the confines of their own milieu. Familial and interpersonal relationships are presented for the first time from the inside out rather than vice versa.

While Chicano writers have made great strides

in presenting a closer, truer view of the Chicano in his own environment, their works remain circumscribed by a masculine perspective. Current works written by Chicanas themselves stand as a milestone in both the literary and cultural history of the Chicana. These writers supersede other portrayals in that they generally reflect a unique, more intimate, and more realistic appraisal than has previously existed. Stereotypical accounts by both social scientists and male writers are shattered by new images of the Chicana that ascribe forceful and independent characteristics to her. A fresh light is cast on male-female relationships, the Chicana as mother, daughter, and grandmother, and the Chicana in relationships with other women.

The Chicana in American Literature

The appearance of the Chicana in American nonfiction dates back to the 1840s and 1850s, when a surge of travelers invaded northern Mexico and recorded observations of the people and the places they saw. These accounts are generally distinguished by the careful attention male travelers in particular pay to the manners and dress of *mexicanas*. Such minutely detailed records might simply arise from a sort of cultural shock the traveler experienced, but an equally plausible explanation would be that Mexican women presented a rather extraordinary sight to the newcomer. Women emerge from the pages of first-hand accounts as predictably exotic and erotic and present the first examples of stereotypical depictions that recur in literature. Although their deficiencies are cited as frequently as their attractions, it is noteworthy that their exotic qualities often triumph when they are compared with their American sisters.

A peculiarly exotic practice that astonished American travelers was cigarillo smoking. When this was coupled with alluring physical features, a heady combination was produced that was nothing short of spectacular. According to Lewis H. Garrard in 1850, "though smoking is repugnant to many ladies, it certainly does enhance the charms of the Mexican *señoritas*, who, with neatly rolled-up shucks between coral lips, perpetrate winning smiles, their magically brilliant eyes the meanwhile searching one's very soul. How dulcet-toned are their voices, which, siren-like, irresistibly draw the willing victim within the giddy vortex of dissipation! And these cigarillos they present with such a grace, and so expressive an eye, so musical a tongue, and so handsome a face, that it is impossible to refuse. To use a Scotch phrase, 'It's na sae bad' " (Garrard 1955, p. 171). The attraction of New Mexican women is so powerful that Garrard proceeds to comment on how romantic the notion of a Mexican wife would be. "Sober reality" prevails, however, and he begins to reassess his reaction with a more temperate and partial eye. "From the depraved moral education of the New Mexicans, there can be no intellectual enjoyment. The only attractions are of the baser sort. From youth accustomed to a life of servitude and vitiated habits, we look in vain for true woman's attraction—modesty—that attribute which encircles as a halo the intelligent, virtuous, and educated woman. Surely 'twas pardonable pride in me to notice, by contrast, the superiority of those of my own country" (ibid.).

Garrard does not remain steadfast in his apparent conclusion that American white women are superior to their brown sisters, however. In a subsequent comparison of the attire worn by the two, the hooded and bonneted attire of the civilized lady suffers when compared with the apparel of the señorita: "A skirt is worn a trifle shorter than the present States fashion, so that it can hardly be called a dress; the figure, above the waist, is invested with a chemise, with short arms; but, so sparing were they of material, . . . the chemises were too low-necked . . . but the graceful señoritas de Taos were pleased to make a prodigal display, which, to my unaccustomed eyes and taste, was uncomely, and, in fact, satiating" (ibid., p. 174).

The attraction-rejection pattern Garrard displays in his description of women is not an uncommon one among Anglo observers. George Wilkins Kendall's response (1844, pp. 318–19) is reminiscent of it, despite the apparent "objectivity" of his appraisal. "On first entering the country, the Anglo-Saxon traveller, who has been used to see the gentler sex of his native land in more full . . . costume, feels not a little astonished at the Eve-like and scanty garments of the females he meets; he thinks that they are but half dressed, and wonders how they can have the indelicacy, or, as he would deem them it at home, brazen impudence, to appear before him in dishabille so immodest." Kendall's analytical mind and roving eye effortlessly merge when the stranger conjures up an explanation via a common Yankee expression that Mexican women "don't know any better." This commonsensical conclusion lends his observer's eye more leniency, and he is quickly weaned from the expectation that women should be clothed from head to heel; scanty dress is then easily reassessed as "really graceful, easy—ay, becoming" attire. The contorting, twisting, confining lines of the corseted American female are discarded in favor of his new-found friends. "The consequence any one may readily imagine: the forms of the gentler sex obtain a roundness, a fullness, which the divinity of tight lacing never allows her votaries. The Mexican belles certainly have studied, too, their personal comfort in the costume they have adopted, and it is impossible to see the prettier of the dark-eyed *señoras* of the northern departments without acknowledging that their personal appearance and attractions are materially enhanced by the *negligé* style" (ibid., p. 319).

Although the "*negligé* style" failed to engender modesty in Mexican women, it was for the most part excused and even appreciated by the traveling male. Puritan sensibilities quickly recovered from the assault of sensuality—manners and dress were acknowledged as different, comfortable, and feminine. However, the graceful undress male observers came to tolerate and even admire failed to make the same impression on a female traveler, Susan Shelby Magoffin.

> It was truly shocking to my modesty to pass such places with
> gentlemen.
>   The women slap about with their arms and necks bare, perhaps
> their bosoms exposed (and they are none of the prettiest or whitest)
> if they are about to cross the little creek that is near all the villages,
> regardless of those about them, they pull their dresses, which in the
> first place but little more than cover their calves—up above their
> knees.... I am constrained to keep my veil drawn closely over my
> face all the time to protect my blushes [Drumm 1926, p. 95]

The outrage the eighteen-year-old newlywed experienced was never altered. In fact, her severe initial comment that "Mexicans were as void of refinement, judgment &c. as the dumb animals" (p. 98) was modified only when, in an actual encounter with them, she could decipher that they called her a "bonita muchachita," a pretty little girl. She then remarked, "And now I have reason and certainly a good one for changing my opinion; they are certainly a very *quick and intelligent people*" (ibid.).

Women approached her carriage, shook hands with her, and offered her food which she found quite palatable. She concluded that "they are decidedly polite, easy in their manners, perfectly free &c" (ibid.). The politeness of Mexicans, who "are looked upon as a half barbarous set by the generality of people" (ibid.), is a quality that made its most lasting impression on the young traveler. She found this attribute manifest in the whole of the population and was especially struck by its embodiment in a young girl, a vegetable vendor, whom she took on as a protégée during her stay in Santa Fe. "She came in and we had a long conversation on matters and things in general, and I found that not more than six years old she is quite conversant in all things. On receiving her pay she bowed most politely, shook hands with a kind *"adios"* and *"me alegro de verte bien"* ["I am glad to see you in good health"]. . . . Just to see the true politeness and ease displayed by that child is truly (amazing), 'twould put many a mother in the U.S. to the blush" (ibid., pp. 130–31).

The Mexican qualities Susan Magoffin focused on rather than physical features are emphasized in other accounts by a doctor, a minister, and a prisoner. Each of these men, by virtue of their occupations or circumstances, presents a different aspect of the Mexican woman. In 1848 Dr. Adolphus Wislizenus, a recent German immigrant who made a "scientific" excursion into northern Mexico, says of the women of New Mexico (1969, p. 27) that they "are active, affectionate, open-hearted, and even faithful when their affections are reciprocated. Though generally not initiated in the art of reading and writing, the females possess nevertheless, a strong common sense, and a natural sympathy for every suffering being, be it friend or foe; which compensates them to some degree for the wants of a refined education."

The Reverend Walter Colton, U.S.N., lived in Monterey, California, for three years from 1847 to 1850. He noted that the character of the Mexican female was marked by singular exhibitions of charity and self-denial. "She pities where others reproach, and succors where others forsake. The motive which prompts this unwearied charity, is a secret within her own soul. . . . Be the cause what it may, it justly retains her within the pale of Christian charity, and entitles her to that sympathy in her own misfortunes which she so largely bestows on the sorrows of others" (Colton 1850, pp. 342–43).

James O. Pattie, who was imprisoned and fell ill for a time in New Mexico, spoke in 1831 of the devotion with which a sergeant's sister ministered to him. He describes her as possessing a "kind and affectionate nature" and says of her, when she made inquiries regarding his well-being, that "she assured me that she would pray for our salvation, and attempt to intercede with the general on our behalf, and that while we remained in prison, she would allow us to suffer nothing, which her power, means or influence could supply." She was true to her promise. Pattie continues that he "suffered for nothing in regard to food or drink. A bed was provided for me, and even a change of clothing. This undeviating kindness greatly endeared her to me" (Pattie 1962, p. 288). This individual instance of an attentive female appears in a more generalized form in Pattie's narrative, when he suggests that women were generally hospitable. "Although appearing as poorly, as I have described, they are not destitute of hospitality; for they brought us food, and invited us into their houses to eat" (p. 55).

Hospitality was indeed a characteristic common to all Mexican women. The earliest American explorer to record observations of New Spain was Zebulon Pike, who toured the area in 1807. He praised the daughters of old men who often invited his lads into their homes and provided them with "victuals and drink, and at night [gave] them the best bed in the house. In short, all their conduct brought to my recollection the hospitality of the ancient patriarchs, and caused me to sigh with regret at the corruption of that noble principle by the polish of modern age" (Pike 1965, p. 600).

First-hand accounts by travelers in northern Mexico provide a spectrum of observations ranging from mode of dress to the social qualities of Mexican women. Given the diversity of commentators and what they chose to record, we can only infer that those who doted on sensual deshabille, for example, make more meaningful statements about themselves than they do about what they saw. It is certainly true that the *mexicana norteña* unfailingly caught the eye of the American traveler, but perhaps what best explains the attention she was given is that she provided a very marked contrast to her puritan Anglo sister of the time.

While travel literature often focused on superficial aspects of the *mexicana*, like her dress or her manner in relation to her fellow beings, American fiction follows a more subterranean course. Under the broad headings of the romantic, psychological, and social Darwinist literary traditions, we find writers who often begin with similiar attention to superficial characteristics but then proceed to delve into deeper strata. Because their portrayals are still governed by typecasting, the stereotypes they produce slight the Chicana to an even greater extent than the nonfictive travel literature we have cited. This might be attributed in part to the fact that superficial cultural clashes had given way to outright conflicts between native inhabitants of the Southwest and the incoming American.

The foremost practitioner of romantic literature who takes early California as her subject is Helen Hunt Jackson. Her most famous work, *Ramona*, was published in 1885. Although the primary impetus for the novel was to offer a social commentary on the plight of Indians subsequent to the American takeover of Southwestern lands, it is at the same time the devoted study of a half-Indian, half-Scottish girl and her stern benefactress.

Ramona is distinguished by her ancestry, her flawless brown beauty, and her enduring sunny nature. She and her benefactress, Señora Moreno, provide an interesting contrast. Ramona is a half-breed whose unhappy conception remains a mystery to her and all those who surround her. The pastoral freshness she is endowed with is amplified by her personal virtues and lovely spirit. She is like a princess in peasant dress who is loved by all the inhabitants of the rancho where she lives. Señora Moreno, on the other hand, is far beyond the time when she was the toast of young men from Monterey to San Diego. She is a California aristocrat whose days of glory are quickly receding with the coming of the Anglo. She has scorned Americans from childhood and is especially indignant at their relentless land grabbing.

The original forty square miles her husband presented her as a bride have been pitifully reduced; despite successful claims and counterclaims, "she still was left in undisputed possession of what would have been thought by any newcomer into the country to be a handsome estate, but which seemed to the despoiled and indignant Señora a pitiful fragment of one. Moreover, she declared that she should never feel secure of a foot of even this." Americans are seen as thieving hounds who rob her of her security. "There was no knowing what might happen any day; and year by year the lines of sadness, resentment, anxiety, and antagonism deepened on the Señora's fast aging face" (H. H. Jackson 1885, p. 18).

Señora Moreno's bitterness at the encroachment on her lands is aggravated by the American takeover of church lands that she regards as almost sacred. Despite the harsh realities she must face, the señora's aristocratic background appears to endow her with uncanny resilience. The external burdens she must bear are balanced by the vigor with which she manages the internal affairs of her estate. She shrewdly manipulates her son, the ostensible master of the rancho, and accounts for every person, animal and product of her land.

In contrast, Ramona is a warm, loving creature whose circumscribed world has had but one intrusion—that is, a stay at a convent as part of her upbringing. The strength the señora's birthright gives her is nonexistent in Ramona until she falls in love with the Indian Alessandro. Revelation of her Indian maternity then empowers her to defy her benefactress and elope with her lover. She becomes as enduring a character as the proud and withered old woman.

Although Jackson's depictions of Ramona and Señora Moreno remain highly romanticized, they nonetheless reveal a quality of resilience that women must certainly have possessed in a period of history when hardships for *californios*, both Mexican and Indian, were very real indeed. Being robbed of one's land as the Indians were and then forced to uproot family and household would try a woman's endurance just as encroachment on long-held land grants would threaten an established way of life.

Whether it was digested as the social commentary Jackson intended it to be or simply received as a tear-jerking romantic piece, *Ramona* enjoyed great popularity at the time of its publication in the mid-1880s. Gertrude Atherton added to the romantic tradition with a novel, *The Californians*, in 1898 and a collection of short stories, *The Splendid Idle Forties*, in 1902. Both works are set in the period prior to and after the Anglo takeover and take the aristocratic class of *californios* as their subject. While Jackson focused on external forces as contributing to the social decline of the Californians, Atherton tends to see their decline as springing from internal psychological decadence. In addition, while the separatist tendencies Mexicans and Indians exhibit in *Ramona* are clearly for purposes of self-preservation, in Atherton self-preservation issues from merging with the conqueror through marital unions. The *californio* elite, if no one else, could be "salvaged" through marriage with the incoming American nouveau riche.

A more psychological assessment of Jackson's Señora Moreno can posit a set of social forces working on a psyche. She has lost her husband in a war with the Americans and is left with a son in his image on whom she dotes excessively; encroachment on her lands robs her of security, and the passing of an old way of life causes her to revert to Catholicism with excessive piety. In short, she is a portrait of personal deterioration caused by external forces and manifested in fanatic devotion to family, household, and faith in the face of change. Her rejection of Ramona also follows from a similar obsessive adherence to tradition. The señora's understanding with her deceased sister (Ramona's adoptive mother) that the girl should marry well, within her class, and with her consent is violated, so Ramona is forced to flee without her blessing. Atherton's Doña Jacoba in "The Conquest of Doña Jacoba" is reminiscent of Señora Moreno. She oversees her estate with the same critical eye and knows the ins and outs of its workings thoroughly. She treats her own children with the same coldness the señora exhibits toward Ramona. But whereas the señora's severity and coldness are externally caused, in Doña Jacoba they are inherent traits of character. Her personality assumes pathological dimensions in two scenes especially. In one, her son Santiago has just returned from study in England. He rushes impetuously to embrace her, but she keeps him away with straight, stiffened arms. She grips his shoulder and guides him to the family chapel to give a prayer of thanks for his safe return. Seven years of study in an English college in a Protestant country have eradicated his memory of the prayers he once knew. Her response is incredulous. " 'God! God! Mother of God! My son says this to me!'

She caught him by the shoulder again and almost hurled him from the room. Then she locked her hand about his arm and dragged him down the sala to his father's room. She took a greenhide reata from the table and brought it down upon his back with long sweeps of her powerful arm, but not another word came from her rigid lips" (Atherton 1902, p. 169). In a similar scene, the same outrage is vented on her daughter Elena. Elena's heart has gone counter to the family's expectation that she marry an Anglo; she has fallen in love with Darío Castañares, who has solicited her hand in marriage and been denied. The fact that she has dared defy the family's wishes by falling in love with the son of an Indian sends her mother into a fury. Doña Jacoba proceeds to her daughter's room. "Doña Jacoba shut the door and towered above her daughter, red spots on her face, her small eyes blazing, an icy sneer on her mouth. She did not speak a word. She caught the girl by her delicate shoulder, jerked her to her feet, and lashed her with the heavy whip until screams mingled with the gay laughter of the parting guests. When she had beaten her until her own arm ached, she flung her on the bed and went out and locked the door" (p. 193). The stereotype of the terrible Latin temper takes an extreme form in this scene. Doña Jacoba's children provoke a violent reaction when their behavior runs counter to her wishes. This reaction is a far cry from the stereotype of docile maternity.

In another story, "The Ears of Twenty Americans," a pathological mother once again surfaces. In this story Doña Eustaquia is a venerated and proud woman of Monterey who refuses to bow down to the Americans who have overrun the city after its official occupation. Loyalty to the former regime is not so demanding, however, as the personal loyalty she demands from her daughter. Despite acknowledgment that socializing with the invaders is inevitable and that her daughter is subject to their admiring advances, Doña Eustaquia permits her to embark on a whirl of social activities. She only asks that she never fall in love with an American. Benicia laughingly replies, "No, mamacita, when I love an American thou shalt have his ears for thy necklace" (ibid., p. 60).

Benicia *does* fall in love with an American, marries him, and bears his child. Her mother refuses to have anything to do with her for a time but then goes to visit her when her grandchild has been born. The daughter asks her mother's forgiveness, declares her love for her husband, and suggests that her mother no longer wants a necklace of American ears. "Doña Eustaquia frowned, then sighed. 'I do not know the American head for which I have not more like than hate, and they are welcome to their ears; but *the spirit* of that wish is in my heart, yet, my child. Our country has been taken from us; we are aliens in our own land; it is the American's. They—holy God!—permit us to live here!' " (p. 126). The invading Americans are not truly forgiven, and sadly, neither is Benicia. Like the wicked stepmother in "Snow White," Doña Eustaquia offers her daughter a poisoned orange to eat, to refresh her. The girl goes into convulsions, and she dies an agonizing death in her mother's arms.

Doña Eustaquia's pathological need to possess her daughter becomes a pathological need to possess jewels in another of Atherton's stories, "The Pearls of Loreto." Ysabel Herrera, the heroine of the story, is a young woman of remarkable beauty. As "La Favorita of Monterey," she is notorious for rejecting would-be suitors except the one who will satisfy her obsession to weigh down her lap with pearls. A young *caballero*, Don Vicente de la Vega, accepts her challenge. He embarks on an arduous trek to the desert town of Loreto, robs a madonna of her treasure, murders a priest in the endeavor, and finally returns to Ysabel with his bounty. "He strode over to her, and flinging his serape from his shoulder opened the mouth of a sack and poured its contents into her lap. Pearls of all sizes and shapes—pearls black and pearls white, pearls pink and pearls faintly blue, pearls like globes and pearls like pears, pearls big as the lobe of Pio Pico's ear, pearls as dainty as bubbles of frost—a lapful of gleaming luminous pearls." The insatiable Ysabel is delighted. "She ran her slim white fingers through the jewels. She took up handfuls and let them run slowly back to her lap. She pressed them to her face; she kissed them with little rapturous cries. She laid them against her breast and watched them chase each other down her black gown" (ibid., pp. 35–36).

Ysabel adorns her dress, her neck, her arms, and her hair with the sacrilegiously acquired pearls and proceeds to stun the guests at a ball with her sinfully enhanced beauty. Her triumph is pathetically short-lived, however. When Don Vicente's crime is revealed by a friar who enters the ballroom, she arrogantly acknowledges it, and the lovers then flee to a waiting ship. Violent coastal waves check their flight, and they are mercilessly dashed against the rocks.

The pride we have highlighted in the previous four tales is largely psychological in nature, but it is also inextricably linked to the stereotypically "Spanish" origins of the characters. Although Jackson and Atherton couch their stories in romantic settings laden with dashing *caballeros*, moonlight serenades, unrequited love, memorable dances, and even more memorable ladies, they create a stereotype of the Spanish temperament that is wholly unflattering to women. Three of the characters we focused on, after all, present a rather sinister portrait of the maternal figure that is quite rare in literature.

The psychological depths these two romantic writers probe may not be immediately apparent to the casual reader, but another aspect of their fictive treatment of women may be. This is typecasting. From the pages of romantic novels and stories come numerous examples of two types, the coquette and the seductress. Both of these types hark back to first-hand accounts which found *mexicanas* appealing, exotic creatures.

Atherton's "Ramble with Eulogia" fully explores the demeanor and power the coquette is capable of displaying toward males. In this story, Eulogia magnetizes the young men at a ball as she makes her entry.

> Eulogia's perfect little figure was clad in a prim white silk gown, but her cold brilliant eyes were like living jewels, her large mouth was as red as the cactus patches on the hills, and a flame burned in either cheek. In a moment she was surrounded by the young men who had been waiting for her. It might be true that twenty girls in the room were more beautiful than she, but she had a quiet manner more effective than animation, a vigorous magnetism of which she was fully aware, and a cool coquetry which piqued and fired the young men who were used to more sentimental flirtations. [Ibid., p. 215]

In the course of the story Eulogia beguiles a young American mining engineer, Charles Rogers. Her mother encourages a liaison because she sees him as an ideal catch, a rich husband for her daughter. Eulogia carries the intrigue to its expected conclusion and does in fact reap a marriage proposal from the engineer. When a friend asks her whether she intends to accept this proposal or another, however, Eulogia calmly replies, "Neither." An animated interview with her mother ensues in which she informs the latter of her decision. " 'Thou wicked little coquette!' cried Doña Pomposa, her voice almost worn out. 'Thou darest repeat to me that thou wilst not marry the Señor Rogers!' 'I will not. It was amusing to be engaged to him for a time, but now I am tired. You can give him what excuse you like, but tell him to go' " (p. 250).

Atherton's rather extreme depiction of a coquette who tramples on men at will takes on a more sophisticated form in Bret Harte and Harvey Fergusson. Maruja of Harte's story of the same name (1896a) is an heiress and an intelligent young woman who ultimately stands to offer a suitor more than he can offer her. She manages to discard suitors with grace. Magdalena of Fergusson's *Conquest of Don Pedro* is an equally unique creature who discards not suitors but a husband. Even before her leave-taking is a reality, her spouse wonders "that he should possess such a charming creature, wondering how truly and securely he did possess her. For Magdalena seemed to belong to life and to the world and to give something of herself to all who came within reach of her voice and hand" (Fergusson 1954, pp. 202–3).

The helpless doubt Magdalena's husband feels is typical of the response the coquette can inspire. Males are generally touched in one form or another by the magically magnetic powers of this creature, though few can touch her in turn or hope to possess her. The powers of the coquette are further heightened in that she is usually not a beauty; her strength derives instead from more purely feminine qualities like social astuteness, personal grace, the ability to submerge herself in others, and an overall tendency to give her personality rather than her passions full rein. It is ironic that this, perhaps the supreme stereotype of the *mexicana*, is applied to the most remarkable women in fiction. Eulogia, Maruja, and Magdalena appear to don the facade of the coquette to advance their own personal growth. And they are among the few fictive characters we shall see who do grow.

Whereas the coquette in literature is defined by a host of feminine traits, the seductress is often a mere compilation of physical ones and represents one of the most regrettable stereotypes fiction has produced. The emphasis writers choose to place on physical features or qualities is aggravated by the fact that these qualities become repeatedly synonymous with what is "Spanish" or "Mexican." In the social Darwinist tradition, such equations degenerate into labeling as a "species," and such species are generally a subspecies of the human race rather than a variation within it.

Bret Harte's "Pupil of Chestnut Ridge" is typical of this treatment. The young girl who is the pupil in question springs from "a lot o' poor Spanish and Injin trash" and is "a trifle dark complected":

> "She is n't a nigger nor an Injin, ye know, but she's kinder a half-Spanish, half-Mexican Injin, what they call 'mes—mes' "—
> "Mestiza," suggested Mr. Brooks; "a half-breed or mongrel."
> [Harte 1896*b*, p. 215]

Concha's racial background is but one aspect of her oddness. Her name, her dress, her features, and her presentation of self are all immediately scrutinized by her young schoolmaster, Mr. Brooks. It is diplomatically suggested to her adopted parents that she should be better dressed so as not "to awaken any suspicion of her race." He also notes that her oval face and small childlike mouth suggest little of "the aboriginal type in her other features," while the quick look of intelligence that comes into her eyes betrays a "slight consciousness of superiority to her protectors."

Young Brooks is at a loss in relating to this creature of strange appearance. Not only do her looks disturb him; he is also mystified by the activities she and the other children participate in during recess. He discovers that she dances for them, and while he is at once fascinated and alienated as he watches her, he ultimately suggests that this is a dubious pastime on school premises. The mixed reactions Brooks experiences to the woman/child Concha are of short duration. He comes to find out that an absence of several days from school is attributed to her elopement with a local boy, Pedro.

The entrancement of the schoolmaster in "A Pupil of Chestnut Ridge" follows a well-trodden path of fascination that frequently leads to actual seduction in fictive works. The gulf that separates Brooks from Concha is reduced to a mere gap in *The Conquest of Don Pedro*, where only the width of a store counter separates Leo Mendez from his object, Doña Lupe Vierra, a New Mexican aristocrat. "She was so close he could smell the perfume she wore, mingled with a vague odor of feminine presence. He felt a stir of desire toward her, and also of antagonism, such as any man may feel toward a provocative woman who stands beyond his reach" (Fergusson 1954, p. 33). This seductress almost assumes masculine characteristics as Leo fantasizes about dancing with her and putting his arms around her. "He had almost given up the hope of even that small favor when suddenly she fixed her commanding glance upon him from clear across the floor. He was impressed by her dramatic command of all the looks and gestures by which women communicate their forbidden wishes and seize the initiative which is supposed to belong to men" (p. 106).

After a fierce consummation of their love, Leo offers a discourse concerning the eroticism of the Mexican female. "Lupe came of a class and race of women for whom sex had been their whole profession and relation to life for centuries, and they had made an art of it and of every phase of it, from the first faint smile of flirtation to the final spasm. She was the heir of a great and erotic tradition but her silky skin and her gift of touch were her own. She was truly an artist of love" (p. 115). Skilled eroticism is assessed by Fergusson to be an inherent trait of the Mexican female. But if Lupe's sexuality is explained by a long tradition of dedication to pleasure, it nonetheless remains on some ethereal plane.

This is in contrast to another character in the novel, Dolores Pino, a purported witch, whose sexuality is typified by its animalistic inclinations. Although Leo is warned about Dolores, he appears helpless before her penetrating gaze. He is put in a trancelike state and reacts as one bewitched. "It seemed to him now that he had become only the carrier of his seed, that his only object and errand in life was to go to this woman and pour himself into her . . . he seemed to be only a walking phallus in search of a home" (p. 66).

With Leo reduced to a "walking phallus," we can only deduce that Dolores is the all-consuming womb. Indeed, the young merchant is compelled by her invitation and enters her silent, darkened hovel. "When he had put his hands upon her she did not laugh any more or say a word, but when he had stripped and mounted her she made a continuous guttural sound deep in her throat. It seemed to have in it nothing of her usual voice or of any human voice but to be a subhuman music of desire, of the pure and innocent lust that is common to man and beast" (p. 67). Dolores's bestial lust and sinister powers over the male represent a low point in portrayals of Mexican women in American literature. Were it not sufficient that she is possessed of sinister and primitive sexual prowess, Fergusson adds that she, like Concha, is a "mongrel" of mixed Navajo and Mexican blood, that she is a child born of rape, nurtured on hate, and a witch to boot. A more unsavory amalgam could hardly be conceived of as an exemplar of Mexican womanhood and femininity.

While Concha's and Dolores's "uniqueness" might be ascribed to their lowly "Injin" and Mexican mixtures, Atherton's Magdalena of *The Californians*, who is a mixture of noble Spanish and New England lineage, does not escape the "unique" label. She is not only introduced as "the unfortunate result of coupled races" and a rather uncomely creature but also suffers from offering a constant contrast to her companion, Helena Belmont. Helena is a budding "pure" American beauty with gifts of eloquence and personal magnetism. A description of Magdalena's physical appearance and demeanor more properly approaches that of a plain spinster than a sixteen-year-old. She "had a pair of dark intelligent eyes to reclaim an uncomely face. Her skin was swarthy, her nose crude, her mouth wide. The outline of her head was fine, and she wore her black hair closely below her ears. Her forehead was large, her expression sad and thoughtful" (Atherton 1898, p. 4).

Magdalena's depiction commences a tragedy that only begins with her ancestry and uncomeliness. Her friend Helena is integral to her progressively sad story. Although both girls are wealthy and have eminent fathers, Helena's is indulgent, while Magdalena's deprives his daughter of such frills as an adequae wardrobe or an education and travel abroad. Helena embarks for Europe, where she is to blossom into young womanhood. Magdalena remains to lead a humdrum existence that keeps her in San Francisco in the winter and Menlo Park in the summer. Her almost assured spinsterhood is surprisingly averted by the appearance of an Easterner, Mr. Trennahan. Trennahan has penetrated Magdalena's homely exterior and promised to give her the happy life she has never had when Helena returns and predictably steals him away. Magdalena's life takes a turn for the worse. Her father becomes a fanatic miser and "imprisons" his wife and daughter in San Francisco with no heat and a pitiful household allowance, and Magdalena remains in this state until a penitent Trennahan returns to reclaim her.

Magdalena's sad tale is a marvel not so much for Atherton's story-telling ability as for the inevitability of the plot. When so pathetic a creature is introduced as the heroine of a work of fiction, preparations for woe upon woe have already been laid. Perhaps the message of Atherton's novel is that as the representative of a deteriorating race, Magdalena is unlikely to find a niche in the unfolding American society, despite her Anglo maternity and her wealth and despite the moments of relief her creator offers along the way.

The austere life Magdalena Yorba is forced to lead in *The Californians* is in striking contrast to the debauched life of Steinbeck's characters in *Tortilla Flat* (1935). Seldom has a more motley crew been assembled than this unhappy collection of men and women who inhabit Tortilla Flat, a suburb of Monterey. A remarkable feature of this novel is that from one cover to another there is no let up in the drinking, whoring, thieving, and eating which the characters are capable of indulging in. Thus the Tortilla Flatters effortlessly join the ranks of social stereotyping as a "subspecies" of the human race. Males in the novel fare especially badly, but the women are by no means spared.

Without exception the women of Tortilla Flat maintain illicit relationships with men. All are single, widowed, or in dubious marital circumstances; and not one is a wife, a sister, or a daughter. Again without exception, all solicit men in one form or another. Among their notorious numbers we find Cornelia Ruiz, a brute of a woman who dispenses with old lovers by beating on them or cutting them up. Arabella, a local whore, is known for receiving gifts of silken underwear and then thanklessly taking up with sailors on the beach rather than with the gift givers. Mrs. Morales keeps herself in lovers because they believe she has a fabled $200 in the bank. The youngest and most noteworthy of Steinbeck's women is Dolores Engracia Ramirez. He says that she is "a lady" and that her conduct is "governed by very strict rules of propriety"—that is, that she does not chase after men. Instead, she hangs over her picket fence and allures passers-by. Her lustiness is reminiscent of Fergusson's Dolores Pino.

> It was a pleasant thing to see her when the beast in her was prowl-
> ing. How she leaned over her front gate! How her voice purred
> drowsily! How her hips moved gently about, now pressing the fence
> again! Who in the world could put so much husky meaning into
> "Ai, amigo. A 'onde vas?"
> It is true that ordinarily her voice was shrill, her face hard and
> sharp as a hatchet, her figure lumpy and her intentions selfish. The
> softer self came into possession only once or twice a week, and then,
> ordinarily, in the evening. [P. 154]

The analogy of the female and a feline in heat reduces her to bestial components, a device Steinbeck shares with Fergusson.

The *mexicana's* sexual aspects have been more subjected to abuse by American writers than any others. Despite the depths to which such treatments have been taken, however, writers do not limit themselves to sexual depictions. Frank Norris's Maria Machapa, for example, is a completely asexual creature, but she nonetheless manages to represent a low form of human life. She appears in *MacTeague* (1924), a novel in the social Darwinist vein which shares elements with Harte's "Pupil of Chestnut Bridge" and Steinbeck's *Tortilla Flat*. In the social chain Norris constructs in this, his masterwork, Maria clearly is its lowest link.

Maria works as a maid for the occupants of a roominghouse in a working-class quarter of San Francisco at about the turn of the century. She inspires a curious reaction from the other characters in the novel. "Now we'll have some fun. It's the girl that takes care of the rooms. She's a greaser, and she's queer in the head. She ain't regularly crazy, but I don't know, she's queer. Y' ought to hear her go on about a gold dinner service she says her folks used to own. Ask her what her name is and see what she'll say" (p. 20). What she says is, "Had a flying squirrel an' let him go."

Little information is given about Maria, but then little is needed to explain her. The labels that identify her—"greaser," "queer," and "crazy"—suffice because not only is she not developed as a character in the novel, she is shy of even being considered a person from the onset. Her trappings of lunacy are reinforced by the vividness with which she is capable of describing the gold dinner service. Whether people believe that the service existed and was owned by her once wealthy Central American family is irrelevant to all save one character, Zerkow the Jewish pawnbroker. Like Maria, Zerkow occupies the lowest rung of Norris's social scale, and so it is appropriate that *he* believes it did and does exist. Their shared lunacy leads to a relationship and their ultimate marital union. Zerkow's expectation that his wife will reveal the whereabouts of the dinner service to him remains unfulfilled in the course of several years. In a desperate and uncontrollable fit of rage, he slits her throat one night and then kills himself.

The progressively bleak picture we have presented in the foregoing pages reveals a pathetic series of depictions of the Chicana in American literature. From the coquettish señorita to the lusty whore to the lunatic, a series of portrayals unfolds that pays little tribute to Mexican femininity. Underscoring this series, which recedes into negativity, is the theme of an encounter between two very different cultures which produces a pattern of initial attraction that quickly gives way to rejection, seduction, and finally, relegation to inferior status of one by the other. In the following section we shall examine how the Chicana fares in Chicano literature.

The Chicana in Chicano Literature

Chicano literature as a corpus is a recently emergent phenomenon of the 1970s which has gained only faint recognition among established literary circles. Works like Villarreal's *Pocho* (1970), Vasquez's *Chicano* (1971), and Villaseñor's *Macho!* (1973) have been published by large, "legitimate" publishing houses and for the most part propagate stereotypical accounts of Chicano culture, whereas more masterful endeavors like Rivera's . . . *and the earth did not part* (1971), Anaya's *Bless Me, Ultima* (1972), and Arias's *Road to Tamazunchale* (1975) have been published by either Chicano presses or obscure American presses. Neglect by the publishing world has been aggravated by a tendency in mainstream literary circles to discount Chicano works as ethnic, esoteric, or of a lower caliber than American works. Moreover, this combination has all too often made it simple to regard Chicano literature as an unacknowledged stepchild of American literature. Nevertheless, despite this reception by publishers and critics, works by Chicano authors continue to be produced, are slowly gaining wider audiences, and certainly provide their own best argument for acknowledged stature.

Chicano literature as a whole can be distinguished from other literature in a number of ways. To begin with, the Chicano or Mexican-
American is taken as its subject and is dealt with in his own milieu. The
detached observer, so typical of American works, is replaced by a more
sophisticated eye and ear that uncover nuances in Chicano culture.
Chicano literature is also characterized by a greater tendency to realism
than has appeared in earlier American work—romanticized landscapes
like pastoral early California or a Spanish arcadia give way to barrios,
migrant camps, and rural towns as common settings. The characters
who people these new environs are themselves more believable than
their literary forebears—they can be fallible and vulnerable as often as
they are resilient and enduring. All in all, Chicano literature attempts
to capture the diversity of the Chicano experience with more empathy,
sophistication, and insight than has been characteristic of American
literature on the same topic.

There might be some temptation, given the foregoing, to assume
that because this literature is written by Chicanos, the authors are
automatically invested with some rare quality of omniscience with regard to their subject matter. This would be misleading. As mentioned
earlier, Chicano writing is not free of stereotyping or typecasting and
is even guilty of propagating a variety of notions about Chicanos and
Chicano culture which Anglo society holds. Just as significantly, although Chicano authors introduce aspects of the Chicana which American literature has overlooked, deficiencies still remain in their
portrayals. Before examining these deficiencies, however, the strides
Chicano writers have made in depictions of the Chicana should be
noted.

As is true of Chicano works in general, those that depict Chicanas
allow for a greater multiplicity of portrayals than we have seen in
American works. Consequently a range of women appear of different
ages, temperaments, personalities, backgrounds, and political and religious persuasions. Another difference between American and Chicano
work is that the former present Chicanas "where they are at" in given
environments, while the latter concern themselves with Chicanas
"where they should be at," with cultural expectations of the female
serving as a more or less constant measuring stick. The theme of the
woman in her place is prevalent in Chicano literature, but it is always
subsumed by the greater theme of rites of passage into manhood. The
ancillary status of women is balanced by the remarkable numbers in
which they appear in literature. Over all, Chicano authors should be
credited with producing literary characters who are truer, more credible,

and more closely akin to what Chicanas may be about than the creations of their American predecessors. But their achievements remain governed by a masculine universe, as are American works, and thus all is not well in Chicano literature. This is especially true of the dichotomization of women into "good" and "bad" camps, a motif that pervades Chicano writing. There are a preponderance of whores and prostitutes who serve as instruments for sexual outlet and hark back to one American depiction in particular.

Fergusson's *Blood of the Conquerors* (1921) dichotomizes women both racially and sexually. The protagonist, Ramon Delcasar, is a young New Mexican lawyer who sets his sights on acquiring an Anglo wife, Julia Roth. In the course of the courtship he maintains a purely carnal relationship with Catalina, the daughter of old Archuleta, a goatherd who Ramon esteems. Ironically, though he deflowers Catalina and is held accountable for this by her father, he refuses to marry her, making a decision that runs counter to his own culture from which he finds himself alienated. "Among the Mexicans, seduction is a crime which, in theory and often in practice, can be atoned only by the shedding of blood. Marriage is the door to freedom for women, but virginity is a thing greatly revered and carefully guarded. The unmarried girl is always watched, often locked up, and he who appropriates her to his own purpose is violating a sacred right and offending her whole family" (p. 143). Ramon's reaction to Catalina's impending maternity rejects her, her father, and cultural tradition. He takes the pregnancy as an offense to himself and broods that he has taken other girls, as has every other man, and that bad luck has unfairly befallen him. After a number of years, when he finally concedes to Julia's inaccessibility, he invites Catalina and their son to join his household, but she comes as a housekeeper, not as a legitimate wife.

The age-old norm that discriminates between women one takes to bed as opposed to those one takes home to mother is effected in Fergusson's novel and assumes even more dramatic proportions in Chicano works, where it surfaces as the good-bad woman syndrome. Prostitutes and loose women are a common fixture in Chicano writing and offer a continual contrast to faithful wives and devoted mothers. A classic treatment of this dichotomy is rendered by Antonio Villarreal in *Pocho* (1970). The opening scenes of the novel introduce us to Juan Rubio, an arrogant, calloused *macho* who has been a soldier in Pancho Villa's army and now returns to Juarez. He struts into a stereotypically outfitted cantina complete with a mariachi band playing sentimental ballads, a young girl dancing a *jarabe tapatío* on a table top, olés, mescal, and a host of whores. He takes a fancy to the young dancer, gruffly informs her that she pleases him, and orders her to sit and drink with him. She nervously obeys, cognizant all the while that her lover is in the room. Juan quickly disposes of this nuisance by killing him and proceeds literally to pull the girl out of the saloon and into a hotel. She dutifully removes his boots and after their love making timidly suggests that he has not asked her her name. "What does that matter?" he retorts. He mentally notes that "in a cantina, as in bed, courtesy was nonexistent" (p. 2). Courtesy is nonexistent and so is treatment merely as a human being, humanity being a quality which is denied whores. In contrast, when Rubio immigrates to Los Angeles and sends for his wife, he reflects about her: "He found a new respect for this woman, who had relentlessly followed him so many miles, and his nurtured ego made him love her for the first time in his life. He stopped his drinking and gambling and learned to be discreet in his love affairs" (p. 28). Juan Rubio as the reformed *macho* who wants to change for his wife's sake suffers many lapses. In another stereotypical scene near the close of the novel he beats Consuelo, threatens to kill her, commands her to get his things together, and abandons her for another woman.

The omnipresent loose woman resurfaces in Edmund Villaseñor's *Macho* (1973). Here she is again a discardable sexual object. Roberto, the protagonist, like Juan Rubio is a migrant who comes to the United States on a quest for money, "the god." His plight as a bracero is briefly alleviated by a live-in arrangement with a *gringa* waitress and by a Chicana girl friend, a deaf-mute. The mute girl remains nameless but is described as ugly, though "young and hungry." Her sexual hunger is part and parcel of the love she bears for Roberto, while his own hunger is measured by the number of times he can perform sexually in their nocturnal encounters.

> They'd get together in the fields between the rows of cotton . . . and Roberto would lay his *sarape* on the soft earth, and he would mount her. . . . One, two, three times a night, night after night, he would mount her, and she would moan and gasp and scratch and say she loved him by patting her heart, . . . and he would mount her again, and this night he took her seven times, until she died that small death so many times that she screamed . . . NO MORE! She was going insane, coming, going, dying, and the woman in her person was busted forever. Open, open, to all a man and a woman should be. [P. 105]

The fantasy of man's supreme sexual power over woman culminates in this passage. The author's encompassing statement that through sexual union "all a man and a woman should be" comes to pass is reduced to absurdity when Roberto regains his senses and remembers he is supposed to be at a poker party to help a comrade out. Ignoring the girl's beseeching moans and gestures, he tears himself away from her and walks away, never to see her again.

In a scene similar to Villarreal's cantina scene, Richard Vasquez again depicts the entrancing power of a young saloon whore. Hector Sandoval, a forty-eight-year-old man, fixates on a young beauty. "He stared, unconsciously going closer as he studied the girls. One in particular fascinated him. She had a low-cut dress, tight, and her full, youthful beauty sang to the eye. Her calves were exposed and shone an even brown. Black shiny hair fell to her shoulders, and her red mouth glistened. She was smiling as she talked to another man. She suddenly threw back her head and laughed, and her heavy full breasts seemed to want to explode" (Vasquez 1970, pp. 41–42).

Whores are an element common to almost all Chicano works, but they can be timid as in *Pocho*, clinging as in *Macho!* taunting as in Vasquez's *Chicano*, or enterprising, as is Rosa, another prostitute in *Chicano*, who helps Julio Salazar embark upon a taco-selling venture. Scarlet women are not exclusively of Mexican origin. A pubescent Anglo tomboy in *Pocho*, Zelda, succumbs to a gang bang rather than be called chicken by her male companions. Young Richard Rubio gains sole rights to her body when he beats her into sharing a hole where they hide during a game of hide-and-seek.

> For fully five minutes, they struggled in the darkness. . . . One of her eyes was badly bruised, and her mouth was bleeding. . . .
> "Jesus!" she said, and was frightened. He opened her shirt and stroked her breast. She stared at him wide-eyed. Then he was tasting the blood in her mouth, and as they sank down together, he could hear the boy who was "it" chanting, "Five, ten, fifteen, twenty. . . ."
> [Villarreal 1970, p. 141]

A soft, corpulent Phyllis Ferguson appears briefly in Raymond Barrio's *Plum Plum Pickers* (1969). Her opulently furnished "magic pad" is maintained through the "fees" she charges migrant workers. Fat, greedy Phyllis offers a sharp contrast to a skinny, aggressive *gabacha* who is humorously depicted in *Macho!*

> He swallowed, huge-eyed, and looked at her . . . truly seeing her for the first time, and his heart was moved with pity. There she was,

undressing, and smiling, and he, Roberto, could now see that her teeth had wires and silver on them. The poor girl. Her teeth were falling out, . . . there she was nude, and she was so skinny. . . . And now, there she was, doing something to her eyes . . . oh, *Dios mio!* she was taking out her eyes and putting them into a little metal tub, and . . . he swallowed. Terrified. There she now came. Naked, arms open, and with no teeth, and no eyes, and he glanced around for escape. . . . [Villaseñor 1973, p. 133]

The array of bad women we have seen parade across the pages of Chicano novels attests to the diversity of forms the male creative spirit can give them. The monolithic stance assumed by characters who partake of their favors is given a poignant turn in Rudolfo Anaya's *Bless Me, Ultima* (1972), where the prostitute is seen through the eyes of a young boy.

Antonio's scanty knowledge of scarlet ladies and good-time houses leaves him with only a vague impression of both. "The house belonged to a woman named Rosie. I knew that Rosie was evil, not evil like a witch, but evil in other ways. Once a priest had preached in Spanish against the women who lived in Rosie's house and so I knew that her place was bad. Also, my mother admonished us to bow our heads when we passed in front of the house" (p. 31). Both admonitions are cast aside in a crisis situation, however, when Antonio is forced to enter the gates of Rosie's house with Narciso to ask for his older brother, Andrew. Antonio appears to lose his innocence through association rather than actual contact as he approaches the house.

> Oh God! my soul groaned and I thought that it would burst and I would die huddled against the evil house. How had I sinned?
> "¿Quién? Who? Ah, Narciso, you!" It was Andrew. He threw open the door. "Come in, come in," he motioned. One arm was around a young girl. She was dressed in a flowing robe, a robe so loose it exposed her pink shoulders and the soft cleft of curving breasts.
> I did not want to see anymore. I pressed by forehead against the cold wood of the porch wall and closed my eyes. I wanted the cold to draw all the heat out of my tired, wet body and make me well again. The day had been so long, it seemed to stretch back to eternity. I only wanted to be home, where it was safe and warm. I wanted to hate Andrew for being with the bad women, but I could not. I only felt tired, and older. [P. 156]

Anaya's allusion to guilt by association introduces a point that needs elaboration. Such guilt is a phenomenon that issues from a culturally dominant, moralistic male perspective that readily condemns the bad woman as a contaminant. Interestingly, males who are involved in clandestine activities are themselves guiltless—"bad" men do not exist in literature, or even elsewhere, perhaps. But if it were not enough that the examples we have cited are laden with derogatory assessments of bad women, we also find that dichotomization does not always adhere to its neat distinctions of good and evil. A purgatorial land exists in Chicano fiction where normally revered daughters are accused of looseness simply by virtue of associations with men—a transgression of cultural strictures. Though this is a minor theme, it occurs in *Pocho*, where Richard's sister, Luz Rubio, is labeled a whore for staying out too late with her boy friend.

> Richard came home . . . to find his house ablaze with lights and his father in a rage. He had never seen him so angry. His face was livid, and when he spoke, saliva sprayed with his words and some trickled down the corner of his mouth.
> "My daughters will not behave like whores!" he shouted. . . . "What hour is this—three o'clock in the morning—for a decent girl to be coming home?" he asked. "Where were you?" [Villarreal 1970, p. 165]

The theme is picked up in a very similar scene in *The Plum Plum Pickers*. Margarita, a high school girl, seeks refuge with a neighbor after being physically abused by her father, Pepe, an old drunkard who accuses her of being intimate with Ramiro Sanchez. Ramiro finds her huddled in a dark orchard as she makes her way to Lupe's.

> Lupe took her in, and later she told him why. Pepe had actually accused her of sleeping with him. Worse, with being pregnant by him. . . . Pepe had grabbed her by the hair of her head and had slammed her again and again against the front door, banging her until she nearly passed out. His own daughter. Go on, yelling at her, get out, get to hell out of here, you puta. You prostitute, puta, the worst possible thing a father could possible [*sic*] call a daughter of his. Dizzy, her head reeling, hurt, grieving, she ran stumbling. . . . [Barrio 1969, p. 192]

As she makes her way from the shack, Margarita hears her mother retaliating in her behalf. " 'You brave borracho. Hitting a grown woman. Doesn't that make you feel brave though. . . . Come on, you coward. For this I raise my children? For this indecency I pick your stupid prunes? Bah—' She spat at him. A sick man, Pepe. Caught between the old and the new. The ideal and the promise" (p. 192).

In the two preceding passages Luz and Margarita are called whores by their fathers and subjected to abuse whether the label is warranted or not. The subject of their true or imagined looseness becomes academic when one looks beyond the quotes to their implications. On the most immediate and elemental level, the scenes are surely denigrating to Chicanas. In addition, however, they provide examples of negative stereotypes of Chicano *men* as raging, brutal drunkards. Relationships between father and daughter, husband and wife, and boy friend and girl friend are also attacked, so that the entire family constellation is brought into question. Finally, Chicano culture itself is reduced to a pathology of violence and foul language.

Despite the negativity of the foregoing, not all depictions of women in Chicano literature follow the same bleak pattern. Recurrent images of the mother, for example, represent a highly positive view of the Chicana. A well-known work that takes the mother as its subject is Jose Montoya's poem, "La jefita."

> When I remember the campos
>   Y las noches and the sounds
> of those nights en carpas o
> Bagones I remember my jefita's
>   Palote
>   Clik-clok; clik-clak-clok
>   Y su tocesita.
>
> (I swear, she never slept!)
>
> Reluctant awakenings a la media
> Noche y la luz prendida,
>
>   PRRRRRRINNNNGGGGGGG!
>
> A noisy chorro missing the
>   Basin.
>
> Que horas son, ama?
> Es tarde mi hijito. Cover up
> Your little brothers.
> Y yo con pena but too sleepy,
>
>   Go to bed little mother!
>
> A maternal reply mingled with
> The hissing of the hot planchas
> Y los frijoles de la hoya
> Boiling musically dando segunda
> A los ruidos nocturnos and
> The snores of the old man

Lulling sounds y los perros

Ladrando—then the familiar
Hallucinations just before sleep.

And my jefita was no more.

But by then it was time to get up!

My old man had a chiflidito
That irritated the world to
Wakefulness.

Wheeeeeeeeeet! Wheeeeeeet!

Arriba, cabrones chavalos,
Huevones!

Y todavia la pinche
Noche oscura

Y la jefita slapping tortillas.

Prieta! Help with the lonches!
Calientale agua a tu 'apa!

(Me la rayo ese! My jefita never slept!)

Y en el fil, pulling her cien
Libras de algoda se conreis
Mi jefita y decia,
That woman—she only complains
in her sleep.

This bilingual poem is a grown man's memory of his mother in a migrant camp as she began the daily ritual of lighting the fire, rolling out tortillas with her rolling pin, and starting breakfast in the darkness while her family slept. Warmth is conveyed through the predictability of her tasks and the mode with which she responds to her children. The tone of the poem also captures the awe with which the young boy marvels at his mother's stamina. She not only maintains a household but pulls her hundred pounds of cotton alongside her husband in the fields. The height of the boy's wonder at his *jefita* comes when he remarks that she is uncomplaining: "she only complains / in her sleep."

Mothers in Chicano literature are universally warm, enduring, and uncomplaining. Their home, whether a tent, a migrant shack, or a house, is their domain, and the hearth is almost synonymous with their maternal soul. Like Montoya, Anaya makes passing reference (1972,

p. 48) to Antonio's mother in the kitchen. "I heard by mother enter her kitchen, her realm in the castle the giants had built. I heard her make the fire glow and sing with the kindling she fed to it."

Ties between mother and son are incredibly strong in Chicano literary works and might be called a trait inherent in Chicano culture itself. A mother's endurance in adversity endows her with strength that sustains her children as well as herself. In literature, adverse situations often take the form of husband-wife conflicts which originate in a husband's irresponsibility with money, drunkenness, or a tendency to womanize. In the scene in *Pocho* cited earlier, Consuelo and Juan Rubio have a nasty fight, after which he leaves her for another woman. Rather than collapsing, Consuelo considers his leave-taking as a victory: "She began to talk of the new life they must make without him, and she sounded almost happy" (Villarreal 1970, p. 171). She gathers comfort from religion, looks for support from her son Richard, and asks him to join the family in going to church. With some apprehension, he refuses, knowing the torment it causes her. A compromise is struck which is at some cost to each of them.

> She accepted her defeat, and it was clear to him that as long as she could keep him by her side, nothing else mattered. Her love for him was so strong that even his renunciation of the eternal life was not too great for her to suffer. It was not too healthy, this thing, she knew. Yet it was bearable, because she realized that she had but a small part of him. She had lost her men—both of them. And already there was a look of mourning on her face—An emblem more convincing than if she had donned black garments. [P. 173]

The loss of a son also takes place in *Macho!* Roberto, frustrated by his family's poverty and his father's daily hanging out at the local cantina, abandons his village and heads for the United States. He rides his horse along the bank of a river while his mother wails her loss on the opposite side.

> And there came Roberto's mother on the other side of the river. Crying, and shouting, and praying, and bellowing like a cow with calf. SHE LOVED HIM. AND SHE WANTED HIM TO STAY HOME. To please, for the mercy of God, not go. Because he'd never return. She just knew it. And for two kilometers she followed on the other side of the moon-bright river, crying her love and fear and heartbreaking sorrow. Roberto began to cry and told her to please go home. But still she came, rosary in hand, bellowing her love. Finally she fell. Exhausted. [Villaseñor 1973, p. 69]

The fierce devotion of Roberto's mother is also displayed in *Chicano*, when young Neftali Sandoval is conscripted into an army that passes through his village. His father claps his hand over his mother's mouth to stifle her screams as she is pulled into their hut. "Lita and Hector Sandoval stayed in their shack all day. Periodically she would begin to wail, and he would comfort her, saying their son would be back. . . . But his face showed the doubt of his own words. Toward evening she went outside and looked about, exhausted from weeping. She sat on a large rock in front of the house and sobbed softly" (Vasquez 1971, p. 31). Her vigil continues far into the night, when Neftali miraculously returns and runs into her waiting arms.

Although the image of the mother in Chicano literature is a consistently positive one, variations do occur, as in the adopted or surrogate mother, for example. In a powerful short story by Octavio I. Romano-V., "A Rosary for Doña Marina" (1969), we are given Señora Marina de la Fuente, a childless woman whose husband left her in middle age. Now an old woman, she houses Lina, the orphaned daughter of a sister, and Pedro, her young second cousin, in her home. Doña Marina is fanatically religious and leads a deliberately routinized and tidy life. Whether her barrenness, abandonment by her husband, or even senility can be suggested as explanations for what ensues in the story the reader is left to decipher for him or herself.

Lina contracts an illness whose symptoms Doña Marina mentally diagnoses as those of early pregnancy. Once she has determined this, she embarks upon an odyssey of the mind that spells disaster for all three characters. Lina is taken to an abortionist to get rid of her nonexistent child, Pedro flees the house, and in a climactic scene Doña Marina takes axe in hand and destroys the bed where the transgressors have "sinned."

> "It was here, here," she screamed as she turned her wrath upon the mattress, digging the axe into the compressed cotton with dull thuds, ripping it asunder. . . . Her hair came undone and it hung loosely draped almost to her waist, the ebony strands hanging loosely down her back and partly in front, over her chest. She continued to flail at the collapsed bed until her arms ached and she could swing the axe no more. Exhausted by her scornful passion, she fell to her knees. The axe fell from her tired hands. With what remained of her ebbing tide of fury she beat on the ruined remnants of the bed with her clenched fists while the resilient black-coiled vortices undulated with a turbulent asymmetry. Her fists beat slower and slower until the immobility of complete exhaustion interceded. She slumped forward,

her long loose black hair draping over the remains of the bed, the cotton, and the still twitching bedsprings. [P. 90]

When her feat is finally accomplished, Doña Marina recoils in horror at what she has done and retreats into religion with even greater fanaticism. Her remorse never completely cleanses her of whatever twisted guilt she may feel. Some years later she comes across a number of family photographs with Pedro in them. She painstakingly scissors him out of group shots, shreds single portraits of him, and then burns them. This final bout of insanity leads the reader to surmise that perhaps Doña Marina bore a sublimated love for her cousin Pedro and that her lapse into madness was caused by what she perceived as a betrayal in his "relationship" with Lina.

The substitute mother in Chicano literature takes a very different form in *Bless Me, Ultima*. Ultima comes into young Antonio's life as both a second mother and an archetypal wellspring for his transformation into manhood. They establish a firm osmotic relationship from the moment they meet. Antonio takes her hands, looks up into her brown eyes, and notes that they are clear and sparkling, like those of a young child.

> "Antonio," she smiled. She took my hand and I felt the power of a whirlwind sweep around me. Her eyes swept the surrounding hills and through them I saw for the first time the wild beauty of our hills and the magic of the green river. My nostrils quivered as I felt the song of the mockingbirds and the drone of the grasshoppers mingle with the pulse of the earth. The four directions of the llano met in me, and the white sun shone on my soul. The granules of sand at my feet and the sun and sky above me seemed to dissolve into one strange, complete being. [Anaya 1972, pp. 10–11]

Through his apprenticeship with Ultima, Antonio gains an intensity of vision not only of the natural world but of the human sphere as well. He is instructed in the use of medicinal herbs and experiences the power of goodness as it triumphs over evil in an exorcism. Ultima is a *bruja*, but a white witch, and a *curandera* (healer) as well. While these define her "professions," they are superseded by what Antonio learns of the feminine universe through her. In a pensive mood, he ruminates about a primitive god in the form of a carp who inundated two former, short-lived worlds with fire and water. He wonders why a forgiving god should not exist. The Virgin Mary forgave those who killed her son. "Perhaps the best god would be like a woman, because only women really knew how to forgive" (p. 130). Antonio's apprenticeship is as much a rite of passage into manhood as an initiation into an androgynous mind and spirit.

In another scene, Antonio and his father speak of understanding as coming from the experiences of life. And understanding, his father says, simply means having sympathy for people. Ultima's power encompasses sympathy, magic, beauty, and goodness. Of her sympathy, his father continues,

> "Ultima has sympathy for people, and it is so complete that with it she can touch their souls and cure them—"
> "That is her magic—" . . .
> And that is what Ultima tried to teach me, that the tragic consequences of life can be overcome by the magical strength that resides in the human heart. [P. 237]

Antonio's relationship with Ultima comes to a close with her imminent death. He approaches her death bed and with sad urgency asks her to bless him. "Her hand touched my forehead and her last words were, 'I bless you in the name of all that is good and strong and beautiful, Antonio. Always have the strength to live. Love life, and if despair enters your heart, look for me in the evenings when the wind is gentle and the owls sing in the hills, I shall be with you—' " (p. 247).

A more permanent link between the feminine spirit and the male realm has probably not been made in Chicano literature. And the positive force with which Anaya forges that link represents a unique high point in depictions of the Chicana. The value of Anaya's portrait of Ultima, moveover, is that she combines archetypal and symbolic functions which are critical to the novel, but she is also very much a woman of flesh and blood who is an exemplar as much for Antonio as for the reader. Her powers, her access to magic, and her belief in positive forces make her a landmark among the characters Chicano fiction has created.

If Ultima can be seen as almost an abstraction of high femininity, Mrs. Rentería of Ron Arias's *Road to Tamazunchale* (1975) would then serve as her down-to-earth analogue. Mrs. Rentería is a spinster who lives in contemporary East Los Angeles. Although Arias's novel is doused with humor, his portrayal of the old maid is marked by pathos. A group of local residents gather to retrieve the unmarred body of David, a young man who has drowned, from a dry river bed. Suggestions are tossed around as to who should house him, and she disagrees, laying claim to him. " 'No!' Mrs. Rentería shouted, unable to control herself any longer. 'He'll stay with me!' Although she had never married, had never been loved by a man, everyone called her Mrs. out of respect, at times even knowing that word could hurt this small, squarish woman . . . 'David is mine!' she shouted for all to hear" (p. 58). Mrs. Rentería bathes, shaves, manicures, and changes David and then clips his hair. He becomes her lover-in-residence and is not only a perfect specimen of manhood but a perfect gentleman as well.

> And not once did he notice her splotchy hands, the graying hair nor the plain, uninspired face. During the warm afternoons David would take her out, arm in arm, to stroll through the lush gardens of his home, somewhere far away to the south. He fed her candies, gave her flowers and eventually spoke of eternity and a breeze that never dies. At night she would come to him dressed as a dream, a sprig of jasmine in her hair, then lay by his side until dawn, awake to his every whisper and touch. [Pp. 60–61]

Just as Ultima expanded the realms of possibility for human goodness, so Arias expands the possibilites of love in his world of fantasy.

In two portraits of Chicano wives, or, more accurately, portraits of a husband and wife, the authors begin on similar ground but achieve very different ends. Barrio's *Plum Plum Pickers* and Tomas Rivera's "Christmas Eve" (Rivera 1971) begin with women in similar circumstances. Lupe and Maria both have a number of small children; they are temporarily housed in a stationary location which is part of their annual migrant route; they are stay-at-home housewives; and both express some frustration about the effects poverty has on themselves, their children, and their lives in general. From these basic points of commonality, their characterizations begin to diverge. Barrio's Lupe is a pensive, brooding woman who carries a secret outrage about her environment. She is sick of a life-style that includes cockroaches, worn linoleum, second-hand clothing, a communal outhouse, lack of running water, no appliances, and a consistently meager income that ties her family to an unfulfilling day-to-day existence. There are no prospects for betterment in the future.

As a frustrated wife, she is subject to outbursts of anger at life's unfairness. The only things that alleviate her distress are a statuette of the Virgen de Guadalupe, a small host of potted plants she cultivates, and a kind-hearted husband who attempts to prod her out of her moodiness. On one occasion he returns to their shack, downs a few glasses of wine, and teases her with compliments. His good mood rankles her, and her bitterness comes flooding forth. "She snapped. She just didn't care any more. Anger shattered her usual selfcontrol [sic] and para-

lyzed her good sense. She slammed clothing into the old cardboard suit-
case that had been standing in the corner" (Barrio 1969, p. 89). She
routs her children out of the house and begins to leave.

> Holding the baby in one arm, the box in the other, she held the screen
> door open for the children to scamper through. As she turned to
> release the door, she felt herself grasped firmly around the waist,
> and lifted clear into the air. The box was snatched from her hand.
> "You put me down!" she screamed, kicking.
> "Not until you promise to behave," said Manuel. [P. 89]

Manuel sets her down and innocently questions her behavior, but "he
really did not see the many hurts and the many complications that
constantly chipped away at her reserve, her resolve, her plans, her
peace of mind, her dreams" (p. 90).

Lupe regains control of herself and decides to make tacos, Manuel's
favorite food; and he goes to the store for tortillas, bringing her back
a gift of potted geraniums. Despite breakdowns such as these, Lupe's
life proceeds in the same way. What Barrio is able to capture so well
here is not the optimism she is denied, or futile escapes from reality,
but a human being coping with an oppressive environment of poverty.
In a sense, this is also a depiction of a modern-day woman's adjustment
to the traditional role of the enduring wife, with all the difficulties of
that adjustment revealed.

Rivera's Maria is also a wife who adjusts to her role. After a history
of having her children receive only nuts and oranges as gifts for Christmas, Maria resolves to buy some small toy for each of them. She approaches her husband with the suggestion.

> "Look viejo, the children would like something for Christmas."
> "What about the oranges and nuts that I bring them?"
> "Well, yes, but they want toys. They won't settle for food.
> They're older now, and they are aware of more things."
> "They're not in need of anything. . . ."
> "Well, yes, but it's different here since they see many things . . .
> come on, let's go buy something for them. . . .
> "I'll go to Kress myself," [Maria said].
> "You?"
> "Yes, me." [1971, p. 129]

Her husband's incredulity at Maria's announcement that she will buy
the toys unveils her phobia of venturing out of the house alone. In a
past incident, she got lost in downtown Wilmar, Minnesota. She re-
affirms her resolve to him, he consents, and together they plot the
route she will take.

She rises extra early the next morning, takes care of her chores, and gets ready. Rivera then resorts to stream of consciousness so that we share her thoughts as she steps out. "I don't know why I'm so timid, my God. Downtown is six blocks away. I just go straight and I turn right when I cross the tracks. Then two blocks and there is Kress. On the way back I walk two blocks and then I turn left and then straight home" (p. 130). But Maria's mental journey to Kress and back home again has just begun. She has inadvertently left out the reality of terrifying obstacles she must encounter. She is mortally afraid of dogs, of being accosted by someone, of traffic, and of crossing the railroad tracks. What would ordinarily be mundane to another pedestrian are nightmarish to her. Even the movements and whistles of trains some distance down the tracks unsettle her, causing her to retreat several times before she finally musters the courage to proceed. Her fears multiply with each block she walks, and by the time she reaches downtown she is in a state of virtual panic. She dreads getting sick, as she did in Wilmar. In a zombie-like trance, she picks out some toys at Kress, puts them in her shopping bag, discovers a wallet, unthinkingly puts that in her bag also, and is promptly arrested by a security officer. The entire experience has gotten so completely out of control that the weeping Maria has a breakdown.

The deliberate, painstaking build-up Rivera gives this scene intensifies the underlying idea that perhaps Maria should not have ventured out in the first place—especially given her past experience in Wilmar. Maybe it was a crazy thing to undertake. She internalizes the notion that it *was* an insane thing to do while her husband reinforces the more "sane" notion that yes, she should have stayed home.

> "I think I'm insane, viejo."
> "That's why I asked if you thought you might get sick as you did in Wilmar."
> "What will become of my children with an insane mother like me? With an insane woman who can't even express herself nor go downtown? . . . What if they send me to the insane asylum? I don't want to leave my children alone. Please, viejo, don't let them send me; don't let them take me, I shouldn't have gone downtown."
> "Well, just stay here in the house and don't leave the yard. There is no need for you to go out anyway. I'll bring everything you need. . . . I'm going to tell the boys not to bother you anymore about Santa Claus. I'll tell them there is no Santa Claus so they won't bother you with that anymore." [Pp. 132–33]

The implications of this final scene between husband and wife are shocking. Although the husband is as well meaning as Lupe's husband, he is feeding Maria's phobias and reinforcing an age-old cultural norm that a woman's place *is* in the home. He is blind to the fact that there is something unhealthy about a timidity in a grown woman that approximates that of a young child. In addition, Maria's imagined insanity is catered to simply because it is not denied. Even the tremendous guilt she feels at not achieving her end is effectively heightened—the myth of Santa will be destroyed. She thus suffers a double burden of mental incompetence and an inability to carry out a simple task. Rivera thus presents us with a portrait that negatively reinforces acquiescence to a circumscribed traditional role, whether that was his intention or not. Unlike Lupe, who copes with an unfriendly environment, Maria's need to engage the real world head on is checked.

Chicano literature reaches a high point of expression in what we shall call the "spirited" woman. As a group, these women are generally young, enterprising, intelligent, and often consciously deviant from established cultural norms; most importantly, they identify with their ethnicity. The choices they make are often at some cost to their families and to themselves, but sometimes not. What perhaps most distinguishes this group from others we have discussed is that they represent a new breed of Chicana. Their very appearance in literary works suggests that male writers are capable of going beyond feminine stereotyping and creating notable examples of what the Chicana can be in literature. As representative of such characters we will discuss Angelina of *Chicano;* Margarita of *The Plum Plum Pickers;* Esperanza, Gloria, Lydia, and a *huelgista* (striker) of *Macho!* and Eva of Carlos Morton's "El Jardin" (1973).

Angelina Sandoval is Neftali's firstborn child, a second-generation Chicana who has been raised in an almost exclusively Chicano neighborhood in a community outside Los Angeles. Her assets of intelligence, ability to get along in school, facility with English, and even her fair skin are constantly begrudged her because they have been denied to her younger brother Gregorio. By rights *he* should have been the eldest child and thus endowed with them. Angelina grows up with the stigma of gender upon her. She is asked to drop out of school to help purchase tools for Gregorio's apprenticeship as a cobbler. When he is killed in the war, Neftali decides to sell the tools rather than pass them on to another son. The scene in which this takes place is too much for Angelina. She stands in the living room and accuses her brother Victorio of cowardice for not demanding what is rightfully his. She also lashes out at her father for interviewing every prospective boy friend who ever came to see her and expresses her resentment that at the age of twenty-three she has been relegated to spinsterhood. Victorio reminds her that their lives have always been governed by the Mexican traditions his father adheres to. She responds, "Oh, crap. I'll tell you how sacred the old traditions are. If things had been really tough, he'd have married me off to the first cholo that came along when I was fifteen. But I was able to work all the time. So that makes him extremely selective in my behalf. Now there's not a guy within ten miles who'll come near me, because he'll have to give a personal history to Dad or my brother. I've had it and I'm getting the hell out of here, and if you guys are smart, you won't come back" (Vasquez 1971, p. 77).

Her resolve to leave is momentarily shaken by her parents' reference to the biblical passage about honoring one's mother and father. Neftali also suggests that *gringo* ways have crept into her thinking. Her eyes well up, she holds back the tears and acknowledges that yes, perhaps that is true. She does carry out her plan to leave, however, and in the course of time she establishes a small taco stand that eventually flourishes into a prosperous Mexican restaurant.

Margarita of *The Plum Plum Pickers* is a rural contrast to Angelina. Although she is bright like Angelina and has the potential to do well in school, her social relations with her Anglo peers are in a constant state of tension. Anglo boys find her attractive and openly flirt with her, while jealous white females either scorn her or challenge her to fights. Margarita maintains her self-control and stays away from Anglos. At the same time, she finds it difficult to identify with her Mexican roots, as she has never been to Mexico and does not share her parents' memories of it. Straddling two worlds yet unable to participate fully in either, she reflects on her status as a Chicana. "What was the good of being born a perfectly good, honest, private, legal citizen of the United States of America if everyone was going to snarl Mexican to your face like it was some hateful word?" (Barrio 1969, p. 70). Margarita casts herself adrift from the real world and roams in a world of make-believe. She has an idle dream that a prince clad in blue will come and take her away. She also resorts to early morning reveries when she communes with nature. Her daydreaming is often punctuated by insightful questions—where did she come from, why is she here? Though she appears as something less than the mistress of her own fate, by the close of the novel she chooses the Mexican side of her identity and smilingly consents to be Ramiro Sanchez's girl friend. Although Margarita chooses to be a Chicana housewife, she will undoubtedly become the mother of a band of Mexican lawyers, teachers, jigsaw-puzzle makers, judges, and even the county supervisor, as Ramiro proposes.

Esperanza, a *huelgista*, and Gloria and Lydia of *Macho!* represent a different aspect of the rural experience. Esperanza is a young Mexican woman whose once fertile farm has been reduced to barrenness by volcanic ash and pollution from a nearby American power plant. The *huelgista* works for César Chávez, and Gloria and Lydia Sanchez are part of a now stable migrant family. A common characteristic of these women is that they all function and hold their own within an almost exclusively male world.

Esperanza, for example, is the protagonist's younger sister who is left in charge of the family when Roberto comes to the United States as a bracero. Roberto has a curious kind of respect for Esperanza, because he accepts her uniqueness as a female. "She was so different from other girls. She was smart and quick, and he liked her as a person, a friend, someone to talk to" (Villaseñor 1973, p. 31). Esperanza reads books, complains about the smallness of the town they live in, and uses strong language to express her discontent with her small world. He recoils at her language. "Esperanza, I forbid you to talk this way. God made you a woman. He had His reasons. You are not to question. Have respect! Is it not bad enough that I broke customs tonight? Ah? Is not once enough?" (p. 31). She responds by smiling,

> and her eyes went large and brown and full of fun and mischief. "If I were a man," she repeated, "I'd break all the customs every day!"
> Roberto began to speak, to anger, but then stopped . . . and held. Saying nothing. His sister was so un-girl-like. It was hopeless. . . . Poor thing . . . she was hopeless. She would never get a husband the way she behaved. Never. Hell, she was already sixteen and still single. [Pp. 31–32]

Roberto's view of his sister is dictated by traditional expectations of women, but he displays a rare kind of tolerance, if not acceptance, of Esperanza as she is rather than as she should be.

Although Roberto is depicted as an outrageously stereotypical *macho*, complete with gun, knife, and an animal-like disposition, his attitude toward his sister allows him to cast a unique eye on women he encounters in the United States. He is impressed by a young *huelgista* as she attempts to summon workers out of the fields.

> It was a Mexican girl on top of the old panel truck, and she was a sight to see. She wore black pants and black boots and had one hand on her hip, another on the bullhorn, and she was screaming, cursing, and laughing. Roberto smiled. There she was, tall and slender, and she was a *toda madre*, a real live mother, and many men stopped

their work. This woman, this girl was not asking them nicely to stop their work and come and join them. No! She was yelling at them, saying they were cowards, not men, if they allowed a *patrón* to rob them of their dignity. [P. 161]

Similarly, he listens as Gloria, the elder of the Sanchez sisters, speaks out against the disparity of wages earned by farmworkers and the mainstream labor force. He passes no judgment on Gloria's brusqueness as she tries to rattle him out of his apathy. He is duly impressed by her articulateness and the fact that she has a scholarship at a junior college. Lydia Sanchez does not share her sister's mental or political zeal, but she is unusual in that she can pick as fast as any man, loves sports, and is on her high school's track team. Both sisters combine their differentness with feminine grace, and both still retain many aspects from their cultural heritage. They cook with their mother, make tortillas, do housework, are polite in their dealings with outsiders, and are clean and tidy. Their awareness of themselves as Chicanas is heightened by the inequalities they see around them daily, and in a very real sense, they represent a merger of liberated and traditional aspects. As such, they come as close to real-life exemplars of a new breed of Chicana as can be found in Chicano literature.

A final figure to be examined is Eva, a character in a play, "El Jardin." Eva is Eve of the Garden of Eden, but a completely contemporary version, and she is of course a unique version as well. Eva is blatantly materialistic, brazenly sensual, and insistent on acquiring knowledge.

In the opening scene, Adán reprimands her for talking to the *serpiente*.

> EVA. He has such a nice slick body . . . he's soooooo
> slllliiiiiiimmmmmyy!
> ADAN. [*Crossing himself.*] ¡Madre mía! ¡Mira que ruca ésta! What difference does his body make? You should judge a man by his spirit!
> EVA. That's your way of thinking ése, I'm more inclined towards the flesh.
> ADAN. It turns you on, huh! Well it doesn't excite me. You are a carnal creature, Eva. . . . Oh Lord. . . . If I catch that snake around here again, ésa, I'm going to wring it around your neck.
> EVA. The way he slides, slithers, on the ground. . . .
> Uuuuummmmmm . . . He's so evil!
> ADAN. ¿Pero cómo puedes ser tan pendeja? Don't you know that he'll lead you into temptation?
> EVA. ALL I KNOW is that he wants to teach me about life, about knowledge. [C. Morton 1973, p. 8]

Adán and Eva continue their bickering, but she remains unmoved by the dangers he warns her of in associating with the serpent. She voices her dissatisfaction with Paradise—everything is so monotonous and so boring! Adán again tries to persuade her that this is the best of all possible worlds. One should not question why they are there.

> Eva. That's just it, you never question. You obey blindly and never think for yourself. You are but an extension of him. Who wears the pantalones around here? We're still wearing diapers. [P. 11]

Eva remains adamant in her insistence to know more. Her headstrong nature is of course the cause of her demise, but what is noteworthy about Morton's character is that in Eva we have an image of a woman who protests, a woman with spirit.

The images of women we have seen in Chicano writing display a variety of harlots, mothers and mother substitutes, wives, sisters, daughters, and spirited women. Depictions range from blanket categorization as good or bad women to more subtle inferences of what is and what is not acceptable female behavior. The stereotyping we saw in American works is somewhat alleviated by Chicano authors who present characters like Ultima, Gloria and Lydia Sanchez, and Eva as unique examples of the Chicana. While these characters are literary milestones, they nonetheless remain ensconced in a male superstructure governed by a male consciousness.

The Chicana in Chicana Literature

Chicana literature, like Chicano literature, has only recently come into existence and shares with it a number of problems. That is, it suffers from a lack of exposure in major publishing circles and is perhaps considered less than legitimate by some critics. Furthermore, although writings by Chicanas are frequently found in Chicano anthologies, journals, newspapers, and literary magazines, a major compilation of their work has yet to emerge.

Although Chicana writers as a group have not attained the prominence their male counterparts have achieved, there exist a host of examples of notable contributions by Chicanas to literature. Despite its limited bulk, Chicana literature has probed deeper and more perceptively into the female situation and psyche than its American and Chicano predecessors.

Chicana writers address themselves to dilemmas of Chicano/American identity, male-female relationships, female roles within the family, and even female-female relationships. These subjects are marked by the intimate urgency of the first-person narrator in many cases; they refute prevalent stereotypes of women; and they allow for surprisingly lifelike characters in real-life situations. Interestingly, specific points in time and space—that is, either a historical backdrop or real locations—are not infrequently missing in Chicana writing. Landscapes or settings can be a more symbolic fabric against which characters and situations are played rather than real geographic entities. At the same time, personal experience and an autobiographical tendency in this fiction does away with detached acounts. Thematically, interfamilial relationships assume rich new dimensions; male-female relationships are conveyed via abstract expression and images; and the new frontier of female relationships is treated with astounding force that pushes back the literary perimeters American and Chicano authors have only begun to define.

If a general statement can be made about Chicana literature, we might say that is touches virtually every aspect of the Chicana experience with remarkable sympathy, intensity, acuity, and realism. Not only is the Chicana voice an urgent one—it ushers from a diversity of women writers who are both young and old, educated and not, content and angry, and naive and experienced. Chicana literature is coming of age, and it captures the realities of the Chicana experience with greater force and dynamism than works that have preceded it. This might suggest that through literature Chicana writers are making headway in breaking oppressive barriers in the greater society and in their culture as well.

Because there are such a great number of Chicana writers, it would be futile to attempt an author-by-author description of works, particularly since many Chicanas are distinguished by the quality rather than the quantity of their works. There will also be glaring omissions of some noteworthy writers. Our focus here, however, will be on the broad topic we have touched upon, of interfamilial and interpersonal relationships.

One theme with which Chicanas have been concerned is assimilation into mainstream Anglo culture. A Chicano writer like Raymond Barrio touches on this in his portrayal of Margarita, who straddled both cultures and finally chose her Chicano side, as does Richard Vasquez in his characterization of Mariana. Margarita and Mariana represent studies of Chicanas who confront and challenge American values and expectations, particularly as those values demand rejection or subordination of their own culture. Barrio's and Vasquez's depictions are thus situations of choice. Acculturation as treated by Chicana writers is cast in a very different light. Its "problematic" aspects are collapsed, and there is little sense of a choice being made. Instead, the insidious and very profound influence of Anglo culture on the language, education, and life-style of the Chicana is acknowledged. Georgia M. Cobos, a writer and teacher, comments on the destructive powers the educational environment can have on the ethnic pride of Chicano children in a poem entitled "Suffer Little Children" (1969).

> Pride and love are lost within the yellow cumulative folder—
> That one which limits and relegates my boys to hoods
> and slaves,
> And my girls to early ugliness and pain.
>
> Pride is gone forever from a well equipped science lab—
> When the young scientist can not read;
> From a geography shelf, from a globe, a map, a bowl of flowers
> When their only purpose is destruction
> And the consequence—a silent unexplained punishment.
>
> Pride runs cold as Andres scribbles their names
> Upon a wall with a broken window.
> THEY BROKE IT! ONCE IN THEY WROTE THE CRY:
> "KNOW ME. I AM SOMEONE!" [P. 37]

Cobos is equally judgmental about insistence that children reject their mother tongue:

> Pride becomes shame
> As the tones of a mother tongue
> Learned from a lullaby or a *consejo*
> Are wrested and snatched
> From babes who would use them. [P. 38]

While Cobos speaks from first-hand experience as a teacher, Mónica Zamora (1974) writes as a student who is puzzled by the passing of a parent-instilled language and culture which is being submerged by Anglo society.

> Ya no aprendo mucho de mi Lengua
> Porque yo cresí en una gringa sociedad.
> A dónde se fue mi Cultura?
> Ojala que podré hallar la. . . .[1]

The impact of acculturation at the elementary and secondary school levels assumes a more sinister aspect at the university level in Adaljiza Sosa Riddell's autobiographical poem, "Como duele." A taunting, mocking dialectical tone is directed at *vatos* (young dudes) from the barrio who have shed their eagle jackets and now strut through the halls of academie or the battlefields of war. The same accusatory tone blames American societal manipulation for their unnatural transplantation out of the barrio.

> ... Where were you when
> I was looking for myself?
> As if I didn't know.
> Where the MAN and
> all his pendejadas
> sent you,
> > To Dartmouth, Los Angeles City College,
> > Barber's School, La Pinta,
> > Korea, and Vietnam; too many of you
> > returned wrapped como enchiladas
> > in red, white, and blue. [Calvillo Schmidt 1973*b*][2]

The fatal merger of the Mexican enchilada with the American flag is a stunning sociopoetic image.

Though the writer herself participates in higher education—"I was at Berkeley"—she was among the few and looked for the few *vatos* there. Her search was not in earnest, however, and she catches herself recognizing that "I'm not even sure / that I really looked for you." This admission makes the writer an accomplice to the crime, a partner, so to speak, who is held accountable for the violation of barrio culture. Another stanza of the poem addresses her male counterpart again but speaks for both in asking where it all has led them.

> I heard from many rucos
> that you
> would never make it.
> You would hold me back;
> From What?
> From what we are today? [Ibid.]

The blatantly accusatory, if not angry, voice Sosa Riddell has directed at the *vatos* and her male counterpart assumes greater subtlety and nuance when she turns it on herself. "They," Anglos, are mocked with a note of sarcasm as her male contemporary becomes a sounding board and deflects blame for her own demise.

> My name was changed, por la ley.
> Pobrecitos, they believed in me,
> That I was white enough

to stay forever,
that I would never find you again.

I found you, Chicano,
but only for a moment,
Never para siempre. [P. 76]

The momentariness with which the writer can relocate herself in her past or reestablish herself on barrio soil beside a Chicano is recognized as that—temporary. They *are* the past. She hypothesizes a personal death of sorts and juxtaposes it with her present state.

Perhaps I died before,
when I said good-bye
al barrio y al Cruiser.
He went to road camp,
por grifa y peleonera.
While I was saved—
for what?

Sosa Riddell's powerful explication of the process of acculturation through education ultimately poses a critical question—what is it all for? The answer is left open-ended, perhaps to suggest the schizoid potential assimilation can have in the Chicana psyche. The final lines of the poem dramatize this potential, and it ends with a compromise consolation which sees her male counterpart caught in the tentacles of acculturation as she is.

Pero sabes, ése,
what keeps me from shattering
into a million fragments?
It's that sometimes,
you are muy gringo, too. [Ibid.]

Though the theme of acculturation in Chicana literature is generally identified as producing a split in loyalties, equated with *malinchismo* (acculturated Chicanas are modern-day traitresses), and carries with it a number of sad consequences, its consequences are always couched in human terms. When removed from the human arena, however, the merging of Mexican and American elements in the mundane world of Chicanos can be innocuous. A poem by Lorenza Calvillo Schmidt (1973a) captures this merger in everyday life through the use of English, Spanish, and Chicano slang.

califas
    baby blue skies
    con patches de white clouds

flat fields running
into famous mountain range.
y yo
    comiendo tacos de frijoles
    heading for the freeway
    california winds. . . .
califas music
    los oldies but goodies
    y yo waiting for a 7-up
    yo yo mi 7-up
    heading for the freeway.

The topic of acculturation has conjured up a variety of responses in Chicana poetry but is essentially a minor theme in their works. A more recurrent one, which is subjected to a greater variety of expression, is that of male-female relationships. Chicana attitudes toward the Chicano decidedly contradict the long honored stereotype of the woman as passive and the male as dominant. Abstractions of the relationship between the two are not uncommon—the male appears as the embodiment of an idea or aspiration—while traditional roles are brought into question in more concrete male-female situations.

A striking poem by Inés Hernández Tovar, "Compañero" (1977), offers an example of the male as an abstraction (here a synonym for solitude).

Sin que te des cuenta
a veces me acuesto contigo
esas pocas veces cuando
    la soledad me acompaña
y la puedo recibir
    calmadamente
Soy celosa
lo sabías?
Me fastidio
    con tareas
    quehaceres
    compromisos
y te quiero ir a buscar
Si no te tengo, si no te encuentro
me encelo
No sé
Es que eres soledad
Y la soledad
es lo que deseo
    más que nada.[3]

Tovar's rendering of the male as both abstract and real is a tribute to her technical virtuosity. Like men, solitude can elude a woman who is burdened by a monotonous routine of housewifely chores. She pursues solitude, covets it, and envies it for the release it can give her, just as a man's freedom outside the boundaries of a home allow him the same release. A very understated element of the poem is that the spontaneous interchange of the male and solitude is experienced by the woman without the male's awareness of it. The enhancement of sympathetic female omniscience recurs in another poem, "Words Unspoken," by Angela de Hoyos (1977).

> You may boast that in your prison
> you have locked me for no reason
> save the fact that in your house
>   there shouts a man
> and I'll stay—NOT to add glory,
> O my conquerer, to your story—
> but because my instinct tells me
>   that perhaps
> underneath all that bravado
> quakes a hopeless desperado
> who longs to win a battle
>   now and then.

De Hoyos's poem is a remarkable piece in that while she uses the metaphor of a house as a prison and sees her man as her keeper and conqueror, at the same time her intuition supplies her with important insights. She is able to peel back the abstract roles of dominance and bravery that govern *machos*, revealing a human being beneath the mask who must wrestle with life's battles. Surprisingly, neither man nor woman suffers from this revelation. It is rare that *machismo* is handled with such insight and understanding as it is in this poem. "Words Unspoken" should stand as an exemplar of *machismo* as it touches the sympathies of the Chicana rather than as it victimizes her.

Another *macho* convention that occurs in all Chicano literature is the *vato*, *ruco*, or *pachuco* of the barrio—the barrio dude. In one of a series of barrio poems, Virginia Granado (1974) takes the *pachuco* as her subject and again, rather than perceiving him as an agent of oppression, pays tribute to him as a positive abstraction—as a Chicano hero. The *pachuco's machismo* is translated as ethnic pride and endurance in the face of discrimination, a function he has served historically. "His shoulders, they carry that pride, wisdom, that machismo that we of 'La Nueva Raza' are discovering now . . . his was always there. . . . He was there the time of the 'zoot suits,' he was there when they weren't allowed to eat in restaurants. . . . He's here now that we're trying to change things." Granado sees the *pachuco* as an instructor in the preservation of her race and culture. While she gladly surrenders to him, it is clear that her submission is motivated by a desire to gain more instruction rather than by simple meekness or acquiescence to his strength.

It is curious that all of the foregoing poems present the male as an anonymous figure, generally identified only as "you." Chicano writers, on the other hand, readily dedicate poems to girl friends, wives, and mothers. A marked preference for anonymity on the part of Chicanas might be attributed not to a reluctance to identify real men in their lives but to lend emphasis to the fact that they are addressing a more abstract entity. They appear to be more preoccupied with considering universal male characteristics as they impinge on women than with how a particular man impinges on the experience of a particular woman. It might be inferred from this that the Chicana writer is as capable of understanding the male spirit and psyche via this method as male writers have been of understanding females. A by-product of this is that it also allows her to transcend personal boundaries and share in the realm of the male on a variety of levels.

An untitled poem by Betsy Tapia (1975b) not only credits the male figure she addresses with an ability to erase desperation she has felt:

> You made all the yesterdays fade
> and my desperation cease for
> the time you smiled. . . .

It also extends his powers beyond the time and space of the poem. He serves as a catalyst for a fuller understanding of her own "halls of darkness."

> I was humbled at the touch of your words
> and I want to remember
> all of my sad days
> that for these few
> I slept with the deepest of dreams
> I walked in the halls of my darkness
> and wanted to see the sunrise
> you embraced. . . .

In "After," another poem (1975a), the poet's distracted thoughts—

> It is the morning after
> tracing the thoughts   with my finger   on the window

—merge with the male to become a "we"—

> How is it we found something in common with the night
> we were on our way　　away

—and gather strength to confront possible separation with painless casualness:

> now I wonder as I leave you
> if I will be erased
> with the next window washing. . . .

Tapia's poems are a distinct account of the feminine psyche's osmotic potential in contact or in unison with the male psyche. A deliberate *non*attempt to control the abstract male figure facilitates an intimate approach to her own consciousness.

Abstract portrayals such as these of the male in Chicana literature are complemented by those which take more true-to-life men as their subject. Although they are more fleshed out, however, the three examples we shall cite bring home cultural mores that mold female attitudes toward the male and vice versa. In a short poem by Bernice Zamora entitled "Pueblo, 1950" (1976, p. 13), the poet succinctly communicates a cultural taboo that bans premarital contact between the sexes. A very real person is addressed.

> I remember you, Fred Montoya.
> You were the first *vato* to ever kiss me.
> I was twelve years old.
> My mother said shame on you,
> my teacher said shame on you, and
> I said shame on me, and nobody
> 　　said a word to you.

Another example, a short story by Caroline Castillo, "Chavalitas mocosas," delightfully and humorously brings home the same message —stay away from boys. In this scene Yoli and Carmen, two school-age sisters, have spied Paul Martin who lives across the alley. Carmen urges Yoli to wave at him.

> We're not supposed to play with boys. Everybody tells us so. They're nasty. Mama, Daddy, Aunty, Lupe, Marina, Gloria: they all say "don't play with boys!" All they want is one thing. It's not our toys. All they want is to kiss us! We gotta watch out when we start school. And slap 'em! We gotta slap 'em if they try anything. Heck yeah we'll slap 'em! I just can't *wait* for school to start!
> "HEY PAUL MARTIN!" [C. Castillo 1974, p. 8]

The restrictions Yoli and Carmen's parents and relatives impose on them derive from the traditional cultural expectation that young women should be chaste when they wed. The longer contract between the sexes is deferred, the better.

The unhappy result of chastity that has been surrendered is dealt with in "Epitaph for 'Maria, Maria, Maria la Vandida,' " a short story written by Sylvia Delgado. The title itself is cryptic, but the following dialogue between Christina and her boy friend David is not.

> "David."
> "What?"
> "My period hasn't come down."
> Pause
> "How late are you?"
> "Two days."
> "Two days! So what!"
> "What if I'm preg . . ."
> "Look, whatever happens its your fault."
> "But you said . . ."
> "Fuck what I said. You could of stopped me."
> "I did try."
> "Sure you did, clawing all over me."
> "David!"
> "What?"
> "That's not true!"
> "What are you crying about? Look I have to go."
> "But . . ."
> "Bye." [Delgado 1972, p. 2]

With no apparent remedy in sight, Christina is left to drag around the house carrying the silent double burden of pregnancy and loss of a boy friend. Her mother's piercing observations cut through her as the story ends.

> "Christina, what's wrong with you? You move around the house like a pregnant cow. Are you still mourning for that boy Daniel?"
> "His name is David. No I'm not."
> "Look you are up to no good. And if I find out whats wrong, boy are you going to be sorry."
> "Oh god,
>   damn,
>   damn." [P. 3]

The themes of acculturation and male-female relationships as expressed by Chicana writers are often intensely personal and self-reflective and offer an inside look at Chicano culture.

Another theme Chicana literature explores with equal powers of perception is the family, particularly the interdynamics of family relationships. In Anaya, Vasquez, and Villaseñor we saw the intimate bond that exists between mother or mother surrogate and son. Two Chicana works, Castillo's "Chavalitas Mocosas" and Rita Gutierrez-Christensen's poem "Eulogy for a Man from Jalostitlan" (1976), present father-daughter relationships. What is interesting is that these works reveal almost polar views of that relationship. The two little girls who are the protagonists of "Chavalitas Mocosas" give a vivid account of a spanking they get from their father, while Gutierrez-Christensen presents a moving portrait of an irreplaceable parent.

Castillo's short story opens with an energetic scene in which a group of little girls are playing in a field dotted with dirt mounds. They stuff dirt in their shoes "to run faster," have races, and play hide-and-seek. The high time they are having is suddenly interrupted by Carmen and Yoli's father, who approaches with a belt in hand. The girls' play area is restricted to their own yard, so they are due to be spanked for going into the field.

> "Here comes your Daddy!" . . .
> Yikes. . . . Uh oh. He's got the cinto. My pecho is starting to hurt. Oh NO. If I start crying even before he hits me I'll get it even harder. He hates to see us cry for no reason. There's that bola in my throat. I can't swallow.
> "Aijjiii!"
> I'm flying. It's cold all over except for in between my legs. I hear Carmen crying.
> "Don't hit us Daddy! PLEASE don't hit us!" She's next.
> "OW! OW! OW! OWEEEE!"
> Hot stings. OWWWWWWWWWWW. He lets me go. On my cola, ow my cola. Oh I HATE HIM! He's got Carmen now. Oooo. Oooo. One-two-three-four-five. Her mouth's getting bigger and bigger. Screaming louder, louder. . . . The hairs on my arm are going up.
> . . . Carmen's screaming and so am I . . . I don't feel like counting 'em. I don't feel like doing nothing. I hate you, you big bully, pig-faced caca. [C. Castillo 1974, p. 6]

The childish outburst of anger Yoli spews at her father underscores an unfairness she senses in the spanking. Though her father may be plagued by the dead-end frustration of a handicapped, unemployed Chicano who has two children and another on the way, these realities have no weight in her own world.

The funny, earthy, and endearing sisters Castillo creates in this story are an enduring contribution to Chicana literature. In contrast to their feisty natures, the speaker in Gutierrez-Christensen's eulogy poignantly documents a father's exemplary life of selfless giving and inspiration for his daughters.

> "Please, no eulogy," I told my sisters.
> "I can't bear to hear a priest saying
> Empty nothings over our father's grave."
> His eulogy was carved in our hearts.
> How could a priest express how one old man
> (He was 47 when I was born and I was his oldest.)
> Raised four little girls into womanhood
> With kindness, wisdom and love? [P. 59]

A widower, the father raised his four daughters through years of migrant poverty. The poem details recollections of meals he made for his children, including oatmeal cookies on chilly days.

> (No matter how hard he coaxed,
> We seldom ate the oatmeal he cooked for breakfast.
> So he made cookies with it instead.) [P. 64]

A Mexican bread pudding, *capirotada*, was prepared in wealthy times;

> When my father felt rich in time and money
> He'd make a capirotada. . . .
> Corn tortillas on the bottom of the pan,
> Alternate layers of French bread, Longhorn cheese,
> Panocha, raisins, canela and canned Pet milk,
> It doesn't taste the same.
> I use to think that what was missing
> Must be the wood stove.

On Christmas Eve he mashed a pumpkin left from Hallowe'en with orange, sugar, cinnamon, and milk. When times were lean again,

> We'd all go quail egg hunting along the railroad tracks.
> On the way we'd pick flowers called Indian Paint Brush.
> My father would sit and make us crowns
> Which we placed on our heads as we hunted for the nests.
> [Ibid.]

Once the proper ratio of eight quail eggs to one hen egg had been gathered, a "migrant's brunch" was concocted with cheese, onion, cilantro, oregano, and "Fresno chiles / Fresh from our garden" scrambled into the eggs. The poor but colorful meals Gutierrez-Christensen serves up in her poem do not detract from the very pronounced poverty she depicts. Bedroom curtains came down for Easter dresses, and the father mended his shoes for an Easter service.

Some fifty years after he left Mexico, his grown daughter and her family take him on a return trip. He comes back full of tales and with a yearning to go again. A heart condition that requires daily medication move his daughters to prevail upon him not to make another trip, but he leaves with some neighbors anyway.

(Loretta carefully counted and packed the little pills.)

> He returned three weeks later
> In a Mexican coffin,
> Dressed in an elegant Mexican suit
> (He always liked nice clothes.)
> A trace of a smile on his face
> And the bottle of pills unopened. [P. 61]

Though the coffin was to remain unopened, his daughter Judy protests, and the mortician gives in to her request.

> He cautioned Judy about the smell, that the lingering odor
> Might create an even greater emotional trauma.
> Judy responded that she understood.
> Her need to touch my father was great............... [P. 67]

A final meeting between father and daughters carries the full force of their feeling for him.

> The next morning my father's coffin was opened.
> There was no smell.
> We touched our father's hands, kissed his face
> And said farewell.
> I, the unbeliever, said to my Catholic sisters
> "There is a Russian proverb that says
> That if the body doesn't smell it means that the person is a
>   saint."
> "Ooooh," my sisters said.
> But didn't we always know that? [Ibid.]

The warm, vivid memories of an extraordinary father Gutierrez-Christensen affords are not duplicated in Chicana literature. The examples we turn to now, of mother-daughter relationships, begin by taking a downbeat turn. Short stories by Guadalupe Valdés-Fallis, "Recuerdo" (1975), and Sylvia Wood, "La Polvadera" (1976), represent relationships in which the mother is unable to fulfill her maternal role either through circumstance or oversight.

"Recuerdo" is about a mother who finds herself in the miserable predicament of accepting or rejecting the offer of an old, fat, smelly lawyer to "take care" of her daughter Maruca. Her predicament is compounded by a look at her own life. She has a slew of children who depend on her, lives with a barely tolerable lover, and has a shanty to live in. Don Lorenzo's "arrangement" with Maruca promises to give her daughter everything she never had—a house, pretty things, security, happiness. Rosa is torn between the repulsion she feels toward the garlic-breathed, greasy lawyer and her desperate need to have her daughter be provided for. When she finally confronts the girl with his proposition, Maruca is incredulous. "The face was pale now, the eyes surprised and angry. 'You want me to go to bed with Don Lorenzo? You want me to let him put his greasy hands all over me, and make love to me? You want that?'" Rosa answers, "Don't you see, I want you to be happy, to be safe. I want you to have pretty things and not to be afraid. I want you to love your babies when you have them, to hear them laugh with full fat stomachs . . . I want you to love life, to be glad that you were born." Maruca responds by asking her mother whether she really believes that sleeping with Don Lorenzo and being happy she was born are synonymous. She looks at Rosa, waiting for an answer, "depending on it." Her mother cannot verbalize the response that screams inside her. "No, no! You will hate it probably, and you will dread his touch on you and his breath smelling of garlic. But it isn't HE, that will make you happy. It's the rest of it." Her daughter's brown eyes continue to plead with her, full of tears, and Rosa finally answers, "Yes, Maruca, it will make you happy." Maruca's sacrifice for the sake of security is complete. Her mother collapses into loneliness and fatigue and tells her to go to church. She watches her as she goes, "prayer book clutched tightly in one hand, hopeful still, trusting still, and so very, very young still. And she wondered if she would change much, really, after Don Lorenzo, and the baby and the house. She wondered if she would still be gay and proud and impatient" (Valdés-Fallis 1975, p. 65).

Rosa's final thoughts have no response. It is all too clear that whatever potential Maruca may have had for gaiety, pride, and impatience is lost forever, just as the tie between mother and daughter is severed.

Wood's "La Polvadera" assigns the mother the same vocation as Rosa's, that of scarlet woman, though she is a gaudy, bedangled creature compared to the dowdy Rosa. The story is narrated by the daughter in a cutting, sarcastic tone of voice.

There are certain advantages to being illegitimate; the obvious one is that when called "hija de puta" or "bastard," unlike others, you don't feel any strong moral or ethical commitment to defend your doubtful lineage.

> My mother was the barrio whore. She was called "la Polvadera" and I never knew if she earned it by her claim that she could raise dust anywhere she danced, or whether it was from all the face and body powder she wore. Probably both. [Wood 1976, p. 92]

Though at first glance it may appear that the daughter finds nothing redeeming either about her mother, herself, or the life they share, this derives from an undercurrent of vulnerability which springs from lack of genuine communication between the two. "We never had any conversations, she and I. She had her dances and lovers and I had my books. We both knew that I would someday leave and never return; so we never discussed it. Once or twice we made attempts to reach each other but the unvoiced feelings were already buried too deep" (p. 93). One attempt at bridging the gap between them is initiated by the mother on New Year's Eve. She suggests that she will stay home, spend the evening with her daughter and make *buñuelos*—tortillas fried to a crisp and eaten with sugar or honey. The gesture breaks through the girl's protective shell as she watches her mother knead the dough for the tortillas. "Her face glowed and her cheeks were naturally pink from the heat of the stove, and she had her hair pulled from her face; and she looked so pretty I wanted to tell her I loved her no matter what" (p. 95). The momentary spell of love is shattered by neighbors who come over and turn the evening into a party. The daughter withdraws, the gap is widened irreparably, and reconciliation becomes hopeless. Like the relationship between Rosa and Maruca, this mother-daughter relationship suffers a premature death.

Valdés-Fallis's and Wood's depictions of mothers represent unique examples in Chicana literature of women who are ill suited or even incapable of motherhood. They dispel a popular stereotype of Chicano mothers as universally gifted with warmth and caring. Three other writers, Judy A. Lucero, Margarita Cota Cardenas, and Guadalupe Castellano, add to a broader definition of motherhood.

Lucero's "Little Girl's Prayer" (1973) laments the separation of a mother and daughter that is imposed rather than chosen, as in the stories above. The poem is especially urgent as Lucero was a *pinta*, a prisoner, herself. With innocent conviction the daughter offers to forfeit gifts in exchange for her mother's presence on Christmas Eve.

> A little girl prayed on Christmas Eve
> with tears in her eyes, She bowed on her knees
> She looked to Heaven ... and said these words ...
>
> "Please God, send my Mommy home on Christmas day ...

I know U love little Girls and Boys . . .
So please . . . send my Mommy instead of Toys."

The mother, in a more philosophic stance of resignation, acknowledges the impossibility of seeing her daughter and can only marvel at what a gift she is to her.

That night in a Prison far away
A lonely prisoner knelt down to pray . . .
On her face was a look of Despair.
as she whispered to God a Solemn Prayer . . .
"Please God . . . watch over my Little Girl . . .
She's the greatest Gift in all the World. . . ."

"Por nosotras," by Cota Cardenas (1977), is a poem in which the mother gently imprisons her daughter with possessiveness. Her over-protectiveness emanates from maternal anxiety about what it is to be a woman in the real world. This may explain her reluctance to let the little girl go out to play. In a larger sense, it is also a reluctance to let her daughter grow up.

beso las negras trencitas
de esta niña que llora en mis brazos
porque no la dejo salir a jugar
hace que pidan los ojos y es que
no sabe que es sólo mi manera brusca
de madre confusa y es que no quiero que la empujen
afuera que no se astille un dedito del pie
saliendo descalza   que no se me vaya muy lejos
de enfrente de la casa   que no aprenda tan pronto
tan pronto que se aprende   NO   ESTO ES MIO   TU NO
PUEDES   VETE A TU CASA   NO   ERES MUJER[4]

Cota Cardenas's poem, like the other works we have discussed in this section, holds the view that motherhood, or the lot of women, is circumscribed. Rosa's own bleak history causes her to impose an unhappy future on Maruca; La Polvadera's need for a good time is an assertion of the freedom she must have at the expense of her daughter; an imprisoned mother's role is already physically defined, and over-protectiveness is as much protection of self as it is protection of a daughter. In contrast to this concept of maternity, Castellano's "To a Mandolin" (1975) provides an overwhelmingly poetic image of motherhood that knows no boundaries.

I would rather be inquisitive
than secretive about my life,

like a storm in my head
where cities of worry and disillusionment
reside. . . .
One day I will enter through your window,
sliding under the rug to find the children
without the happy homes. [P. 145]

The ambitious outlook—that free of worry and disillusionment, the speaker can soothe the plight of all children with unhappy homes—moves to a more specific yet still idealized expectation for her own children.

I want to watch my children gliding in a river
with cool feathers for oars, . . .
I want to enter their impressionable little minds.
the spaces which are great orators. . . . [P. 146]

In other words, the mother's great capacities for optimism are earmarked for an easy transfer to her children. Castellano's poetic energy may be a flight of maternal fantasy, but her poem nonetheless suggests an interesting contrast to her more earth-bound sisters.

The margins of primary familial relationships are further expanded in Chicana literature in the form of a secondary grandmother-granddaughter role. Though it would seem that this relationship is more tenuous or less noteworthy than the others, in fact it has a very real place in Chicano families and reflects the idea that the Chicano family accommodates extended family bonds. Whereas mothers and fathers must all too often respond to the daily rigors of life, grandmothers are more removed from such pressures and can provide a different experience for their granddaughters.

"Las dos hermanas," a story of two sisters by Rosalie Otero Peralta (1975), is told by a young granddaughter and great-niece of the two women. The story focuses on the close relationship the two elderly sisters have maintained throughout their lives. The narrator functions as an inside observer who relates the dynamics of their relationship. She describes her grandmother thus: "My grandmother Teresina was the dominant one, her dark hair neatly intertwined into a braid that she wound into a chignon and pinned to the back of her head with large bone hairpins. Today, being Sunday, she had waved the sides of her hair with her old curling iron and donned her silves filigree earrings. As she talked, her penetrating hazel eyes would capture the minutest detail through green tinted wire-framed spectacles" (p. 67). Teresina might dominate her sister Marcelina, but at critical points in the latter's

Fig. 6   Anonymous elderly woman. Courtesy of
Marian E. Luna, Riverside County Office on
Aging, California.

life, her dominance has had positive effects. As the plot unfolds it is revealed that contrary to Teresina's counsel, Marcelina married a womanizing widower many years her senior who had a number of small children. After some years Marcelina discovered one day that he was intimate with Juana, the next-door neighbor. Marcelina being naturally weak, her stronger sister intervened on her behalf and arranged a separation through the local priest—this despite the pressures of gossip that surrounded the incident. The granddaughter is given only bits and pieces of what has transpired, but as more information is gathered, she gains more and more respect for her grandmother.

The events of Marcelina's life have a gradually wearing effect on her, and she becomes ill. Teresina's distress at the seriousness of the illness moves her to take her granddaughter aside and tell her the whole story of her sister's unhappy life. By confiding in her granddaughter, she begins to forge a new relationship that will help them both cope with Aunt Nina's impending death.

The closeness Teresina's granddaughter begins to feel toward her is reflected by Theresa in Estela Portillo Trambley's "Paris Gown," in which the granddaughter meets her grandmother Clotilde for the first time.

> Theresa had anticipated this after dinner *tete a tete*. In her mind there were so many things unclear about this woman who had left her home in Mexico so long ago. . . . The stories about her numerous marriages, her travels, her artistic ventures, and the famous names that frequented her salon were many. But no one had ever discussed how she got to Paris in the first place when the women of her time had had small freedoms. Her life abroad had become scandal in epic to the clan of women in aristocratic circles back home. There was a daring in her grandmother's eyes. [Portillo Trambley 1975, p. 1]

The mystery surrounding her grandmother does indeed center on how she got to Paris in the first place. On the way to learning from her grandmother how it happened, Theresa is transfigured by the very presence of the seemingly ageless Clotilde. "Theresa sat silent. She had suddenly glimpsed into a beautiful clear depth in a human being. She felt sudden love and admiration for her grandmother. Clotilde's fragile, ember quality of spirit grew and filled the room. . . . Theresa felt Clotilde had a deep and lasting comprehension of her place in the universe. How fresh and open was the world in this room. Theresa felt that the room itself was a composite of what Clotilde had become in the life process" (pp. 1–2). Theresa's observation that the room is a composite of Clotilde is an excellent illustration of a note made at the beginning of this section regarding some Chicana writers' use of setting. The author often transforms a place into a symbolic organ for the presentation of her characters. Here, Clotilde, like the room, has become eternally fresh and open to life's experiences. She is so open, in fact, that as she embarks on an explanation of how she got to Paris, she does not spare her granddaughter in using sophisticated language or offering a philosophic rationale for her flight. Theresa's state of mind is so receptive that she effortlessly joins the plane from which her grandmother speaks. By the end of the story, when Clotilde's reasons for leaving Mexico are reduced to a wish for feminine freedom and equality, Theresa is fully capable of understanding such an explanation. Moreover, in the course of one afternoon, Theresa's soul and psyche have so grown that they begin to merge with her grandmother's. It is no accident that Portillo Trambley refers to her as a woman in the last line of the story—"Both women looked out the window and caught the full colors of life" (p. 9).

The strong bonds between grandmother and granddaughter surface again in another of Portillo Trambley's short stories, "Rain of Scorpions" (1975). In a powerful scene in which the small house Lupe and her grandmother share threatens to be inundated by a mud slide riddled with scorpions, the sturdy young woman takes the frail old woman on her back and struggles arduously to get her to safer, higher ground.

Interfamilial relationships among women embrace a variety of settings and situations and take different forms. It is noteworthy that in all the preceding examples women relate to one another in a nonstereotypical way and are themselves nonstereotypical. That is, neither meekness nor passivity characteristically typifies mothers, daughters, or grandmothers, and there is a predisposition to relate to one another on the same plane, regardless of age. A norm of assertiveness and individuality appears to prevail, so that no types or categories of women exist. Such a norm, even in adverse circumstances, reveals a significant stride Chicana literature has made over American and Chicano literature. Chicana writers provide a wealth of portrayals that see women for the first time as strong, decisive, idealistic creatures who attempt to modify or cope with their environments. Life-styles, such as that of whores, do not contain women like Rosa or La Polvadera. They are neither the unidimensional nor the stereotypical scarlet women we have seen in American and Chicano literature. In addition to taking a new look at whores, Chicana writers make us witnesses as young girls become young women under the empathetic tutelage of their grandmothers and the universally warm Chicana mother is scrutinized with new vigor and insight. All of these characterizations are a new species.

If it can be said that Chicana writers radically modify depictions of women through a look at interfamilial dynamics, it might then be suggested that they achieve a complete breakthrough when their depictions venture outside family and cultural structures. Women as they embrace women are a new phenomenon in Chicano literature as a whole, and the women in the examples we shall cite are compelled to lean on one another not because of family ties but for very different reasons. As a case in point, Sylvia Gonzales's poem "Woman and Woman" (1974) presents the gravitation together of two women for the purpose of sheltering one another from abstractions like cold, fear, and want.

> A flame flickers . . .
> Do you dare?
> There's fire in your eyes.
> Warmth . . .
> Warmth in your eyes. . . .
> Take shelter in your sister's arms
> And while she comforts you
> Linger there awhile,
> Soothing each other's fears
> In discovery of each other [P. 65]

Two works by Estela Portillo Trambley, "The Day of the Swallows" (1969: a play) and "If It Weren't for the Honeysuckle" (1975, a short story), take the solace women can provide for each other a step farther.

Josefa of "The Day of the Swallows" is as intricately wrought a character as Portillo Trambley has created and embodies a complexity of facets and tensions. On one hand Josefa is endowed with marvelous feminine attributes—she is regal looking, a pious Christian woman, and a gifted lace maker, and she is known for her ready charity in taking unfortunate souls into her home. On the other hand, Josefa is a high priestess in the cults of light, beauty, and physical passion. Her house is a cathedral of light whose furniture is bedecked with beautiful handmade lace and embroidery. Religion and beauty do not combine to make Josefa a total being, however, for she is driven by physical passions. Because men have no place in her world and thus cannot cater to her needs, she has taken as a lover Alysea, a young woman who lives with her. Josefa's complex nature can only be maintained if all the elements of her existence are kept in perfect balance. Her peace is disrupted by

men, however. David, another member of the household, discovers the
two women one night; Tomás, a local drunk, also recalls seeing the
two women emerge from a night swim in the waters of a nearby lake;
and a young man, Eduardo, woos Alysea and threatens to carry her off.

In a series of actions Josefa attempts to cement her crumbling world.
She ruthlessly cuts David's tongue out, holds her own against Tomás's
threats of blackmail, and implores Alysea not to succumb to Eduardo's
advances—he has already caused the death of another woman. All is to
no avail. Josefa ultimately confesses the enormity of her sins to a priest,
realizes she can no longer be the example to the community she once
was, and commits suicide.

The power of Portillo Trambley's portrayal of Josefa does not lie in
the components of Josefa's remarkable character, her actions, or even in
the fact that she has a homosexual relationship with Alysea. It derives
instead from the defiant feminine attitude she assumes, that discounts
men as necessary to personal fulfillment. She speaks to Eduardo of
desires she has had that are so intense they are painful.

> JOSEFA. . . . Does it surprise you that I speak of desire? Oh, yes . . .
> I felt it . . . to my fingertips . . . it was so real, the beautiful need . . .
> the lights of the barrio were far off in another world . . . this always
> affected me . . . I became another being far from my kind . . . even my
> desire was a special suffering. . . .
> EDUARDO. You still did not marry.
> JOSEFA. What does that have to do with desire? my desire . . .
> like my being . . . became a purer grain. It was more than someone
> to see or touch . . . or embrace . . . it was a need for a pouring of
> self . . . a gentleness . . . a faith. I did not want the callous Indian
> youth . . . with hot breath and awkward hands . . . a taking without
> feeling . . . no, not that! I wanted so much more. . . . [Portillo
> Trambley 1969, p. 167]

Josefa looks for and finds more in the things she surrounds herself
with, in Alysea, because she is an extraordinary woman. The feminine
force with which she imbues her world and touches the people and
things in it is, ironically, both powerful and fragile at the same time.
The radiance with which she tries to touch Alysea, like the warning
she tries to impart about the wiles of men, is unsuccessful. Alysea's
flight with Eduardo represents a symbolic undermining of a critical
component in Josefa's world. And with the loss of even one touchstone
in her life, Josefa's doom is inevitable.

Josefa's tragic fall is countered by the triumph of three women in
"If It Weren't for the Honeysuckle." Beatriz, much like Josefa, is a

paragon of feminine strength who derives this strength not from the ethereal worlds of light and beauty but from the earthly world of fertility and greenness. Beatriz too nurtures her green world independently of men save one, Robles. Robles is the serpent in her garden.

Beatriz married Robles as a young girl to escape the daily drudgery of washing for her nine brothers. He is a lecher who already had a wife and six children, yet knowing this, Beatriz chose to go with him anyway. As his visits to her begin to subside and he brings a younger "wife," Sofa, to live with her, Beatriz begins to find an order in her life that gives her joy. All goes well, despite two traumatic occasions when in drunken fits Robles cripples Sofa by breaking her hip and kills Sofa's cat by dashing its head against a wall. These two events are stoically borne by the two women until Robles introduces a third female into their household—Lucretia is a waif of a girl whom Robles rescues from a cholera-ridden house. Beatriz and Sofa take her in, and as they nurse her back to health, an unspoken pact is sealed between them. Beatriz silently vows that Lucretia will not become still another of Robles's victims, and Sofa joins in the pact when she learns the cold truth about her cat's disappearance.

A plot to murder Robles emerges from two sources. The first, in classic Portillo Trambley fashion, comes via natural symbolism. As Beatriz is absorbed pruning back a honeysuckle vine one day, she discovers three Amanitas, poison mushrooms.

> As she lifted them to find the main artery, the one to be salvaged from the rest that would be cut away, she saw them.
>
> Three white, fruiting Amanitas . . . full blown, forming the usual fairy ring. The ring was completed by smaller stumps of spores that had failed fruition. But these three . . . these beautiful three were blown reproductions of a whiteness found in dreams. Beatriz stared in fascination. An excitement grew in her. In the back of her mind, there was something. She looked up at the climbing honeysuckle and felt a triumphal presence. . . . These three were a gift from the honeysuckle. Beatriz did not doubt. She touched them with a growing assurity; then, she swiftly cut them with the small hatchet and put them in the pocket of her apron. Her concentration came back to the present chore. She continued clipping the smaller vines that grew out of the main stem in brilliant timbre . . . trumpets of freedom . . . trumpets of freedom. . . . [Portillo Trambley 1975, p. 103]

The natural world's symbolic imperative for Robles's death, which supplies Beatriz with the three Amanitas, one for each woman in the story, is reinforced by her own mental conviction that he should be killed.

"The gall drowned Beatriz. One memory upon the other of a man who crushed the soul between his teeth. She felt the back of her mind for the thought that was a mortal gesture against the kind of death that Robles brought with him every time. She was suddenly very tired of scooping up the fragments of broken things and broken spirits. An operative evil had to be destroyed" (p. 105). The motive for killing Robles—that Lucretia's innocence should be preserved—is reinforced by a more universal conception that women should not be victimized by the "swollen poison" of men that Robles personifies. In what can almost be called a chant, the inequality he represents is echoed and reechoed.

> It had been decreed long ago by man-made laws that living things were not equal. It had been decreed that women should be posses-sions, slaves, pawns in the hands of men with ways of beasts. It had been decreed that women were to be walloped effigies to burn upon the altars of men. It had been decreed by the superiority of brute strength that women should be no more than durable spectacles to prove a fearful potency that was a shudder and a blow. It had been decreed . . . how long ago? . . . that women should approve of a manhood that simply wasn't there . . . the subservient female loneli-ness . . . It had been decreed. [P. 106]

Beatriz, Sofa, and Lucretia form a triad of defiance against the decree. Robles is given a bowl of chicken soup with Amanitas in it. He lapses into a coma, and with the silence that follows his death rattle, stillness, peace, and the "bright design" are once again restored in the feminine green world.

Seven

Chicana Feminism

We have seen that examples of extraordinary or exemplary women abound in Mexican and Chicano history, from La Malinche and Sor Juana Inés de la Cruz to Lucía González Parsons. Let us now focus on the emergence of Chicana feminism in the twentieth century, when there developed a distinctive feminine consciousness and the delineation of women's issues and concerns in Mexico as well as the United States. Special attention must be given to the Mexican revolution of 1910, because it was undoubtedly the most significant catalyst in the growth of Mexican-Chicana feminism. Prior to the revolution, women excelled in various endeavors, but their primary objective was not the liberation of women per se. In the earlier fight for Mexican independence from Spain, for example, women like Doña Josefa Ortiz de Domínguez are rightly called *heroinas*. Yet these women were fighting for the liberation of all Mexicans from Spanish rule, not for the liberation of women from masculine control.

In this chapter, our basic aim is to show how the roots of contemporary Chicana feminism can be traced to the Mexican revolution and its twentieth-century Chicana precursors. In addition, we will isolate the unique or distinctive characteristics of Chicana feminism and analyze its relation to Anglo feminism and the Chicano movement.

The Role of Women in the Mexican Revolution

Any significant social upheaval such as the Mexican revolution can be divided into at least three basic stages: (1) episodes preceding and leading up to it, (2) the event itself, and (3) its results or consequences (Mendieta Alatorre 1961, p. 14). This tripartite classification will serve as the basis upon which our discussion of the role of women in the revolution will be organized. We will first examine women who are best termed "precursors" because their most significant contributions took place just prior to 1910, although many also played significant parts in one or both of the other stages as well. Next, we will discuss the role of women in the revolution itself. Finally, we will attempt to isolate important societal changes which came in the aftermath of the war.

Feminine Precursors of the Revolution (1900–1909)

In order to appreciate fully the role played by women in the period immediately preceding 1910, one must have some awareness of the sociopolitical conditions of the time. The end of the war of reform in 1867 brought with it the successful expulsion of the French and a return to home rule. The presidency of Benito Juárez introduced a liberal constitution and the promise of a liberal and democratic government. The promise was short-lived, however, as the ascendance of Porfirio Díaz to the presidency in 1876 was to signal the beginning of a thirty-four-year dictatorship that ended with the revolution and his expulsion. Díaz consolidated not only his own power but the power of wealthy landowners as well at the expense of the masses, who were brutally exploited. The exploitation of Indians was so great that it culminated in the Indian wars of the early 1890s, during which thousands of them were either killed or deported. As the rich grew richer, the poor naturally grew poorer. Most *peones* were landless and forced to work for subsistence wages under the *hacienda* system (Silva Herzog 1960, p. 40). By 1910 it is estimated that almost half of Mexico was in the hands of 3,000 families and the real wages of a *peon* were about one-quarter of what they had been in 1800 (Parkes 1969, p. 306). Foreign investment was encouraged by according many privileges to foreign capital. American business interests owned three-fourths of the mines and more than half of the oil fields, and they held substantial interests in many other industries.

Discontent grew rapidly, and by the turn of the century the seeds of rebellion had taken root. One of the most significant avenues of protest against the Díaz regime was the free press. Signs of journalistic opposition were evident as early as the 1880s; the official response was organized harassment. A contemporary observer noted, "La primera persecución sistemática de la prensa independiente principia a fines de 1885 y se prolonga durante 1886; su objeto evidente fue rodear de silencio los comicios celebrados en junio de este año, para propiciar la elevación al Congreso de hombres incondicionales de la dictadura."[1] Many journalists sought refuge in the United States, where they continued to write in protest of the Díaz regime. Adolfo Carrillo founded *La república* in San Francisco and Ignacio Ramírez *El mundo* in Brownsville. With the founding of *Regeneración* by the brothers Ricardo and Enrique Flores Magón, the period of intense press resistance was initiated.

Women were in the forefront of this resistance. They founded and edited radical newspapers, formed feminist organizations, and helped to establish revolutionary groups, with the aim of liberating the masses and granting the vote and other political rights to women. Though harassed by government forces and frequently imprisoned or exiled, they continued the revolutionary struggle. The four women discussed here—Juana Gutiérrez de Mendosa, Elisa Acuña y Rossetti, Dolores Jiménez y Muro, and Sara Estela Ramírez—were examples of those who were both founders of Mexican feminism and precursors of Chicana feminism.

Juana Belén Gutiérrez de Mendoza was born in Durango in 1875. She attended normal school and started a career in teaching (one of the few professions then open to women), but the two driving forces in her life were to help educate poor Indian children and to secure more rights and benefits for agricultural and industrial workers (Siller 1975). In her lifetime she distinguished herself as a teacher, labor organizer, radical journalist and champion of human liberties.

At fifteen she married Cirilo Mendoza, a miner from Guanajuato whom she taught to read and write. Her career as a journalist started in Parral, Chihuahua, where she worked for a liberal and independent newspaper called *La voz de Ocampo* (Rodríguez Cabo 1937, p. 18). Having won the respect and admiration of her fellow revolutionaries, in 1901 she founded her own newspaper, *Vésper*, acquiring the money to buy a printing press by selling some goats that she owned. *Vésper* was dedicated to defending the rights of miners and was strongly anticlerical (Siller 1975). Its subtitle was apt: *Justicia y Libertad*. Juana established a very close relationship with the Magón brothers and the publication of *Vésper* was heralded by *Regeneración:* "Ahora que muchos hombres flaquean y por cobardía se retiran de la lucha, por considerarse sin fuerzas para la reivindicación de nuestras libertades . . . aparece la mujer animosa y valiente, dispuesta a luchar por nuestros principios, que la debilidad de muchos hombres ha permitido que se pisoteen y se les escupa. La señora Juana B. Gutiérrez de Mendoza acaba de fundar en Guanajuato un periódico liberal, *Vésper*, destinado a la defensa de las instituciones liberales y democráticas."[2]

Juana's opposition to the dictator led to her arrest on several occasions. She was imprisoned for her activities against the government in 1902 and again in 1903; and *Vésper* was confiscated along with other radical newspapers. This did not dampen her revolutionary fervor; in prison she met and collaborated with other women, including Dolores Jiménez y Muro, Inés Malváez, and Elisa Acuña y Rossetti. Even in prison Juana continued to direct a newspaper called *Fiat lux*.

Her imprisonment created a furor among her supporters, and she was released on the understanding that she would leave the country; traveling to San Antonio, Texas, with Elisa Acuña and Camilo Arriaga, an anti-Diaz radical leader, with the intent of republishing *Vésper*. The paper appeared again in 1910 in full suport of Madero, though only one issue was published (Siller 1975). During the revolution Juana served with distinction under Zapata and earned his esteem; she had troops directly under her command and achieved the rank of colonel (Rodríguez Cabo 1937, pp. 18–19).

Juana Mendoza lived for many more years, publishing *Alma mexicana* in her later years. Even in old age she continued her work: "Treinta y cinco años de incesante lucha y sesenta de vida ponen a cualquiera fuera de combate, o por lo menos sirven para justificar indiferencias o disfrazar cobardías. . . . Yo tengo ese derecho, pero no tengo el rincón. En todos los rincones del mundo está viviendo un dolor . . . y, yo no tengo indiferencia para ver, ni cobardía para huir, ni mansedumbre para acomodarme allí."[3]

Another outstanding woman and collaborator with Juana Mendoza was Elisa Acuña y Rossetti (d. 1946). Also a teacher by training, Elisa was a coeditor of *Vésper*, and helped found the feminist organization Hijas de Cuauhtémoc. Young Elisa shocked the Magón brothers when she appeared at the offices of *El hijo del Ahuizote*, another Magón paper, and declared herself a liberal, offering her services in the struggle to liberate the Mexican people (Mendieta Alatorre 1961, p. 34). The Magón brothers were very impressed and invited her to sit on the board of directors of the Centro Director de la Confederación de Clubes Liberales de la Republica (or Ponciano Arriaga), a liberal group founded by Camilo Arriaga. She was also an active member of Redención, the

first anticlerical organization which was established by the liberal Santiago de la Hoz and the Magón brothers (Rodríguez Cabo 1937, p. 16).
During the revolution Elisa staunchly supported Madero, and she
founded a newspaper, *La guillotina*, which became an effective vehicle
for combating Huerta, Madero's treacherous successor. Like the
Magóns and many other members of the radical press, she was forced
to flee the country but returned, joining Zapata's forces and participating in an extensive propaganda campaign on his behalf in Puebla.
In addition, Elisa assumed important administrative positions in several
feminist groups, including the Liga Pan-Americana de Mujeres and
Consejo Feminista.

Dolores Jiménez y Muro (1850–1925), another revolutionary precursor, occupied a position equal in importance to that of any other
woman. Her writing spanned politics and literature, published under
the pseudonyms "Espartaco" in her political writing and "Anima" in
her literary work (ibid., p. 17). Jiménez y Muro helped edit *Diario del
hogar*, *El libertario*, and *Tierra y justicia* and served as president of the
Hijas de Cuauhtémoc. Shortly after the organization was formed,
Dolores was imprisoned, and it was there that she laid the groundwork
for a new feminist group with a more clearly defined plan of action,
Regeneración y concordia. The group called for betterment of conditions for Indians and the proletariat, elevation of the economic as well as
moral and intellectual status of women, and unification of all revolutionary forces (ibid.).

Jiménez y Muro also became a strong supporter of Zapata during the
revolution, serving in his army and accompanying several of his chiefs
during important campaigns in the Sierra de Guerrero. It was during
these campaigns that she wrote the preface to Zapata's "Plan de Ayala."
She died many years later in near poverty and anonymity. Only months
before her death did she receive token recognition for her efforts, in the
form of a small pension granted by the subsecretary of education, Gil-
berto Valenzuela (ibid., p. 18).

The last woman to be highlighted here, Sara Estela Ramírez, is from
a Chicana perspective perhaps the most important. Until very recently
her contributions as a Chicana were not recognized (E. Zamora 1976,
p. 4), but while she may not have attained the fame of other precursors
of the revolution, she is important to Chicanas because she joined the
struggle for liberation of her *raza* on both sides of the border.

Like Jiménez y Muro, Sara Estela was both a literary figure and a
political activist. Born in 1881 at Villa de Progreso in the state of
Coahuila, she was graduated from a teacher's college in Saltillo. At the
age of seventeen she went to live in Laredo, Texas, where she was em-

ployed as a Spanish teacher (ibid.). She became involved in opposition politics on both sides of the border, serving as the official representative of Ricardo Flores Magón and his Partido Liberal Mexicano. Sarita was also active in Regeneración y Concordia and Ponciano Arriaga and worked as a journalist for *La corregidora,* where she fought for "la libertad espiritual y económica de la mujer" (Rascón 1975, p. 154).

Although Sarita died early, at the age of twenty-nine, during her twelve years in Laredo she distinguished herself as a teacher, poetess, labor organizer, and defender of human rights. Her accomplishments were such that she was eulogized at her funeral as "the most illustrious Mexican woman of Texas" and "La Musa Texana" (E. Zamora 1976, p. 4). Much of her writing encouraged "mutualism" and the organization of labor, but she also addressed feminist issues, as evidenced by her poem "¡Surge!" dedicated to *la mujer* (ibid., p. 5):

> ¡Surge! Surge a la vida, a la actividad, a la belleza de vivir realmente; pero surge radiante y poderosa, bella de cualidades, esplendente de virtudes, fuerte de energías.
>
> Tú, la reina mundo Diosa de la adoración universal; tú, la soberana a quien se rinde vasallaje, no te encierres así en tu templo de Dios, ni en tu camarín de cortesana triunfadora.
>
> Eso es indigno de tí, antes que Diosa y Reina, se madre, se mujer.
>
> Una mujer que lo es verdaderamente, es más que diosa y que reina. No te embriague el incienso en el altar, ni el aplauso en el escenario, hay algo más noble y más grande que todo eso.
>
> Los dioses son arrojados de los templos; los reyes son echados de sus tronos, la mujer es siempre la mujer.
>
> Los Dioses viven lo que sus creyentes quieren. Los reyes viven mientras no son destronados; la mujer vive siempre y este es el secreto de su dicha, vivir.
>
> Solo la acción es vida; sentir que se vive, es la más hermosa sensación.
>
> Surge, pues, a las bellezas de la vida; pero surge así, bella de cualidades, esplendente de virtudes, fuerte de energías.[4]

Women and the Revolution

The revolution was undoubtedly one of the most significant social upheavals of all time, not only because it was sparked by the widespread and relatively spontaneous protest of the masses but in addition because it generated numerous and profound social changes. Perhaps the most significant of these changes, although one which is not generally recognized, was the alteration of traditional sex roles. Many of the real and promised changes of the revolution were to be short-lived,[5] but its effects on the status of women were long-ranging and permanent.

By the time of the revolution the belief that women were inferior and should be subordinate to men was clearly established. Although pre-Columbian society was characterized by a clear-cut division of labor, in which men were concerned with agriculture and war and women with sewing, embroidery, and other domestic activities, women's position relative to men's was more nearly equal than it was after the conquest. Spanish colonization replaced a communal society with a more individualistic system that revolved around nuclear families. Previously women had participated in all aspects of Aztec society and were provided by the community with food and shelter in return; now they were to be protected and cared for by one man in exchange for their domestic, procreative, and sexual services. No longer were there available to women institutions like the *calpulli*, a governing unit made up of "a cultural group based on blood lineage and on the territory it occupied" (Peterson 1959, p. 112). It was a clan of interrelated families with its own name, emblem, patron god, and government, and it held communal lands for all its members. In the *calpulli* a woman "tenía la obligación de reunirse periódicamente en asambleas, para tratar sus problemas específicos de madre y trabajadora. Discutían la reglamentación a que se sometía la asistencia educativa, que ella prestaba al hijo hasta los 5 años de edad, . . . planteaba los asuntos de su barrio en función de la familia. . . . Su opinión y funciones eran respetadas y tan importantes como la de los hombres; es decir, no había discriminación y se reconocía su capacidad como madre, productora y administradora eficiente."[6]

Now religion became an important instrument for perpetuating the subordination of women. The children of *caciques* and other influential persons, for instance, were indoctrinated to reject traditional Indian values and beliefs. The Franciscan fathers saw the Christianization of the family, the basic unit of human society, as essential to the conversion of the indigenous population (Kasuhiro Kobayashi 1973, p. 451). In 1529 they founded in Texcoco the first house for instruction in religious doctrine for daughters of influential persons, as well as others who wished to enter. Girls were separated from the influence of the family and community to be instructed in the faith and taught about the "good life" (Rascón 1975, p. 149). The actual intent, however, was not to teach or instruct them, even in a rudimentary manner, but to prepare them for their matrimonial duties, making them perpetuators of the faith and good mothers and wives (Kasuhiro Kobayashi 1973, p. 456). By 1534 these convent houses were established in eight localities, although the conversion efforts were resisted by many Indians who preferred the communal way of life (Rascón 1975, p. 149).

By the nineteenth century the subordination of women had been so successful that their duties in society centered almost exclusively around domestic activities. The ideal role for women was the care and nurturance of children, and their daily work revolved around home and family (Turner 1971, p. 133). Education was also an almost exclusively male prerogative, and women were excluded from most professions except teaching; and when employed outside the home, they assumed the most menial and lowest-paying jobs. Denied significant participation in other institutions, women's sphere of influence was limited largely to the perpetuation of traditional cultural and religious values via the home and the church. It is revealing that one of the few organized efforts by women to influence the political order during the nineteenth century came in the form of an 1857 petition by some 500 Guadalajara women calling for more power to be granted to the church (ibid.).

Yet the Industrial Revolution had introduced the need for cheap unskilled labor, and by the middle of the century enterprising capitalists had become familiar with the advantages of female labor. Many factories, especially textile and tobacco, were able to profit by exploiting women and young children. As early as 1860 women were hired to work in factories in Puebla, Tlaxcala, Querétaro, Veracruz, Mexico City, and other cities because they worked harder and for less pay than men. Married women or unmarried women with children were preferred, since they were forced out of economic necessity to accept the fourteen- to eighteen-hour work day and the low wage, which was frequently paid not in cash but in goods and articles in the company store.

Excesses and abuses were common, and many abortions and much infant mortality were caused by the inadequate and unsanitary conditions under which women were forced to labor. So extensive were these abuses that they affected population growth: "La 'disminución de la multiplicación de [las] unidades' provenía de los continuos abortos, sobre todo en las fábricas de tabaco por ser ese elemento altamente nocivo para el embarazo, a la mortalidad infantil provocada por la falta de salud de la mujer, la cual tenía quen privarse de amamantarlo para retornar cuanto antes a su trabajo, a las enfermedades pulmonares de los niños que se sometían prematuramente a jornadas agotadoras en las condiciones más antihigiénicas, etcétera."[7]

Such exploitation predisposed many women to support late nineteenth-century efforts to organize workers and safeguard their rights. As early as 1880 Carmen Huerta presided over the Second Congress of Workers (ibid.). Strikes were prevalent in the 1880s, and although not successful in bettering working conditions, they helped to increase awareness of their situation among workers in general and women workers in particular.

On the eve of the revolution, the economic exploitation of women was even more severe than the exploitation of men. In 1910 only about 9 percent of all Mexican women were gainfully employed (Moreno 1958, p. 240). Without money to feed themselves or their families, women were forced either to work for long hours and under miserable conditions in the factory or to seek other alternatives. Faced with the choice of starvation or prostitution, many elected the latter. Luis Lara y Pardo (1908, p. 22) found that in 1905 about 120 out of every 1,000 women between the ages of fifteen and thirty were registered as prostitutes with the department of health. This statistic of course excludes the thousands of unregistered prostitutes. Prostitution was thus one of the few occupations open to women in the prerevolutionary period, and during the revolution itself it is estimated that the number of prostitutes actually increased.

The belief that women were inferior and hence incapable of assuming important positions was perpetuated not only by organized religion but by the government itself.[8] The Díaz regime had come under the influence of the *científicos,* or positivists who adopted Social Darwinist doctrines and positivism to "explain" or, more accurately, to justify social inequities. Andrés Molina Enríquez, in his "Apunte científico sobre los orígenes orgánicos de la patria," a work recently described as an excellent example of the sociology of that time, saw reproduction as the most fundamental function of women, along with providing a method for the expulsion of cellular excesses of men in a natural manner (Rascón 1975, p. 151). He warned against the evils of female employment, which would have dire consequences for society: "la sociedad se perjudica con el trabajo de las mujeres, tanto por el aumento de incapaces que tiene que venir a sostener, cuanto por la disminución de la multiplicación de sus unidades" ("Society is harmed by the employment of women, as much for the increase in the incapable which it must come to support as for the decrease in the reproduction of its numbers," ibid.). These arguments were used to mask the economic exploitation of women and to encourage their participation in such occupations as those of seamstress in factories that made uniforms for the army and domestic worker, at even lower wages.

The Mexican revolution enabled women to become involved not only in the protests of the Mexican population as a whole but in the expression of exclusively feminine issues, for these forms of exploitation were closely intertwined. As noted, militant women founded revolutionary magazines and newspapers. Organizations whose goal was to bring about equality for women also emerged, like the Hijas de Cuauhtémoc, Hijas de Anáhuac, Hijas del Pueblo, and Regeneración y Concordia. As early as 1906 groups such as the Admiradoras de Juárez demanded legal rights for women, including the vote. They also attacked the theories of Molina Enríquez and other apologists for the exploitation and subordination of women (ibid., p. 154).

The revolution broke down traditional sex roles, and women fought side by side with men: "La técnica militar permitió que la mujer portara armas sin dificultad y es así como las soldaderas vinieron a pelear al lado de los hombres en los ejércitos revolucionarios. . . . los soldados, tanto federales como revolucionarios, llevaron a sus mujeres consigo en los carros de ferrocarril que transportaban a los beligerantes de una parte a otra de México."[9] Not only did women fight alongside men, but they were forced to assume many jobs customarily reserved for men, demonstrating that they were just as capable of executing them as men. The participation of women was so extensive that the *New York Times* (May 10, 1911) reported with wonderment that "women have taken a spectacular part in the revolution." They were in charge of medicine, munitions, clothing, food, mail, and information concerning the enemy on the front lines. They also worked as secretaries, train dispatchers, telegraph operators, pharmacists, reporters, nurses, teachers, and businesswomen (Turner 1971, p. 134). In short, the revolution did much to equalize relations between the sexes: "Durante la Revolución Mexicana de 1910 los hombres se vieron unidos en una nueva relación con la mujer, ya que ésta jugó un papel nada familiar como compañera y pareja. Por primera vez en la historia de México desarrolló en gran escala sus aptitudes al lado de los hombres, y gano reconocimiento como compañera, consorte y pareja."[10]

While "La Adelita," "La Valentina," and other real and mythical *soldaderas* were immortalized in *corridos* (ballads) and folklore, such portrayals have tended to emphasize the supportive and dependent role played by women. Juana Alegría (1975, p. 131), for example, notes that "cuando las soldaderas acompañan a sus hombres, generalmente ignoran las razones por las que éstos van a la batalla. Ellas no saben de ideas politicas y ni siquiera de razones económicas. . . . Lo que, en cambio, estas mujeres sí saben a la perfección es que tienen un hombre al que pertenecen, puesto que es el que las provee económicamente y

Fig. 7 A *soldadera*. Taken from the *Historia gráfica de la revolución mexicana* by Gustavo Casasola, published by Trillas Editorial, S.A., Mexico City.

también las maltrata y les pega, con el que tienen relaciones sexuales y las embaraza, y al que sirven incondicionalmente."[11] Aramoni (1965, p. 234) notes similarly that she "makes the tortillas and cooks for the man, sleeps with him and satisfies him sexually, and passes him the cartridges that will destroy the men who lie on the other side of the trenches. . . ."

While the *soldaderas* played an important supporting and morale-boosting role, such romantic characterizations minimize the active role played by other women in the hostilities. Many, such as Juana Gutiérrez de Mendoza and Dolores Jiménez y Muro, became colonels, and the former confronted Zapata directly in order to impede abuses of the troops (Rascón 1975, p. 156). Other women were used in espionage. Aurelia Rodríguez, a resident of Puebla and supporter of Madero, was imprisoned in that city as a result of such a mission. When she was forced to abandon her newborn child, it died because she could not nurse it (Rodríguez Cabo 1937, p. 20). Women like Margarita Neri assumed military posts and had hundreds of men under their command (*New York Times*, May 10, 1911). According to Rascón (1975, pp. 155–56), it was not uncommon for women to occupy such posts: "No son raros los casos de mujeres que ocupan puestos de mando, como el de Carmen Alanís, que se levanta en armas en Casas Grandes, Chihuahua, y participa en la toma de Ciudad Juárez con 300 hombres bajo sus órdenes; Ramona Flores, que ocupa el cargo de jefe del estado mayor de un general carrancista que operaba en el noroeste. Ella había armado un contingente con la herencia de su marido, muerto en la rebelión maderista."[12] Other women were able to fight with the troops, but only disguised as men. Some of these women were eventually recognized, and Carmen Amelia Flores and Limbania Fernández also rose to the rank of colonel (ibid., p. 156).

The participation of women in the hostilities was not always voluntary, however. Victoriano Huerta's agents forcibly recruited women to work in gunpowder factories (O'Shaughnessy 1916, p. 58). Also separated from their families by the Huerta government were 300 peasant women from the state of Morelos, sent to Quintana Roo in the expectation that they would form a colony with men who had been exiled to that region for military service. The action caused the soldiers to mutiny, and the women were returned to Veracruz, where they were abandoned on the beach without food or clothing, hundreds of miles from their families. There almost all of the women gave birth (ibid., 124–25). The *huertistas* also forced women, many of them wives and daughters of revolutionaries, to travel ahead of the trains which contained government troops so that they might avert derailments and attacks (Turner 1971, p. 135).

It seems fitting that a discussion of the role played by women in the revolution should end with the women of Puebla, for their courageous actions most vividly symbolize the support among Mexican women for the revolutionary effort. There was a great deal of support for Madero among women, but this was especially true in Puebla. We will focus here on the contributions of some of these supporters, namely, the Serdán women and the Narváez sisters.

In 1910, while Porfirio Díaz made preparations for the centennial anniversary of independence from Spain, he and Ramón Corral were declared president and vice-president of Mexico. But the announcement met with considerable opposition among those who wished to bring the dictatorship to an end. Madero had been actively campaigning for the presidency, confronting Díaz and warning, "If the peace is broken, you will be held responsible before the civilized world" (Batalla de Bassols 1960, p. 8). Madero issued a call to arms, declaring the elections null and void, but he was arrested and transported to San Luis Potosí for trial. He managed to escape to the United States and from there issued another general call to arms to the Mexican people, in his famous "Plan de San Luis."

The plan called for the mobilization of arms to commence on November 20, 1910. Aquiles Serdán, a close ally of Madero, had recently returned to Puebla from San Antonio, Texas, where he had conferred with Madero. The government forces in Puebla, fearing that the Serdán household had been turned into an arsenal, ordered a siege of the house (Mendieta Alatorre 1961, p. 53). Aquiles Serdán had every opportunity to escape but he chose instead to stay and defend the arms that had been placed in his trust, confident that sympathizers would come to his aid. Although greatly outnumbered, Aquiles, the women in the household, and a handful of supporters valiantly defended the arms. Carmen Serdán, Aquiles's sister, was the most courageous of all. Wounded and under enemy fire, she went onto the main balcony of the house, exhorting her compatriots and curious onlookers to take up arms (*New York Times*, May 10, 1911): "Carmen, en el paroxismo de la desesperación, al cerciorarse de que los comprometidos no respondían a la señal convenida, pese a las bombas lanzadas, . . . y dirigiéndose a los curiosos que estaban cerca de Santa Teresa, los arengó, agitando en la diestra un rifle."[13] Aquiles was killed in the siege, and the Serdán women— Carmen Alariste viuda de Serdán, Filomena del Valle de Serdán (Aquiles's wife), and his sister Carmen—were incarcerated, taken first to the jail at Merced and later to the municipal hospital of San Pedro, where Aquiles's daughter, Sara, was born. After being wounded and taken prisoner, Carmen Serdán is reputed to have said to the police chief of Puebla, "Cowards, twenty against four hundred!" (Saénz Royo 1954, p. 39).

The martyrdom of the Serdán family was not in vain, as they served as inspiration to thousands of others. Just days after the death of Aquiles Serdán the Narváez sisters, Guadalupe and Rosa y María, established a center in support of *maderismo* in Puebla. For many years they coordinated an operation that manufactured and distributed arms to revolutionary forces through intricate channels for contraband. The Narváez sisters had initiated their revolutionary activities as early as 1909, and they, along with other women of Puebla, continued them well into the revolution (Mendieta Alatorre 1961, p. 55).

The Revolution and Women's Rights

The revolution signaled the emergence of a distinctive feminist movement which sought to bring about the legal, social, and political liberation of women. While rank-and-file women assumed nontraditional roles, feminist writers and speakers provided the ideological underpinnings for the movement. They established feminist organizations and publications, wrote newsletters, distributed literature, held conferences, marches, and protests, and otherwise pressured for full political rights for women. Despite the many contributions of women during the revolution there was still substantial opposition to women's suffrage and other feminist demands. Yet they continued their fight for equality, and the postrevolutionary period brought to fruition many feminist goals.

Although the Mexican feminist and suffrage movements were well developed by the time of the revolution, the myth persists that Mexican feminism is a much more recent phenomenon that owes much of its impetus to the suffrage movement in Europe and the United States. A leading expert on the subject, Ward M. Morton, observed that

woman suffrage is a recent issue in Mexican politics. The traditional lack of concern about political rights for Mexican women was the reflection of a society hardly conscious that such a problem existed. . . . The nineteenth-century feminist movements in Europe and the United States produced only faint echoes in Mexico. No Mexican counterparts of Susan B. Anthony or Mrs. Henry Fawcett emerged in Porfirian Mexico. . . .

World War I did much to advance the cause of women's rights because of the increased feminine participation in national life demanded by wartime activities in the nations involved. It resulted in an upsurge of demands for women's rights in Europe and the United States which produced an echo in Mexico. [Morton 1962, pp. 1–3]

Such a limited and culturally ethnocentric view does not conceive of the possibility of a Mexican feminism that is endemic and need not turn to other cultures or movements for guidance and inspiration. Mexican women had their own civil war and their own oppression; they did not need World War I or the feminist movement abroad to inspire them.

Demands of equal rights for women were voiced in Mexico as early as 1821 by feminist groups of the period (Rascón 1975, p. 140), and Morton himself (1962, p. 2) acknowledges that in 1878 a socialist journal, *La internacional*, advocated "the emancipation, rehabilitation, and integral education of women" as one item on a twelve-point program. Another group, the Admiradoras de Juárez, was founded in 1904 and two years later demanded legal rights and the vote for women (Rascón 1975, p. 154). In May 1911 a petition signed by several hundred women demanding the vote was presented to interim President De la Barra. It noted that the constitution of 1857 did not specifically exclude them from voting since it made no reference to the gender of voters (*New York Times*, June 1, 1911). Similarly, the Liga Feminista Cuauhtémoc issued a manifesto calling for the complete economic, physical, intellectual, and moral emancipation of women and asked that they be granted full political rights (Velarde 1926, pp. 307–8). Women's suffrage and other issues were advanced by these organizations and by numerous publications containing feminist articles and reports. *Revista de revistas*, for example, published fourteen articles in 1913 and 1914 on women's equality and included such issues as feminism in Europe, Japan, and the United States; feminist literature; and theoretical justification for the moral, intellectual, and legal emancipation of women (Turner 1971, p. 137).

Madero had substantial support from women and appeared sympathetic to them but did little to advance their rights during his brief tenure (W. M. Morton 1962, p. 2). When Venustiano Carranza ascended to power, on the other hand, he proved to be an active ally of women. How much of this sympathy was self-generated and how much resulted from feminist pressure is not clear. What *is* clear is that Hermila Galindo de Topete, his personal secretary and a prominent feminist in her own right, had a tremendous impact on Carranza's policies.

Hermila Galindo's involvement in feminist issues predated the revolution. In fact, feminism was a lifetime concern for her. She was a journalist and an intellectual, versed in psychology, sociology, and revolutionary ideology (Saénz Royo 1954, pp. 64–65). Her influence led to the Carranza Decree of December 29, 1914, which legalized divorce under certain conditions, and his amendment of the civil code in January of the following year to incorporate this change (Turner 1971, p. 139). She was also allowed to distribute feminist literature in Veracruz, Tabasco, Campeche, Yucatán, San Luis Potosí, Coahuila, and Nuevo León. At a congress of teachers in March of 1915, Hermila Galindo "ascended the tribune to make known the ideas which she held in defense of women and with beautiful phrases and concepts no less beautiful she spoke of the great power of feminine sentiments and of the influence which Mexican women were exerting in order to bring about the triumph of the cause of the people, the Constitutionalist cause" (Saénz Royo 1954, p. 65). Her speech, "La reivindicación de la mujer mexicana," was published in the great daily *El dictamen* and caused considerable controversy, but Carranza steadfastly supported his personal secretary against her detractors and intensified his advocacy of women's equality.

On September 16, 1915, Hermila Galindo joined Artemisa Saénz Royo and other women in founding *Mujer moderna,* a feminist magazine which also supported populist causes and a revolutionary program and was viewed favorably by Carranza (Saénz Royo 1954, p. 66).

Hermila was influential in initiating the First International Congress of Women held in Mérida, Yucatán, in January 1916, under the auspices of General Salvador Alvarado, Constitutionalist governor of Yucatán (Grupo de Voluntarias del INFONAVIT 1975). Although unable to attend because she was on a mission for Carranza outside the country, Hermila submitted a paper entitled "La mujer en el porvenir" ("The Woman in the Future") which aroused opposition and was labeled immoral by its opponents.

However, while Carranza did not directly exclude women from participation in the election of deputies or membership in the constitutional congress which met in Querétaro in December 1916 and January 1917, his decree of September 14, 1916, effectively continued their disfranchisement. It limited electors to those eligible to run for deputy under the constitution of 1857 and invoked a national election law which restricted voting to males (Morton 1962, p. 5).

Upon her return from a trip to Cuba, Hermila sent the following message to the constitutional congress, urging them to grant full political rights to women:

The nation and the world are dependent upon your labors, gentlemen Deputies, and I have great hopes for this new code in which will be reflected your patriotism and sense of justice as popular representatives, forming yourselves into political parties with legitimate aspirations but without personal selfishness in order that the woman who has not been excluded from the active part of the revolution will not be excluded from the political part and, consequently, will achieve from the new situation, rights, which even though incipient, will put her on the path toward her own advancement, from which will flow the advancement of the fatherland. [Saénz Royo 1954, p. 69]

Despite her fervent and eloquent plea, the all-male congress failed to give serious consideration to the question of women's suffrage, accepting articles 34 and 35 of the constitution proposed by Carranza without change. These articles simply reiterated the provisions of the 1857 constitution which made no reference to sex. The interpretation was made, however, that its drafters intended to exclude women, since women lacked a political conscience: "Las actividades de la mujer mexicana han estado restringidas tradicionalmente al hogar y la familia, no han desarrollado una conciencia política y no ven además la necesidad de participar en los asuntos públicos. Esto se demuestra en la ausencia de movimientos colectivos para ese propósito." That women had participated extensively in the revolution was not considered sufficient reason to grant them political rights as a "class": "El hecho de que algunas mujeres excepcionales tengan las condiciones necesarias para ejercer satisfactoriamente los derechos políticos no funda la conclusión de que éstos deban concederse a la mujer como *clase*. La dificultad de hacer la selección autoriza la negativa."[14]

Although the framers of the constitution of 1917 denied women the vote, they did appear to have made some important concessions to working women. Article 123 provided for maternity leave and protected women from work at night and in certain dangerous and demanding occupations. Specifically, a woman was (1) not to engage in physically demanding work after the sixth month of pregnancy, (2) to be given a one-month maternity leave at full pay after giving birth and not lose any employment rights or privileges during her absence, (3) to be provided with two extra half-hour rest periods for the purpose of breast feeding until her child was weaned, (4) to be prohibited from night work in industry, and (5) to receive equal pay for equal work without regard to sex or nationality (Pérez 1975, p. 45). These provisions were revised and amended by the constitutional reform of 1974.

Article 123 was based on lofty ideals and promised to raise Mexico to a leadership position among nations with respect to safeguards it provided for working women. But the gains were more apparent than real; in practice many of these so-called safeguards worked to discriminate against women and severely limited their employment opportunities. The same legislation which protected them also restricted their ability to compete with men for jobs (ibid.; and Rodríguez Cabo 1937, p. 26). The veil of "protection," for example, closed doors to employment considered dangerous or harmful and to night-time work in industry.

Shortly after the constitution of 1917 was adopted, Carranza expanded his divorce degree of 1914 by issuing a law concerning family relations which affirmed a woman's right not only to divorce but to alimony and the management and ownership of property (Morton 1962, pp. 8–9). While this gave women marital equality on paper, it gave insufficient protection to unwed mothers or children born out of wedlock. The right of divorce, moreover, was largely an empty one in a society where formal marriages were the exception rather than the rule and where children were frequently the product of informal or casual sexual unions (Rodríguez Cabo 1937, p. 27). The law further penalized women for illicit sexual relations through its prohibition of abortion.

Despite its limitations, the constitution of 1917 was a first step in providing equal legal rights for women. The civil codes of 1870 and 1884 had recognized the judicial rights of single women, with some limitations, but they had severely restricted the legal rights of the married woman. Without her husband's consent, she could not participate in trials, enter into contracts, acquire or dispose of titles, or mortgage property (Mexico, Comité Ejecutivo 1960, p. 7). The constitution of 1917 affirmed that a person's basic legal rights and guarantees shall not be abridged because of one's sex. Among its guarantees were universal and free education for all and freedom of choice in the selection of one's work or profession, and in addition, basic rights such as freedom of written expression and of association were guaranteed regardless of sex.

The rights of women were further extended by the civil code of 1928 (article 2), which specifically stated that "la capacidad jurídica es igual para el hombre y la mujer; en consecuencia, la mujer no queda sometida por razón de su sexo a restricción alguna en la adquisición y ejercicio de sus derechos civiles."[15]

Women thus came to be formally and categorically defined as equal under the law but with a few state and local exceptions, they were still to be denied the vote until 1953. Yucatán in 1922 was the first state to grant the right to vote in state and local elections, but the right was nullified after the assassination of Governor Carrillo Puerto in January 1924 (W. M. Morton 1962, p. 9). San Luis Potosí granted women who could read and write the right to vote in local elections in 1923, and in 1925 Chiapas became the first state to grant complete political rights to women effectively in state and local elections.

The postrevolutionary period proved to be a paradoxical one for Mexican women. At the same time that women's equality was opposed and suffrage was effectively denied them, the feminist movement flourished. Numerous groups and organizations, and publications as well, arose to advance the rights of women. Undoubtedly the most important feminist organization to emerge in the postrevolutionary period was the Frente Unico pro Derechos de la Mujer (FUPDM) (Rascón 1975; p. 160). The FUPDM consolidated other organizations and isolated basic issues that united all women literate or illiterate, communist or Catholic, urban or rural, and at one point had a membership in excess of 50,000. In 1935 the Frente was formally established at a national congress held at the Hidalgo theater in Mexico City and attended by women from every state in the republic. The comprehensive program of action which emerged from the Congress called for:

1. The unlimited right of women to vote and hold office;
2. Modification of the nation's civil codes to provide them equal rights with men;
3. Modification of the federal work law with the intent of making feminine employment compatible with maternity;
4. Modification of the agrarian code so that all women who met the same requirements that applied to men would be able to inherit land;
5. A judicial statute covering female employees of the state;
6. Incorporation of indigenous [Indian] women into the social and political life of the country;
7. Establishment of work centers for unemployed women;
8. Total improvement and protection of infancy and childhood; and
9. Ample or expanded culture [i.e., education] for women. [Rascón 1975, p. 161]

Despite the popularity of such groups, however, some women, frustrated by the continued opposition to feminism and women's equality, chose more radical alternatives. In 1936 a group of women headed by the illustrious Juana Gutiérrez de Mendoza called for the formation of a separate feminist republic. These socialist women felt that the capitalist system breeds antagonism between the sexes and perpetuates the subordination of women (ibid., p. 147).

Twentieth-Century Precursors of Chicana Feminism

Just as it is commonly assumed that Mexican feminism derived directly from the suffrage movements in the United States and Europe, it is assumed that Chicana feminism is a by-product of Anglo feminism. But a firm basis for the emergence of the contemporary Chicana feminist movement was laid during the early part of the century by Chicanas themselves.

The Mexican revolution is important to Chicanas because it provided many female models and a rich feminist legacy and also gave great impetus to Chicana feminism. It was during this period that a significant interchange developed between feminists on both sides of the border.

Many persons opposed to the Díaz regime were either imprisoned or forced to flee the country. In the United States, these Mexican revolutionaries were forced to deal with the colonial oppression of the Chicano. Since the Mexican revolution sought to rid Mexico of Anglo imperialism, the oppression of Chicanos by American industry showed that *mexicanos* were oppressed on both sides of the border. The result was the free exchange of ideas between persons and the development of a liberation movement that transcended national boundaries. Equally significant was the fact that many of these exiled persons were imbued with a truly revolutionary ideology that sought the liberation of all oppressed people—the poor, Indians, and workers, as well as women. The Magón brothers were especially important catalysts in this transnational struggle.

Ricardo and Enrique Flores Magón were central figures in the Mexican revolution, the American labor movement, and the Chicano's struggle for liberation. After they founded *Regeneración*, which first apeared on August 7, 1900, they helped to establish the Partido Liberal Mexicano (PLM), a party which was to have a strong influence on the course of the revolution.

In 1904 they were forced to cross over into the United States, where they continued to publish *Regeneración* in San Antonio. The radical paper enjoyed a broad readership among Mexicans and Chicanos (Silva Herzog 1960, p. 156) and continued to foment opposition to the dictator. While in the United States the Magóns worked as farm laborers and dishwashers (Gómez-Quiñones 1973, p. 27) and quickly became involved in efforts to organize workers on issues such as poor working conditions, discrimination, police brutality, and the lynching of Mexicans (Acuña 1972, p. 156).

One of the central tenets of the PLM was the liberation of women. The influence of the *magonistas* was evident in the "Plan político y social" signed in the Sierra de Guerrero in March 1911. It touched on such problems as urban reform, higher salaries for both sexes, and improvement of the indigenous race, points which were central to the *partido* and to the feminist group Regeneración y Concordia (Rascón 1975, p. 156). Nowhere is the commitment of the PLM to the liberation of women more clearly expressed, however, than in Ricardo's own essay, "A la mujer," an eloquent call to action for women to rebel against their economic and social oppression:

> Compañeras, do not fear the revolution. You constitute one-half of the human species and what affects humanity affects you as an integral part of it. If men are slaves, you are too. Bondage does not recognize sex; the infamy that degrades men equally degrades you. You cannot escape the shame of oppression. The same forces which conquer men strangle you.
>
> We must stand in solidarity in the grand contest for freedom and happiness. Are you mothers? Are you wives? Are you sisters? Are you daughters? Your duty is to help man. . . . Man's bondage is yours and perhaps yours is more sorrowful, more sinister, and more infamous. [Flores Magón 1910, p. 3]

These views were much more than idle rhetoric, for women played a prominent part in the PLM (Silva Herzog 1960, p. 64). Women like Modesta Abascal and Silvina Rembao in Mexico, Andrea and Teresa Villareal in Texas, and María Talavera and Francisca Mendoza in Los Angeles were staunch and important supporters (Gómez-Quiñones 1973, p. 27). Other women like Sara Estela Ramírez, Juana Gutiérrez de Mendoza, Dolores Jiménez y Muro, Elisa Acuña y Rossetti, Guadalupe Rojo de Alvarado, and Inés Malváez were also instrumental in the party. This active participation demonstrates that "within our revolutionary tradition there have been serious and progressive statements on women's rights" (preface to Flores Magón 1910, p. 2).

The PLM elicited broad support among Chicanas throughout the Southwest. Several *tejana* workers (Margarita Endejos, Domitila Acuña Severina Garza, María Cisneros, Concepción Martínez, and Carmen Lujan) wrote to Magón in support of his efforts. They described themselves as "trabajadoras emancipadas de las necias preocupaciones que han tenido a la humanidad esclavizada. . . . Si los hombres no han abierto los ojos para ver claro, nosotros las mujeres no nos dejamos embabucar por los politicastros. Compañero Magón: duro con el burges que desea encumbrarse para tenernos á los trabajadores con el mismo yugo que por siglos hemos padecido."[16] Another Chicana from San Antonio, María González, helped to raise funds for the PLM (Cotera 1976, p. 68). María was also involved in providing financial aid to political prisoners from Mexico (Cotera 1973, p. 32).

In addition to individual women, several groups and organizations arose in support of the PLM. *La mujer moderna*, published by Andrea and Teresa Villareal, was sympathetic to its program. The Leona Vicario club raised money for the "Partido," as did the Liberal Union of Mexican Women (Gómez-Quiñones 1973, p. 40).

There was great concern at this time with the overall oppression of Chicanos. Lynchings and beatings were common occurrences along the border (see Morales 1972, pp. 13–14). Nicasio Idar, a liberal journalist and editor of *La cronica,* and his daughter Jovita, a writer for the paper, organized the Primer Congreso Mexicanista in Laredo on September 11–12, 1911 (Limón 1974). The purpose of the congress was to hold workshops and discussions on many issues of concern, including criminal justice, the organization of workers, education, and the status of women. Women participated actively in all aspects of the congress from its inception to its conclusion. Hortencia Moncaya spoke about abuses of the criminal justice system and specifically about the lynching of Chicanos. She was commended for her address by the Agrupación Protectora de San Antonio, an organization that called her a true descendant of Doña Josefa Ortiz de Domínguez and Leona Vicario (ibid., p. 95). Special concern was expressed over the education of women and their role in the liberation of Chicanos. Soledad Peña expressed the view that "it is necessary that all of us understand our duty and that we take a proper course of action. I, like you, believe that the best way of complying with our duty is to educate women; to instruct her and to encourage and to give her due respect" (ibid.). In return for this respect, she vowed that women would follow the example of their Mexican forebears.

The same women who had helped to organize the Congreso founded the Liga Femenil Mexicanista on October 15, 1911, which was committed to the struggle "por la raza y para la raza" (by the race and for the race," ibid., p. 98).

In the decades to follow, Chicanas would distinguish themselves in many areas, but their contributions would go unrecognized. Blocked from participation in higher education and politics, most of them participated at the grass-roots level. They helped to organize Chicano workers, sought to provide better educational opportunities for Chicano children, protested the abuses and injustices of the legal and judicial system, and participated in establishing "mutualist" groups.

As a response to Anglo oppression, many *mutualista* societies emerged—organizations of Chicanos that sought to provide each other with mutual support and protection for such things as burial services, health, protection against abuses by police and the law, and illegal deportations. In addition, they served a social function; balls and other social affairs gave them the opportunity to discuss mutual problems (Taylor 1930, p. 64). Those organizations that enjoyed the greatest longevity and vitality included "provision for the involvement of members' families in the activities of the organization, either through the establishment of women's and young persons' auxiliaries or through regular group social activities in which the members' families can participate. . . . No matter how achieved there is little doubt that family involvement is crucial to the success of a Mexican American organization" (Tirado 1970, pp. 73–74). One of the earliest of these groups, the Alianza HispanoAmericano, formed in Tucson in 1894, had a clear social function and contained auxiliaries for women and youth (ibid., p. 55). Women were among the founders of the Sociedad Funeraria Miguel Hidalgo of Crystal City, Texas, and they continue to play an important part in the operation of the organization (Cotera 1976, p. 73). Another mutualist group, the Orden Caballeros de America, was founded in 1929 by María L. Hernández and her husband.

María Hernández is one of the most eminent Chicanas of the period, and her active political life, which spans more than half a century is a tribute to contemporary Chicanas, but she has not received the recognition and attention she deserves (Cotera 1976, pp. 74–82). Though born in Mexico, María has devoted her life to the social and civic development of Chicanos, distinguishing herself as both orator and author (Hernández 1945). Her efforts on behalf of her people were applauded by Romula Murguia: "Es del esfuerzo inaudito, admirable, digno de tomarse como ejemplo de lo que se trata aquí; puesto al servicio de su raza por una luchadora, tal vez desconocida para muchos, pero enamorada de la sinceridad, deseosa de alcanzar para los suyos los beneficios de la lucha social que sacude al mundo a través de todas las edades."[17] María Hernández's writing contains significant statements on a diversity of topics including society, politics, religion, economics, and women, and her involvement in local political issues is vast. In 1934 she was active in the Liga de Defensa Escolar in San Antonio, a group which sought to improve educational opportunities and facilities for Chicano children (Cotera 1976, p. 79). Not only has she served as an effective spokeswoman for the Chicano community in the areas of education and civil rights, but she has been actively involved in other areas of politics. Even at an advanced age, she has traveled extensively in support of the Partido de la Raza Unida in Texas (Cotera 1976, pp. 80–81). Her commitment to activism on behalf of Chicanos is well reflected in her own words: "I feel my husband and I have worked very hard since 1924 for the betterment of our people. I feel we have not accomplished very much because of our limited resources. But when a person dedicates his life to the movement, that in itself is worth more than money" (Herrera and Lizcano 1974, p. 19).

María Hernández has demonstrated the importance of family unity and cooperation between men and women in the Chicano struggle. Although a feminist and leader in her own right, she is always quick to point to the importance of family unity in the movement and to acknowledge the help of her husband, Don Pedro, "whom she describes as enlightened, committed and liberated in every way, and who has never done anything but to encourage her participation in the affairs of the community" (Cotera 1976, pp. 81–82).

While Doña María Hernández was distinguishing herself in the areas of education and civil rights, another Chicana, Jovita Gonzáles, was making important contributions in literature. Born in Roma, Texas, a descendant of the first settlers of the area, Jovita was one of the first Chicanas to write in English about Chicano culture (Paredes and Paredes 1972, p. 8). Her work has been important in its depiction of Chicano folklore, such as her sketches "Among My People" (Gonzáles 1972b) and "With the Coming of the Barbwire, Came Hunger" (Gonzáles 1972a). A regular contributor to the *Annals of the Texas Folklore Society*, she served as its president in the 1930s, the first Mexican-American to be so recognized (Paredes and Paredes 1972, p. 8).

Jovita did not limit her writing to discussion of Chicano culture and traditions; she also addressed the exploitation and mistreatment of Chicanos. Of special concern to her was the killing of Mexicans along the border. She noted that in the early 1920s between 100 and 300 Mexicans were executed without benefit of trial or formal charges (McWilliams 1968, p. 113). Much of her writing was concerned with the increased tension and hatred that developed between *mexicanos* and *tejanos*. She wrote that "the friendly feeling which had slowly developed between the old American and Mexican families [was] . . . replaced by a feeling of hate, distrust and jealousy" (ibid., p. 87).

Another area where Chicanas have made important contributions is the labor movement. Although not typically in positions of power or formal leadership, many rank-and-file Chicanas were actively involved in the struggle to organize Chicano workers. In the 1930s, for example, Chicanas helped to organize the International Ladies Garmentworkers Union in Texas. They composed about one-third of the work force in this industry, and although there was considerable conflict between them and the Anglo organizers, Chicanas were instrumental in ILGWU organizational efforts (Green 1971, p. 152).

The 1930s was a period of intense organizational activity in agribusiness. Since agricultural work frequently involved the entire family, Chicanas, like the *soldaderas* of the revolution, worked beside men in the fields and on the picket line. The importance of the family unit is poignantly illustrated by Ernesto Galarza's autobiographical account of the migration of a Mexican family to the United States, *Barrio Boy* (1971). The family—a mother, her son, and her two brothers—move as a unit from the village of Jalcocotán (Jalco) in Nayarit until they finally settle in a barrio in Sacramento. Cohesion is strong as the family remains a basic source of emotional and physical support, and family members left in Mexico are helped to come to the United States. Galarza describes the sense of family unit which remains intact across the migration:

> "Ours remained a Mexican family. I never lost the sense that we were the same, from Jalco to Sacramento. There was the polished cedar box, taken out now and then from the closet to display our heirlooms. I had lost the rifle shells of the revolution, and Tio Tonche, too, was gone. But there was the butterfly sarape, the one I had worn through the Battle of Puebla; a black lace mantilla Doña Henriqueta modeled for us; bits of embroidery and lace she had made, the tin pictures of my grandparents; my report card signed by Señorita Bustamente and Don Salvador; letters from Aunt Esther. ... When our mementos were laid out on the bed I plunged my head into the empty box and took deep breaths of the aroma of *puro cedro*, pure Jalcocotán mixed with camphor. [P. 237]

The strong familistic orientation of Chicanos facilitated their exploitation by capitalists, who found it much more profitable to hire entire families than individual laborers. American employers preferred men with wives and children not only because of their greater stability and because more hands were secured but because families provided cheaper labor (González 1976, p. 13). A study of the sugar beet fields of the South Platte Valley of Colorado by Paul S. Taylor (1930, pp. 95–235) demonstrates the extent to which the sugar beet industry relied on female and child labor. The Great Western Sugar Company favored the recruitment of families because they provided a cheap,

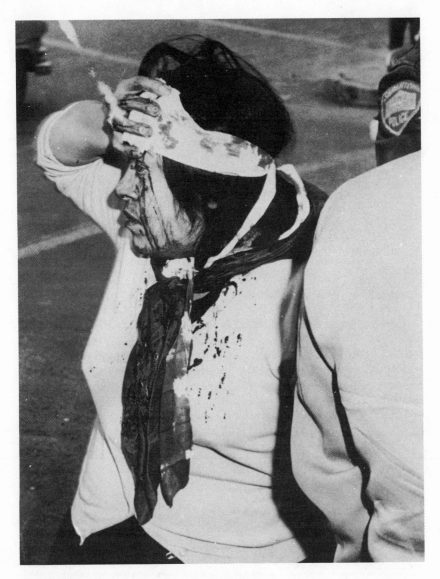

Fig. 8 Janie Lozano, Tex-son Manufacturing Company strike, 1959. Courtesy of the University of Texas at Arlington Library, Division of Archives and Manuscripts.

stable, and self-perpetuating work force. Families were more apt to settle permanently, and company policy encouraged the establishment of Mexican *colonias* by pressuring growers to provide housing for beet workers.

Landowners also tended to prefer Mexican tenant sharecroppers. Unlike white wives and children, families of Mexican tenant farmers typically worked in the fields, providing a greater return for the landowner (González 1976, p. 25). A study by Ruth Allen of 294 Mexican farm women in Texas, most belonging to tenant families ("croppers" or "halvers"), found that although women as a rule worked in the fields, they did not obtain economic independence. Even those women hired out as wage laborers were not paid directly; the wage paid was a family wage and collected by the husband, father, or brother (Allen 1931, p. 137). Allen was appalled not only by this practice but by the apparent subservience of Mexican women:

> If the migration of a people is to be effective, it must be a migration of families. Because it is such a movement of families, the penetration of Texas by the Mexican peon is effective and, shall we say, fear inspiring. The Mexican woman has been taught as her guide to conduct the vow of the Moabitess, "Where thou goest, I will go." Up and down the road she follows the men of her family. . . . She brings with her across the Rio Grande traditions of feminine subservience which seem strange in twentieth century America. And here, these habits are probably strengthened . . . for she has fewer contacts with the new civilization . . . and her ignorance of the English language is greater. [Ibid., p. 131]

Although many Chicanas worked in the fields, their employment extended to other areas. As early as 1900–1907, Victor S. Clark reported (1908, p. 495), Chicanas were employed in canneries, candy and clothing factories, the packing of crackers, and clerical positions. Clark maintained, nonetheless, that Mexican women did not usually work in factories or as domestic servants in the United States, in part because husbands and fathers were protective of them and opposed female employment outside the home (pp. 495–96). A study by Mario Garcia (1976) of Mexican women who migrated to El Paso with their families found that in 1900 an estimated 18 percent of these families had a woman in the labor force, and a full 15.5 percent were headed by women. By 1920 one-third of the immigrant labor force consisted of women, most employed as servants and laundresses. Thus, in addition to agriculture, Chicanas were primarily employed in textile and light manufacturing industries, in clerical work, and in service and domestic work.

Chicanas who worked in such employment were frequently subjected to violence as they joined the struggle to organize workers. In October 1933, in the midst of the depression, the Cannery and Agricultural Workers Industrial Union (CAWIU) organized a strike in the San Joaquin Valley near Visalia. The agricultural labor bureau announced that it was willing to pay $.60 per 100 pounds of cotton, but the organizers demanded $1 (Acuña 1972, p. 163). In addition to low wages, the workers were protesting racism and poor work and health conditions. Tension mounted, and the growers responded to the worker's demands by ambushing them as they left a meeting. They shot into the crowd, killing Delfino Dávila and Dolores Hernández and wounding many others (ibid.).

While many Chicanas have been active in labor organizing, their activities are not well documented. The San Antonio pecan shellers strike of 1938 is significant because it clearly shows that Chicana workers were as oppressed as their male conterparts and that they actively resisted their oppression and exploitation. The trend in the pecan industry in the 1920s was toward mechanization, and entrepreneurs in San Antonio learned that they could maximize profits by hiring cheap Mexican labor: "The great depression of 1929 made the labor supply available at wages so low that entire families had to work at pecan shelling in an effort to obtain the minimum amount of food and shelter needed for survival. The Southern Company found that it could operate at a greater profit by paying those wages rather than by installing and maintaining machinery" (Walker 1965, p. 46). Like agribusiness, the industry worked through contractors who hired the crackers and pickers. It was not uncommon for entire families to work at home (Menefee and Cassmore 1940, p. 9), and many of the workers in the plants were also women and children. Working conditions were poor and unsanitary as ventilation and lighting were inadequate, "workers were crowded elbow to elbow on long wooden benches without backs, and little attention was given to sanitation" (Walker 1965, p. 47). Wages were unbelievably low: workers earned an average of $2.73 per week in 1938 (Menefee and Cassmore 1940, p. 9).

In November 1937 a representative of the United Cannery, Agricultural, Packing, and Allied Workers of America (UCAPAWA), a union chartered by the CIO, went to San Antonio in an attempt to organize the pecan workers. When the Southern Pecan Shelling Company announced on February 1, 1938 that they would reduce wages from $.06

and $.07 per pound for pieces and halves, respectively, to $.05 and $.06, thousands of pecan shellers went on strike at 130 plants throughout San Antonio.

The strike was opposed by the city fathers and the chief of police, Owen Kilday, who used every available means, legal or not, to stop the strike (ibid. 1940, p. 17). Hundreds of picketers were arrested for violating archaic ordinances; they were tear gassed and beaten. Those arrested were kept in deplorable conditions. Thirty-three women were placed in cells designed to hold six. They were thrown in with prostitutes and forced to share a single toilet and drinking cup, even though 90 percent of the prostitutes were reportedly infected with venereal disease (Acuña 1972, p. 166).

The union was finally recognized by an arbitration board, but the victory was short-lived. Rather than meet the minimum wage of $.25 per hour established by the Fair Labor Standards Act, the company elected to close its doors (Walker 1965, p. 55). Eventually it reopened, opting to mechanize and thus displacing thousands of Mexican workers.

One of the leaders of the pecan shellers strike was the young and vivacious Emma Tenayuca. Although only nineteen, Emma was elected to a leadership position in the UCAPAWA union. Like Lucía González and Teresita Urrea, she challenged powerful interest groups while demanding justice for the oppressed. An avowed Communist, Emma joined the Communist party and married the state local party organizer. In time she was named director of the Communist party for the state of Texas. During the heat of the strike, Emma was singled out for abuse as a troublemaker and Communist agitator. According to Acuña (1972, p. 166), "The special target of the city officials was Mrs. Emma Tenayuca Brooks, 'a fiery little Mexican woman about twenty years old,' who was a leader among the strikers and allegedly an admitted Communist. Although the union leadership replaced her, the attacks continued."

Another Chicana in the UCAPAWA was Luisa Moreno. Although technically a Central American by birth, she was a Chicana at heart, having come to the United States at an early age and received part of her education here. One of her first organizational activities took place in New York City in the early 1930s, where she led a protest against the ruthless and cold-blooded police murder of a Mexican named Gonzalo González. González was one of many Latinos savagely attacked by the New York police as they picketed the racist film *Under a Texas Moon*.

Later Luisa served as editor of the UCAPAWA newspaper and assumed a prominent position within the union, traveling extensively to organize workers and establish study groups. These groups were

Fig. 9   Emma Tenayuca (Texas Civil Liberties
Union publication, "San Antonio: The Cradle and
the Coffin of Texas Liberty"). Courtesy of the
Texas Civil Liberties Union and the University of
Texas at Arlington Library, Division of Archives
and Manuscripts.

designed to instruct the workers in reading and writing, civil and political rights, organization, and even Marxist theory.

One of her greatest accomplishments came in 1938 with the organization of the first National Congress of the Spanish Speaking People (Acuña 1972, p. 197). She successfully gained support from a broad cross-section of the Latino population. Many segments of organized labor in addition to UCAPAWA were represented, including the stevedores, copper miners, butchers and meat packers, seamstresses, and construction workers. The congress was set for April 1938 in Albuquerque, but before it convened the House of Representatives Un-American Activities Committee swept into the city, arousing a campaign of hysteria against it. The congress was described as Communist inspired, and pressure was placed on local Chicano leaders to oppose the conference. The end result was that the site was moved to Los Angeles. Despite this opposition and Red-baiting by the media, the delegates were able to push through "a radical and progressive platform. Workers were to be organized, and a newspaper and newsletter were to be published. Legislative priorities were set down, and stands were taken against oppressive laws, immigration officials, vigilantes, and police brutality. The right of farm workers to organize was demanded. . . . In short, the conference dedicated itself to 'the economic and social and cultural betterment of the Mexican people . . .' " (ibid.).

Luisa Moreno obtained a respected position in organized labor, demonstrating great intellect and a facility for organizing workers. She received many honors, including election as international vice-president of UCAPAWA, state vice-president of the CIO, and chairwoman of the California committee against discrimination in the labor movement. Among her most important accomplishments were the organizing of cotton workers in South Texas, pecan shellers in San Antonio, beet workers in Colorado and Michigan, and over 60,000 cannery workers in California.

Because of her political activism, Luisa was deported at the height of the anti-Mexicanism and the Red scare which prevailed in the 1950s. She went initially to Mexico but moved on to Cuba, where she became an active participant in the early years of the revolution. Today she resides in Guadalajara, and despite advanced age her revolutionary fervor does not waver. She remains committed to the liberation of Chicanos and to the cause of workers throughout the world.

The accomplishments of Chicanas in this century are numerous, and they continue to the present day. Rather than listing these many accomplishments, let us focus on a woman whose life and career symbolize the dedication of Chicanas to the organization of workers and the liberation of her people—Dolores Huerta.

Although Dolores Huerta works in the background and does not enjoy the publicity of César Chávez, her contributions to the United Farm Workers have been substantial, and as vice-president of the union and chief negotiator, her position in the union is secondary only to that of César himself. Dolores Huerta's origins can be traced back to the 1600s in New Mexico (Huerta 1974, p. 284). Her father worked as a migrant worker, traveling from New Mexico to Wyoming with the changing seasons. As a child she moved to Stockton, California, where she grew up and attended school. Dolores excelled in school and was especially proficient in writing but was discouraged by her teachers and the racism which prevailed: "When I was in high school I got straight A's in all of my compositions. . . . I used to be able to write really nice, poetry and everything. But the teacher told me at the end of the year that she couldn't give me an A because she knew that somebody was writing my papers for me. That really discouraged me, because I used to stay up all night and think, and try to make every paper different" (ibid., pp. 284–85).

In the late 1950s Dolores was still living in Stockton when she met Fred Ross, who was forming the Community Service Organization (CSO). Ross directed her attention to the idea of registering Chicano voters, and she became involved in CSO efforts to bring this about. She had worked for two years registering voters and fighting police brutality before meeting Chávez.

In 1960 César suggested sending her to Sacramento to lobby for important legislation. She headed the legislative program in 1961, lobbying for benefits like old-age pensions for noncitizens, the right to register voters door to door, the right to take driver's examinations in Spanish, and disability insurance for farm workers (ibid., p. 286).

Throughout a long and distinguished career, Dolores Huerta has worked quietly and effectively behind the scenes lobbying and negotiating on behalf of farm workers. She has proved to be a tenacious and articulate spokesman for the union, challenging skilled and well-paid lawyers with her own innate abilities. Although an outstandingly talented woman, she appears to arouse little hostility or resentment in men: "There's been no reaction from the farm workers to my role as a woman within the union. They will appreciate anybody who will come in and help them. In terms of the leadership itself I get very little friction from anybody, really. Anyone who can do the job is welcome to come in and share the suffering" (p. 286). Despite her many accomplishments and high position, Dolores Huerta appears unaffected. She considers herself just another worker in the movement: "The fact that I get publicity is sort of a by-product of the union. But there's an awful lot of people who have worked continuously since the union started, a lot of women, for example, who nobody even knows" (ibid.). Huerta's humility and quiet dedication is characteristic of the many men and women who, in her words, "son los soldados razos del movimiento" ("are the common soldiers of the movement"), (ibid.).

The Birth of Chicana Feminism

Despite the vast achievements of the precursors of Chicana feminism, a clearly defined movement to liberate Chicanas did not evolve until very recently, a product of the 1970s. Chicana feminism is not impervious to Anglo feminism, but its roots are in Mexican-Chicana feminism. There is thus no need to go outside of Mexican-Chicano culture and traditions to explain its emergence.

The rise of the Chicana movement can be seen as the response to the frustration that comes when hard work and dedication to a cause go unrecognized. For years the Chicana worked side by side with her man with the hope of bettering conditions for *la raza*, subordinating her own personal needs and wants to the good of the whole. As the Chicano movement unfolded in the late 1960s, it became increasingly clear that these needs and concerns were not being recognized or met. The *movimiento* called for an end to the oppression of Chicanos—discrimination, racism, poverty—goals which Chicanas supported unequivocally; but it did not propose basic changes in male-female relations or in the overall status of women. As in the revolution, women were welcomed into the movement to work side by side with their *hermanos;* but unlike their revolutionary sisters, they still found themselves relegated to subordinate positions. The more important and prestigious jobs were assumed by men; *las mujeres* were expected to cook the beans, make the tortillas, do clerical work, care for the children, and satisfy their men's sexual needs. Like the *soldaderas*, they were expected to be totally devoted and to provide for all of the men's needs—social, psychological, emotional, and physical. Sexual taboos were relaxed in the heat of the *movimiento*, but ultimately women who gave themselves for the cause ran the risk of being labeled *putas*, or whores. One Chicana has aptly described this predicament:

When a freshman male comes to MECHA [Movimiento Estudiantil Chicano de Aztlan—a Chicano student organization in California], he is approached and welcomed. He is taught by observation that the Chicanas are only useful in areas of clerical and sexual activities. When something must be done there is always a Chicana there to do the work. "It is her place and duty to stand behind and back up her Macho!" . . . Another aspect of the MACHO attitude is their lack of respect for Chicanas. They play their games, plotting girl against girl for their own benefit. . . . They use the movement and Chicanismo to take her to bed. And when she refuses, she is a *vendida* [sell-out] because she is not looking after the welfare of her men. [Vidal 1971, pp. 5–6]

Faced with this internal oppression, many Chicanas began to question their role in the *movimiento* and to demand an equal voice. They wanted to make speeches, hold office, and take part in shaping the direction and future of *la causa*. But when women expressed these concerns, they were chastised for rocking the boat and not presenting a unified front. At the same time that Chicanos were calling for the rekindling of ethnic pride and identity, Chicanas who pointed to the rich legacy of feminism and female participation in *raza* revolutionary movements were discounted as *vendidas* or as women's libbers. Feminism was seen not as something organic to the culture but as an Anglo trick to divide the Chicano movement (Vidal 1971, p. 7; and Nieto-Gómez 1971, p. 9).

Extreme pressure was placed on Chicanas to forgo their demands and concerns as women. Enriqueta Longauex y Vasquez (1970, p. 379) describes the pressure felt by women at the first Chicano Youth Conference held in Denver in 1969. After attending one of the workshops held to discuss the role of women in the movement, she was dismayed to learn that

> when the time came for the women to report to the full conference, the only thing that the workshop representative had to say was this: "It was the consensus of the group that the Chicana woman does not want to be liberated."
>
> As a woman who has been faced with living as a member of the Mexican-American minority group, as a breadwinner and a mother raising children, living in housing projects and having much concern for other humans plus much community involvement, I felt this as quite a blow. I could have cried. Surely we could at least have come up with something to add to that statement. . . . Then I understood why the statement had been made and realized that going along with

the feelings of the men at the convention was perhaps the best thing to do at the time.

For as disappointing as this action was to Enriqueta and other Chicanas, it had a positive function and appears to have served as a major catalyst in the Chicana movement. The Denver youth conference dramatized the plight of the Chicana, providing a rallying point for feminists. It became clear that the Chicana faced oppression not only at the hands of Anglo society but within her own culture. Many Chicanas condemned the actions of the Denver youth conference, rejecting the philosophy that a woman's place is in the home as a mother of a large family. Their response to the charge that they betrayed their culture and heritage was, "Our culture, hell!" (Flores 1971*b*, p. 1). Groups of Chicanas emerged spontaneously throughout the country to express their concerns. From local groups on college campuses to national conferences, a clear and consistent voice was heard—Chicanas *did* wish to be liberated, and they *did not* consider birth control, abortions, day care, or sex discrimination to be only white women's liberation issues (ibid.). A genuine Chicana movement appeared; communication was maintained through interpersonal networks, women's conferences, caucuses within Chicano conferences, and various publications. There were numerous newsletters and even a Chicana journal, *Encuentro femenil*. Other periodicals, such as *El grito del norte, Regeneración, El grito*, and *De colores*, devoted special issues to the Chicana.[18]

In addition, several feminist groups and organizations were established. The Hijas de Cuauhtémoc, a Chicana feminist group patterned after the parent group in Mexico, sought to educate and liberate Chicanas and founded *Encuentro femenil*. The Comision Femenil Mexicana was established at the National Mexican American Issues Conference in the fall of 1970. Its aim was to organize women so that they could assume leadership positions within the Chicano movement and in the community at large. One of its main projects was the Chicana Service Action Center, the first employment center to provide meaningful employment opportunities and job training for Mexican-American women. In 1974 the Mexican American Legal Defense and Educational Fund (MALDEF) launched the Chicana Rights Project. The specific focus of this research and litigation project was on the needs of Chicanas, compiling information on their educational and employment problems and promoting litigation on their behalf (MALDEF 1977). The Conferencia de Mujeres por la Raza held in Houston in 1971 symbolized this new spirit. The conference focused attention on many issues which are frequently labeled white women's issues and challenged the assumption that the only place for the woman in the *movimiento* is in the home. There was widespread feeling that a woman has a right to a large family, if she wants one, but to stipulate this as a tenet of the *movimiento* is to condemn women to washing diapers and staying at home (Flores 1971*b*, p. 1). It was argued, moreover, that when this concept is stripped of its verbage and intellectual romanticism, it "means continued inequality and suppression of women" (ibid., p. 2).

The feminists' demands caused considerable controversy not only between men and women but among women themselves. Women tended to fall into one of two camps, loyalists and *feministas* (see Nieto-Gómez 1974). The loyalists felt that there was no need for a separate Chicana movement. If women were oppressed, it was because all Chicanos were oppressed by Anglo society. The fact that men oppressed women was the fault of a racist society that oppressed them economically and socially. Feminism, moreover, was Anglo inspired and could only work to split Chicanos. At the 1971 Houston conference, for example, women who felt that the YWCA (which hosted the conference) was using it as a way to advance their own goals and to divide the movement walked out. An anonymous writer articulates the concerns of the loyalists: "I am concerned with the direction that the Chicanas are taking in the movement. The words such as liberation, sexism, male chauvinism . . . plus the theme of individualism is a concept of the Anglo society; terms prevalent in the Anglo Woman's movement. The familia has always been our strength in our culture. But it seems evident . . . that [you] are not concerned with the familia, but are influenced by the Anglo woman's movement" (cited ibid., p. 35). The feminists were seen as individualistic and selfish because they were said to place their own needs above those of the group.

The *feministas* countered that they were not bra burners or man haters and that they were not *agabachadas* ("Anglocized"), as suggested. They pointed to the abundant Mexican-Chicana feminist heritage. Marta Cotera, for example, admonished those who sought to discredit Chicana feminists as anti*raza*, noting "a long, beautiful history of mexicano feminism which is not Anglo inspired, imposed or oriented. . . . We have a rich legacy of heroines and activists in social movements, and armed rebellions from which we can draw models to emulate" (Cotera 1973, p. 30). Feminists argued that it was both unfair and illogical to ask Chicanas to ignore or hold in abeyance their objections to oppression as women (Nieto-Gómez 1974, p. 37). Liberation will only come when Chicano men and women join together in the struggle to end their mutual oppression, for sexism and racism are closely interwoven. Feminists are not traitors to their culture but active agents in the struggle for human liberation. They are supporters of the culture who follow the ideals and examples set down by their feminists forebears, it was argued. Longauex y Vasquez's view of the role of women in the movement (1970, p. 384) was shared by many Chicana feminists: "When a family is involved in a human rights movement, as is the Mexican-American family, there is little room for a woman's liberation movement alone. . . . The Mexican-American-movement demands are such that, with the liberation of La Raza, we must have a total liberation. The woman must help liberate the man and the man must look upon this liberation with the woman at his side, not behind him, following, but alongside of him, leading."

Because of the harassment experienced by feminists, most eschewed affiliation with the Anglo women's movement. Not wishing to divide the movement or to be termed *vendidas*, Chicanas frequently set their concerns as women aside. They believed that "con mi raza todo, fuera de mi raza nada" ("with my people everything, without my people nothing"). The result was that potential gains made by Chicanas were neutralized or minimized. They were not incorporated into the platforms of groups or organizations, and their needs were not reflected in the goals of the Chicano movement. The overall effect of the "women's libbers" label was thus negative. According to Marta Cotera, "Unfortunately, the only effect that Anglo feminism has had on the Chicana has been negative. Suddenly, mujeres involved in the struggle for social justice, who have always advocated more and stronger woman, and family participation in all political activities, are suspect. They are suspected of assimilating into the feminist ideology of an alien culture, that actively seeks our continued domination" (1973, p. 30).

Disillusioned with the resistance to feminism, some Chicanas looked to the emerging women's movement in the late 1960s. Women after all shared a mutual oppression, one that was universal and perhaps more insidious than the oppression of racial and ethnic minorities. With women's issues becoming more clear-cut, Chicanas found that they shared them with others. Other women were more receptive to these problems than their *carnales*. They too were interested in such issues as birth control, abortion, forced sterilization, rape, welfare, working mothers, day care, and sexual discrimination in employment. But Chicanas soon learned that white women were insensitive to their special concerns as minority women. They were in agreement on basic "women's issues," but not on their interpretation or implementation

Cultural differences prevailed: "When a Chicana talks about birth control and abortion she does so in the context of understanding the cultural genocidal acts of this country. When a Chicana demands child care centers she includes in these demands that they be bilingual and bicultural.... If she is a Chicana on welfare she may be even more adamant about being able to select the staff at the child care center so her child will not become a drop-out at the age of two years old because of the staff's prejudices" (Nieto-Gómez, 1974, p. 41). The Anglo women's movement showed itself to be indifferent to the unique needs of Chicanas, assuming that it could unite all women in the struggle against sexism but minimizing or neglecting the issues of racism and poverty. This resulted in a sort of maternal chauvinism that asked Chicanas to subordinate or minimize their needs as members of a racially oppressed group for the greater cause—the universal oppression of women across racial, national, and economic groups. What Anglo feminists failed to see was that it was not possible for Chicanas to conceive of a separate women's movement independent of their racial-cultural struggle, just as it had not been possible for them to separate their problems as women from their racial oppression.

Chicanas found that the Anglo women's movement not only neglected racism but that it too was racist. In their perception Anglo women reflected the attitudes of the dominant society: "Unfortunately many of these women focus on the maleness of our present social system as though, by implication, a female-dominated white America would have taken a more reasonable course. Chicanas have no more faith in white women than white men.... We're oppressed by a system that serves white power and depends upon a white majority for its survival and perpetuation. In our struggle we identify our men, not white women, as our natural allies" (Hancock 1971, p. 6). Chicanas became understandably leery of the Anglo women's movement. As long as Chicanos were oppressed as a people, could Chicanas really share in the accomplishments of Anglo feminism? Were Anglo women really concerned with the unique problems faced by minority women or did they simply want to bring a few black and brown faces into the fold? In short, was the white feminist concern with Chicanas another example of tokenism? These questions were raised because all too often Chicanas found that white middle-class women were the primary beneficiaries of the gains made by social minorities: "Minorities are working hard, pressuring the system for equal opportunity. Suddenly, the hereto [sic] silent Anglo woman emerges clamoring for her political, social, and economic rights.... Priorities are shifted, programs are opened up.

Women will be heard above other minorities. Women—white women —the wives, lovers and mothers of those in power, of course will be heard above the clamor of male and female minorities" (Cotera 1972, p. 25). Since white women were less of a threat to white men than either Chicanos or Chicanas, they were more likely to be accepted and incorporated when minority restrictions were lowered. White women were hired before Chicano men, who in turn were hired before Chicanas (Nieto-Gómez 1974, p. 42; Sosa Riddell 1974, p. 162). Why should a Chicana support the Anglo women's movement if she was still the last to be hired and the first to be fired? To her it made little difference if she was unemployed because she was a woman or because she was a Chicana.

With the benefit of hindsight, the Anglo feminist chauvinism and lack of sensitivity experienced by Chicanas appear especially ironic when one considers that the difficulties encountered by Chicana and Anglo feminists in the late 1960s were not totally dissimilar, and in fact their developments were parallel in significant respects. Much of the impetus for separate feminist and women's rights movements in the middle and late 1960s came from the resistance encountered to the concerns of women, first during the civil rights movement and then in the antiwar and New Left movements. This opposition and insensitivity to feminist concerns was voiced by Stokeley Carmichael in his famous comment, "The only position for women in SNCC is prone." Just as Chicanas were ridiculed for being *agabachadas* and splitting the movement, so were Anglo feminists ridiculed and chastised for introducing disruption in the New Left and drawing attention away from the real issue, which was the Vietnam war (Lockwood Carden 1974, p. 62). Early expressions of feminist concerns had been similarly quashed within the civil rights movement by a call for black power and black nationalism. Feminists were asked to subordinate their needs to the "real" issues. They too were expected to cook, do clerical work, provide sexual release for men; be supportive of men, in other words. Maren Lockwood Carden (ibid., p. 60) describes the plight of feminists: "Although most nascent feminists at first discussed their complaints in private, a few were willing to state them in public. Feminists had already spoken publicly at the December 1965 SDS national convention. Despite the ridicule with which their remarks were then received, they returned the following year with the demand that the convention members accept a plank supporting women's liberation. The women who made this proposal were 'pelted with tomatoes and thrown out of the convention.'" In a manner reminiscent of the loyalists and *feministas*, Anglo feminists split into two groups, according to whether they saw themselves primarily as feminists or members of the New Left (ibid., p. 61). As identification with feminism increased, so did the intensity of response from the men. A number of incidents at which feminist speakers were jeered and ridiculed led women to recognition of the need for a separate and independent feminist movement that was more responsive to them. In January 1969 at the counterinaugural demonstration, for example, Marilyn Salzman-Webb gave a mildly feminist, strongly pro-Left speech which was badly received. She was booed and greeted with shouts and such remarks as "Take her off the stage and fuck her" (ibid., p. 62). Women were shocked and upset. The response of Chicanos to feminism appeared mild by comparison.

Liberation Chicana Style

Chicana feminists hold that liberation will come neither from the Anglo women's movement nor from the Chicano movement but from a unique Chicana movement that works closely or in conjunction with the *movimiento* but is not subordinate to it. Liberation can only come for the Chicana when her triple oppression ends. Gains made by women's liberation may help to reduce or eliminate the universal oppression of women, but they will have little impact on Chicanas as long as Chicanos remain a colonized people. Her discrimination and exploitation will result from racism rather than sexism. Chicana feminists therefore differ from their Anglo counterparts in that they hold that Chicanas cannot be free until all Chicanos are free.

Since Chicanos are a colonized group, the position of Chicanas cannot be divorced from its historical context. This colonial heritage has had an important impact not only on Chicanos as a people but on women. Throughout history *la mujer* has been victimized by both sexism and racism. It is commonly assumed that the physical and spiritual conquest of Mexico gave rise to the cult of *machismo* (Paz 1961). Unable to protect their women from the rape and plunder that accompanied the conquest, males developed an overly masculine and aggressive response to them. The cult of *machismo* is thus said to be a compensation for powerlessness and weakness, a futile attempt to prove one's masculinity. La Malinche symbolizes the violated mother who gave herself to the conqueror and thereby is alleged to have emasculated the male. The conquest and downfall of a people are blamed on a solitary woman. The Chicana who marries an Anglo is similarly La Malinche incarnate.

Chicana feminists are seeking not only to redefine the role of La Malinche and to recognize her as a great woman but to uncover the source of their oppression. She is a positive symbol because "malinche" has become identified with "vendido," or traitor—labels which Chicana feminists have also endured.

While Chicana feminists recognize that independent and assertive women have been unjustly termed *vendidas* and that their cultural heritage has been male dominated, they are not ready to blame all of the ills of Mexican culture on *machismo*. Chicanas have a rich tradition of feminism, and "the passive, submissive Mexican woman is a creation of social scientists and journalists who have taken for granted the idea that women are dependent and unproductive creatures" (Baca Zinn 1976, p. 19). This stereotype of Chicanas has been perpetuated by Anglos and has its complement in the docile, passive Mexican-American male depicted by social scientists (Romano 1973*a*, 1973*b*). If Chicanos are lazy, and dependent, it is argued that their women will exhibit these traits even more prominently. Anglos have been too quick to dismiss the problems of Chicanos and other minorities as emanating from within their own culture. *Machismo* fits into the colonial mentality of the conqueror. It is a mechanism for shifting the focus away from Anglo oppression to alleged pathologies within Chicano culture. The universal oppression of women is ignored, and *machismo* becomes a quaint custom practiced by Mexicans and Chicanos. It is as if the oppression of women is somehow peculiar to Mexican culture. Anglos fail to recognize that the Anglo women's movement was also motivated by male oppression—a reaction to white *machismo*.

The concept of *machismo* is undergoing reanalysis and redefinition. One interpretation is that *macho* attitudes are not a reflection of the internalization of impotence and powerlessness but, rather, "that aggressive behavior of Chicano males has been both an affirmation of Mexican cultural identity and an expression of their conscious rejection of the dominant society's definition of Mexicans as passive, lazy, and indifferent" (Baca Zinn 1975, p. 23). Another interpretation of Chicano *machismo* is that it is not simply the expression of male pride but a political expression of ethnic identity that transcends gender: "The essence of machismo, of being macho, is as much a symbolic principle of the Chicano revolt as it is a guideline for the conduct of family life, male-female relationships, and personal self-esteem. . . . The Chicano revolt is a manifestation of Mexican Americans exerting their manhood and womanhood against the anglo society. Macho, in other words, can no longer relate merely to manhood but must relate to nationhood as well" (Rendón 1972, p. 104).

Las feministas are also reexamining the stereotypical role of the woman in the family. Whereas the female is typically seen as submissive, docile, and relegated to the home, the *macho* is viewed as actively resisting oppression and colonization. A feminist interpretation of *la mujer* redefines her role as one of equally active resistance to colonization. As the center of the family and mainstay of the culture and tradition, the Chicana has helped counter the pervasive encroachment of colonial institutions. The Chicano family has proved remarkably impervious to external forces. As the primary source of preservation of cultural values and language, this resilience is a tribute to the woman. Her domestic role, then, is not passive.

It is ironic that Chicana feminists are stigmatized as *vendidas*, not only because the woman has been the mainstay of the culture but also because Chicana feminists have consistently opposed separatism either from their men or from their culture (Cotera 1972; Nieto-Gómez 1974; Sosa Riddell 1974; Espinosa-Larsen 1972; and Baca Zinn 1975). Chicanas have been unjustly compared with Anglo women, and the comparison has been an effective device for keeping Chicanas quiet and stifling their demands (Nieto-Gómez 1971). Aware of colonial oppression, they reject Anglo feminism for the very reason that Anglos neglect the issue of racism. The Chicana feminist seeks to eradicate poverty and racism as well as sexism. Total liberation will come only when Chicanas and Chicanos can join as equal partners in the mutual struggle against oppression. There is a new force and determination in the contemporary Chicana which will not permit her to subordinate or compromise her principles: "The issue of equality, freedom and self-determination of the Chicana—like the right of self-determination, equality and liberation of the Mexican community—*is not negotiable.* . . . FREEDOM IS FOR EVERYONE" (Flores 1971*a*).

Notes

One | **La Chicana: An Introduction**

1. E.g., see La Rue 1970*a*, 1970*b*; King 1975; and Almquist 1975.

2. Our emphasis on the religious underpinnings of the conquest should not obscure the importance of other factors. Economic and political forces undoubtedly play an equally prominent role. Both the Spanish crown and the *conquistadores* saw the expeditions as an opportunity to gain wealth and power. The point is simply that whatever the initial motives, once the conquest was underway religion became a primary force in justifying the subordination and exploitation of the indigenous population. It provided a ready-made theodicy (Berger 1967, p. 53), as it were, to explain and legitimize the physical and cultural oppression of a "heathen people."

3. "Our Lord God (by design) has kept this half of the world in darkness until our times, and by his divine ordinance he has willed that it be illuminated by the Roman Catholic church, with the intent not that its natives be destroyed or tyrannized but that the darkness of idolatry they have lived in be enlightened, that they be introduced into the Catholic church and instructed in the Christian religion, and that they may attain the kingdom of heaven, dying in the faith as true Christians" (Sahagún 1946, 3:10).

4. "In this very great and very important enterprise, our Lord God willed that a path be blazed and that the wall with which this godlessness was surrounded and enclosed be pulled down; through the figure and deeds of the valiant captain D. Hernando Cortés, our Lord performed many miracles in the conquest" (ibid.).

5. "Heed that it has been said that our lord Quetzalcóatl has arrived; go and receive him and listen attentively to what he tells you; take care that you forget nothing of what he tells you. These are the jewels you are to present him with on my behalf, all of which are priestly adornments that befit him" (Sahagún 1946, 3:20–21).

6. For discussions of internal colonialism, see Moore 1970; Acuña 1972, p. 3; Barrera, Muñoz, and Ornelas 1972, p. 483; Blauner 1969, 1972; and Almaguer 1971.

Two   Cultural Heritage I: Mexico

1. For stereotypical accounts of Mexican women in the United States, see Fisher 1876, p. 46; Hulbert 1933, p. 240; McMurtrie 1943, p. 4; Secrest 1967a, pp. 5–8, 1967b, p. 28; Garrard 1955, p. 171; and Kendall 1844, p. 319.

2. "You should be inside the home, as the heart is inside the body; you should not tread outside the home, nor should you make it a habit to go anywhere; you should be like the ashes that cover the hearth of the home; our Lord inters us in this place; you should work here, and your job should be to carry water and to grind the corn on the metate; you should sweat there, next to the ashes and the hearth" (Sahagún 1946, 1:603–4).

3. "Our Lord gave us the laughter, dreams, eating, and drinking with which we were created and live; he also gave us the function of procreation with which to increase our numbers on the earth; all of these things give our life a fleeting joy, so that later we may grieve with continual cries and sorrows" (ibid., p. 532).

4. "May it never happen, my daughter, that you put cosmetics on your face or that you put paint on it or on your lips to look pleasing; for this is the mark of carnal, common prostitutes . . . those shameless ones who have lost their modesty, if not their senses, who run around in drunkenness and madness; . . . adorn yourself, wash yourself, and wash your clothes so that your husband will not desert you . . . because if you wash yourself and your clothing daily, it will be said of you that you are very clean and very delicate" (ibid., p. 540).

5. "I, an unfortunate and miserable old woman, do not know what has moved you to select me, who have neither judgment nor ability, nor do I know how to do things pleasing to our Lord; why, I am foolish and ignorant; many servants of our Lord abound, and they are knowledgeable, prudent, experienced, and well versed; these our Lord has instructed with his spirit and inspiration, and he has authorized them to practice this vocation" (ibid., p. 586).

6. "Awaken then, and arise, my daughter; for it is day, it has dawned, the whiteness of the morning has begun, and swallows and all the other birds sing. Arise, my daughter, and compose yourself; go to that good place that is the home of your father and your mother, the sun; for all who dwell there

rejoice and are content and joyful; go to your father the sun, and may your sisters the celestial women carry you there" (ibid., p. 597).

7. There has been considerable discussion and controversy surrounding the origins of her name. For a detailed discussion, see Rodríguez 1935, pp. 3–8. Although there is general agreement about her first name, this is not the case regarding Tenepal. Some argue that it is familial and others that it is a derivative of "tenextli," which means "cal," or "lime," because she is said to have been as "white as lime." Rodríguez (pp. 7–8) maintains that it is a derivation of "tempalli," which means "lips," and that "tenepal" was used to signify a person who speaks a lot and with much animation. He concludes that "this name was given to Doña Marina as a result of her quality of intelligence and of speaking various dialects" (p. 8).

8. E.g., "Malintzin, Marina, Malinche. Madre nuestra putísima . . . en el pecado concebida . . . llena eres de rencor . . . el demonio es contigo . . . maldita eres entre todas las mujeres . . . y maldito es el fruto de tu vientre" ("Malintzin, Marina, Malinche. Our whorish mother . . . conceived in sin . . . thou art full of rancor . . . the devil is with thee . . . cursed art thou among women . . . and cursed is the fruit of thy womb," p. 175).

9. The stanzas can be translated thus:

> The curse of offering foreigners
> Our faith, our culture,
> Our bread, our money,
> Remains with us. . . .
>
> Today, at the height of the twentieth century,
> Fair-haired ones [foreigners] keep arriving,
> And we open our homes to them
> And we call them our friends. . . .
>
> Oh, curse of Malinche!
> Sickness of the present,
> When will you leave my country?
> When will you free my people?

10. "Why do we exact so much conviction from her, then? A slave's mentality is conditioned to obey a master, and Hernán Cortés was Marina's master; there was no reason to disobey him" (p. 74).

11. "She had no reason to be faithful or to show loyalty to anyone. At the moment when circumstances proved propitious for her, she was true to herself, putting her intelligence at the disposal not so much of Hernán Cortés as of the historical events it befell her to live" (p. 75).

12. "A convent for women in colonial America was a sacred place, but cheerful; devout, but entertaining. One or two hundred nuns lived there, each with her maid or slave, . . . with little girls as students. There was gossip, tell me and I'll tell thees, the coming and going of maids, games, and the hubbub of little girls" (De la Maza 1967, p. 18).

13. "Had to be considered not only as a house of virtue and prayer far

from the worries of daily life but also as a superior center for culture, for love of the most refined letters and the Latin humanities, as a prestigious refuge."

14. "Resolving that if it grew to the same length again before I learned such-and-such a thing I had set out to learn, I would cut it again . . . because it made no sense to me to have a head adorned with hair if it was devoid of knowledge" (Alegría 1978, p. 108).

15. "She answered each of them fully and correctly. And so it was that Juana's urbanity and talents awakened suspicion and fear. As they had never seen such a phenomenon, the theologians wondered if all that knowledge or, rather, that unusual eagerness to learn was 'inspired,' that is to say, God given—from the devil—or 'acquired' " (De la Maza 1967, p. 16).

16. "Convenience, and not for religious reasons; she looked to the cloister, as she says herself, as a place where she could be removed from matrimony without destroying her decency or impairing her reputation" (ibid., p. 567).

17. "God does not want knowledge in women that inspires arrogance (pride) . . . the knowledge you have subdued is the most trying though pleasant holocaust that has arisen in the trials of religion . . . what a pity it is that such a great intellect should lower itself to acquiring, vile, earthly knowledge with no desire to fathom celestial knowledge; it has humbled itself to the earth, yet considering what transpires in hell, it should beware of going any lower" (De la Maza 1967, pp. 49–50).

18. "During the war of insurrection, Mexican women overran our cities and battlefields like protective goddesses, now announcing the beginning of our independence, now enlivening with their own love a greater, more sacred love; their unexpected heroic feats now touched on the mythical; now, finally, they spilled their own blood, not content with having offered the blood of their sons" (González Obregón 1900, p. 635).

19. "Making them appear to be bandits of the worst species, sacrilegious heretics, tigers eager to drink human blood, furies unleashed from hell . . . excommunicating them so they were outside the bosom of the church and abandoning them to eternal damnation" (G. García 1910, p. 98).

Four   The Woman in the Family

1. We are aware of the numerous criticisms that have been leveled against functionalism. Although we employ some of the vocabulary of functionalism, we do not subscribe to a pure functionalist perspective. For a discussion of this and related issues treated in this chapter, see Mirandé 1975, pp. 375–78.

2. For a more detailed discussion of the traditional Chinese family, see Levy 1968; Leslie 1973, pp. 80–122; Ho 1965; Lee 1953; and Huang 1976.

3. For a discussion of the family, women, and child care in Red China, see Sidel 1973.

4. As economic conditions have improved and the community has gained stability, the strong antifamilistic sentiment seems to be waning. As children born in the kibbutz reach adulthood and establish families, a full-scale three-generational structure has developed. Kin ties have apparently become more important, and relatively stable and cohesive kin networks are emerging (ibid., pp. 280–81). Contacts with relatives are maintained, and children assume responsibility for sick or aging parents (Talmon 1961). There is also evidence of a return to a more traditional role for the female (Firestone 1972, pp. 214–15). In short, the family seems to have regained some of the functions that were lost during the revolutionary phase of the kibbutzim.

5. "One should not walk slowly, for it was a sign of pomposity, nor in a hurry, for it indicated restlessness; and the head should be carried neither too high nor too low, nor should it be turned, or look to one side or the other; the face should be neither smiling nor vexed but should look serene" (Bonilla García 1959, p. 263).

6. "Fine; it has been decided that the young man will be happy to marry her, though he may have to suffer poverty and travail for this; it appears that he has taken a fancy to her although she can do nothing, nor is she expert in carrying out her feminine vocation" (Sahagún 1946, 1:564).

7. "You have ceased to be a young girl now and have begun to be a mature woman; leave your youthfulness and childishness behind. . . . You will rise at night, sweep the house, and light the fire before daybreak; you will have to get up every day. Daughter, do not embarrass or dishonor us, your father and your mother; your grandparents who are deceased cannot come tell you to perform your duties; we speak on their behalf" (ibid., p. 566).

8. "Our daughter, we, your mothers who are here and your parents, wish to console you; be strong, dear daughter, and do not be pained by the matrimonial burden you take upon your shoulders. . . . Your husband has given you the five cotton blankets you see here so that you can trade in the market; you can buy chili, salt, pitch pine, and wood to cook food with. This is a custom the elders left with us; work and perform your feminine duties by yourself, dear daughter; no one should help you; we are leaving now; be dutiful and prosperous as we would wish you to be" (ibid., p. 568).

9. "Take care that you do not give your body to any man [other than your husband] . . . take care that in no way are you known by more than one man. . . . When God decides that you should take a husband, . . . don't defy him; see that at no time nor in any place you betray him, for that is called adultery" (Sahagún 1946, 1:541–42).

10. "You are all present, masters and teachers of the young men. Do not be grieved because your brother, our son, wishes to part company with you; he now desires to take a wife; here he is; this ax is a sign of how he wishes to separate himself from your company" (Sahagún 1946, 1:563).

11. So impressed was Las Casas with the manner in which noble girls were reared by the Aztecs that he likened them to novitiates in a convent:

"Better reared, more decent, more mortified and quiet, without having made a profession of silence, and more sane and temperate one can[not] train the novitiates in the convents to be" (p. 157).

12. "My loving daughter, you see how you are going to your husband . . . you know that it is customary for the women to go and follow their husbands and that they be with them and live in their houses. . . . Be advised, my daughter, to be not defective or ill bred; you should live in a manner that makes you an example to other women" (Las Casas 1974, p. 159).

13. Goodman and Beman (1971, p. 111) found that nearly all of the parental generation in their Houston sample claimed at least one such relationship, and quite often they claimed two, three, or more.

14. The Spanish institution of *compadrazgo* was apparently adopted by the Indians during the colonial period as widespread epidemics led to massive depopulation and left many children orphaned (Gibson 1966, p. 142). Godparents thus originally functioned as parental substitutes.

15. "When God decides that you should take a husband . . . do not contemn him . . . do not defy him; God, who is everywhere, will see you; he will be angry with you; he will avenge himself as he wishes; or you will befoul yourself at his command, or be blinded, or your body will rot, or you will be stricken by poverty because you dared hurl yourself into defiance of your husband, for which fortune will kill you or hold you beneath her feet and cast you into hell" (Sahagún 1946, 1:541–42).

Five   Work, Education, and the Chicana

1. The Labor Department defines as unemployed all those "who did not work during the survey week, who made specific efforts to find a job within the past 4 weeks, and who were available for work during the survey weeks (except for temporary illness). Also included as unemployed are those who did not work at all, were available for work, and (a) were waiting to be called back to a job from which they had been laid off; or (b) were waiting to report to a new wage or salary job within 30 days" (ibid., pp. 31–32).

2. It is significant that there were so few Chicanas who attended or completed college that the Bureau of the Census considers the number too small to compute their median income (ibid.).

3. Their higher rates of widowed and divorced status are probably due mostly to the fact that widowed and divorced men are more likely to remarry and that women live longer than men.

4. Movimiento Estudiantil Chicano de Aztlán. This is a Chicano student political organization found in many high schools and colleges in California.

5. Available data indicate that these "gains" have been modest indeed. Spanish-surnamed persons accounted for only 1.6 percent of all enrollment in higher education in 1968, 2.1 percent in 1970, and 2.3 percent in 1972

(López, Madrid-Barela, and Flores Macías 1976, p. 20). Since persons of Mexican origin account for fewer than 60 percent of all Spanish-surnamed persons and their level of educational attainment is lower than that of most other Spanish-surnamed groups, Chicano enrollment is a much smaller proportion of all enrollment in higher education.

Six   Images in Literature

1. "I don't learn a lot about my Language any more / Because I grew up in a *gringo* society. / Where has my culture gone? / I hope I will find it. . . ."

2. Through correspondence Sosa Riddell has indicated that *El grito* erroneously attributed her poem "Como duele" to another writer.

3.

> Companion,
> without your noticing it
> I sometimes lie down with you
> those few times
>   solitude accompanies me
> and I receive it calmly
> I'm jealous
> did you know that?
> I tire
>   of tasks
>   housework
>   obligations
> and I want to go look for you
> If I don't have you, if I don't find you
> I get jealous
> I don't know
> It's that you are solitude
> And solitude
> is what I desire
>   more than anything.

4.

> I kiss this little girl's black braids
> who cries in my arms
> because I won't let her go out to play
> she makes her eyes plead with me but
> she doesn't understand that this is just the brusque manner
> of a confused mother and it's just that I don't want her pushed
> outdoors, she may get a sticker on her little toes
> going out barefoot   I don't want her to stray too far
> from the front of the house   may she not learn too quickly
> what is so quickly learned   NO   YOU ARE MINE   YOU
> CAN'T   GO HOME   NO   YOU ARE A WOMAN

Seven   Chicana Feminism

1. "The first systematic persecution of the independent press starts toward the end of 1885 and continues into 1886, its obvious goal being to cloak in secrecy the elections held in June of this year in order to facilitate the election of men unconditionally supportive of the dictatorship" (cited in Mendieta Alatorre 1961, p. 29).

2. "Now when many men grow feeble and through cowardice withdraw from the struggle, considering themselves insufficiently strong to recover our liberties, . . . there appears a spirited and valiant woman, ready to fight for principles which the weakness of many men has permitted to be trampled and spat upon. Madam Juana B. Gutiérrez de Mendoza has just founded *Vésper* in Guanajuato, a liberal paper destined to defend liberal and democratic institutions" (cited in Mendieta Alatorre 1961, p. 32).

3. "Thirty-five years of incessant struggle and sixty of life will place anyone outside the combat; or at least they serve to justify indifference or veil cowardice. . . . I have that right, but I have no corner to retreat into. In all the corners of the world an anguish lives . . . and I do not have the indifference to see, the cowardice to flee, or the meekness to accept it" (cited in Mendieta Alatorre 1961, p. 33). Death came at last in 1946 to Juana, at the age of seventy-one.

4. The poem can be translated as follows:

> Surge! Surge to life to liveliness, to the beauty of truly living; but surge radiantly and powerfully, beautiful in your qualities, resplendent in your virtues, full in your energies.
>
> You, queen of the world, Goddess of universal adoration; you, the sovereign to whom servitude is rendered, do not lock yourself in your temple of God or in your triumphant courtesan's boudoir.
>
> A true woman is more than a Goddess or Queen. Do not let the incense of the altar or the applause of the stage intoxicate you; there is something greater and more noble than all that.
>
> Gods are cast from the temples, kings are thrust from their thrones; but woman is always woman.
>
> Gods live what their believers desire, kings live as long as they are not dethroned; woman always lives, and this is the secret of her happiness, to live.
>
> Only action is life; to feel that one lives, that is the loveliest sensation.
>
> Surge, then, to the beauty of life; but surge beautifully in your qualities, resplendent in your virtues, full in your energies.

5. The issue of whether or not the Mexican revolution is dead is one which is still debated; see, e.g., Ross 1972.

6. "Was obligated to meet periodically in assemblies to discuss her specific problems as mother and worker. They discussed a regulation which re-

quired that she assist in the education of her child until five years of age . . . she planned the affairs of the community in the functioning of the family. . . . Her opinion and functions were respected and as important as those of men; that is, there was no discrimination, and her capacity as mother, producer, and efficient administrator were recognized" (Zendeja 1962, p. 9).

7. "The decline in population growth resulted from continuous abortions, especially in the tobacco factories, since that substance is highly noxious to pregnancy; infant mortality brought on by the poor health of the mother, who had to forgo nursing the child so that she could return to work as soon as possible; and lung diseases among children who were prematurely subjected to long and exhausting work days under the most unsanitary conditions, etc." (Rascón 1975, p. 152).

8. The subordination of women was also veiled by rhetoric which eulogized their roles as wives and mothers and made a virtue out of domesticity; see, e.g., Sanz 1907.

9. "Military technology permitted women to carry arms without difficulty, and this is how the *soldaderas* came to fight at the side of the men in the revolutionary armies. . . . The soldiers, federal troops as well as the revolutionaries, brought their women with them on the railroad cars which transported the belligerents from one part of Mexico to another" (Turner 1971, pp. 132–33).

10. "During the Mexican revolution of 1910 the men saw themselves united in a new relation with the woman, now that she assumed a totally unfamiliar role as partner and equal. For the first time in the history of Mexico, she developed her abilities on a grand scale at the side of men and gained recognition as companion, consort, and equal" (ibid., p. 135).

11. "When the *soldaderas* accompany their men, they are ignorant of the reasons why the men go to battle. They do not know anything about political ideas or even about economic factors. . . . Instead, what these women do know very well is that they have a man to whom they belong, inasmuch as he is the one who provides for them economically and also mistreats and hits them, the one they have sexual relations with and who gets them pregnant, and the one they serve unconditionally."

12. "Cases in which women occupy command positions are not rare, like the one of Carmen Alanís, who rises to arms in Casas Grandes, Chihuahua, and participates in the capture of Ciudad Juárez with 300 men under her command; Ramona Flores who occupies the position of chief-of-staff under a *carrancista* general operating out of the northeast. She had armed a contingent with the inheritance left by her husband, who died in the *maderista* rebellion."

13. "Carmen, in a paroxysm of desperation, realizing that those committed to the cause were not responding to the agreed-upon signal, cursed the hurling bombs . . . and, addressing the onlookers who were near Santa Teresa, harangued them, while shaking a rifle in her right hand" (Mendieta Alatorre 1961, p. 53).

14. "The activities of the Mexican woman have traditionally been restricted to the home and the family; they have not developed a political conscience, and they do not see, moreover, the need to participate in public affairs. This is demonstrated by the absence of collective movements to that end. . . . The fact that some exceptional women have the necessary qualities to exercise political rights satisfactorily does not support the conclusion that these rights should be given to women as a *class*. The difficulty in making the choice supports a negative conclusion" (Rascón 1975, p. 157).

15. "Juridical capacity is the same for the man and the woman; consequently, the woman should not be subjected because of her sex to any restriction in the acquisition or exercise of her civil rights" (Mexico, Comité Ejecutivo 1960, pp. 11–12).

16. "Workers who are free of the foolish preoccupations which have held humanity in bondage . . . if men have not opened their eyes to see clearly, we women will not allow ourselves to be deceived by the politicasters. Comrade Magón: be hard on the bourgeois who wishes to elevate himself in order to keep us, the workers, in the same yoke we have endured for centuries" (Gómez-Quiñones 1973, p. 86).

17. "It is about an admirable, extraordinary effort by an exemplar worthy of being emulated that I speak. It is about this fighter, called upon to serve her people [but] unknown to many, whose passion for truth and desire to obtain for her people the benefits of a social struggle that has shaken the earth through all time, that I speak" (ibid., p. 5).

18. Several women have served as editors of major periodicals. *El grito del norte* was edited during its first five years by two Chicana feminists, Betita Martínez and Enriqueta Vasquez. Francisca Flores served as editor of *Regeneración* and Anna Nieto-Gómez and Adelaida del Castillo as editors of *Encuentro femenil,* the second oldest Chicana feminist journal. The first such journal was *Mujer moderna,* published in the 1910s (Cotera 1976, pp. 164–65).

Glossary of
Spanish Terms

adelantado	title formerly given to the governor of a province
agabachado (-a)	"Anglocized," Americanized
agorero	diviner
a toda madre	"a real live mother," fantastic, "out of sight"
Aztlán	mythical land of the north from which the Aztecs are said to have originated, used today by Chicanos to refer to the American Southwest
baile	dance
barrio	neighborhood
bracero	contract laborer brought to the United States for a temporary period
bruja	witch
caballero	young horseman, gentleman
cacique	Indian chief
californio (-a)	Californian
cantina	saloon, bar
capirotada	Mexican bread pudding
carnal	brother
carnalismo	brotherhood
carrancista	follower of Carranza
casta	mixing of Indian and Spanish blood
colonia	neighborhood
comadre	name by which parents address their child's god-mother
	commander
	~~hich parents address their child's godfather
	~~ortés's men
	~~lexico of Spanish parents
	~~)f a map

familia	family
fandango	dance
gabacha	Anglo-American female
gachupines	Spaniards
gringo (-a)	Anglo-American
hacendero	owner of a *hacienda*
hacienda	large estate and lands
hembra	female
hembrismo	womanhood
hermana	sister
heroina	heroine
huelgista	striker
huertista	follower of Huerta
huipil	smock
indio (-a)	Indian
insurgentes	insurgents, rebels
jarabe tapatió	regional dance from Jalisco, Mexico
jefita	mother, (lit.) little boss
junta	assembly of people
llano	plain, plains
machismo	manliness, masculinity
macho	male, masculine
maderista	supporter of Madero
malinchismo	concept in Mexican and Chicano culture which equates selling out, in whatever form, with Malinche's selling out to Cortés
mariachi	Mexican folk band, originally from the state of Jalisco
mescal	intoxicating drink made from a cactus plant
mestizaje	mixing of Indian and Spanish blood
metate	curved stone used as a pestle
mexica	tribe of Indians
mexicano (-a)	Mexican
mexicano norteño	person from northern Mexico
mujer	woman
monte	card game
pachuco	term used in the 1940s to refer to Chicanos who wore zoot suits; see *vato*
partera	midwife
patria	country
patrón	boss
peninsulares	Spaniards born in Spain
peon	modern-day serf
pobres, los	the poor
pocho	"Anglocized" or Americanized Mexic

presidio	fort
rancho	ranch
raza, la	literally race of man; used by Mexicans and Chicanos to refer to themselves
realista	royalist, loyalist
ricos, los	the rich
ruco	older man, father
sarape (serape)	narrow blanket
soldadera	woman soldier
vato	young dude
viuda	widow
vizcaíno	person from the area around the Bay of Biscay

Bibliography

Acuña, Rodolfo. 1972. *Occupied America: The Chicano's Struggle toward Liberation*. San Francisco: Canfield.

Alegría, Juana Armanda. 1975. *Psicología de las mexicanas*. 2d ed. Mexico City: Samo.

Allen, Ruth A. 1931. "Mexican Peon Women in Texas." *Sociology and Social Research* 16 (November–December): 131–42.

Almaguer, Tomás. 1971. "Toward the Study of Chicano Colonialism." *Aztlán: Chicano Journal of the Social Sciences and the Arts* 2 (Spring): 7–71.

Almquist, Elizabeth M. 1975. "Untangling the Effects of Race and Sex: The Disadvantaged Status of Black Women." *Social Science Quarterly* 56 (June): 129–42.

Alvirez, David, and Bean, Frank D. 1976. "The Mexican American Family." Pp. 271–92 in *Ethnic Families in America*, ed. Charles H. Mindel and Robert W. Habenstein. New York: Elsevier.

Anaya, Rudolfo A. 1972. *Bless Me, Ultima*. Berkeley: Quinto Sol.

Aramoni, Aniceto. 1965. *Psicoanálisis de la dinámica de un pueblo*. Mexico City: Costa-Amic.

Arias, Ron. 1975. *The Road to Tamazunchale*. Reno: West Coast Poetry Review.

Ashbaugh, Carolyn. 1976. *Lucy Parsons*. Chicago: Kerr.

Atherton Gertrude. 1898. *The Californians*. New York: Macmillan.

———. 1902. *The Splendid Idle Forties*. New York: Stokes.

Baca Zinn, Maxine. 1975. "Political Familism: Toward Sex Role Equality in Chicano Families." *Aztlán: Chicano Journal of the Social Sciences and the Arts* 6 (Spring): 13–26.

————. 1976. "Chicanas: Power and Control in the Domestic Sphere." *De colores* 2 (3): 19–31.

Bancroft, Hubert Howe. 1886. *The Works of Hubert Howe Bancroft.* Vol. 18, *History of California.* Vol. 1, *1542–1800.* San Francisco: History Co.

Bandelier, Adolphe Francis. 1879. *On the Social Organization and Mode of Government of the Ancient Mexicans.* Salem: Salem Press.

Barrera, Mario; Muñoz, Carlos; and Ornelas, Charles. 1972. "The Barrio as an Internal Colony." In *Urban Affairs Annual Reviews,* ed. Harlan H. Hahn, 6:465–98. Beverly Hills: Sage.

Barrio, Raymond. 1969. *The Plum Plum Pickers.* Sunnyvale, Calif.: Ventura.

Batalla de Bassols, Clementina. 1960. *La mujer en la revolución mexicana.* Mexico City: Instituto de Intercambio Cultural Mexicano-Ruso.

Berger, Peter L. 1967. *The Sacred Canopy: Elements of a Sociological Theory of Religion.* Garden City, N.Y.: Anchor.

Bermúdez, María Elvira. 1955. *La vida familiar del mexicano.* Mexico City: Robredo.

Blacker, Irwin R., and Rosen, Harry M. 1962. *Conquest: Dispatches of Cortez from the New World.* New York: Grosset & Dunlap.

Blanco, Iris. 1977. "Participación de las mujeres en la sociedad prehispánica." Pp. 48–81 in *Essays on la mujer,* ed. Rosaura Sánchez and Rosa Martinez Cruz. Anthology no. 1. Los Angeles: UCLA Chicano Studies Center Publications.

Blauner, Robert. 1969. "Internal Colonialism and Ghetto Revolt." *Social Problems* 16 (Spring): 393–408.

————. 1972. "Colonized and Immigrant Minorities." Pp. 51–81 in *Racial Oppression in America.* New York: Harper & Row.

Bolton, Herbert Eugene. 1908. *Spanish Exploration in the Southwest, 1542–1706.* New York: Barnes & Noble.

————. 1930a. *Anza's California Expeditions.* Vol. 1, *An Outpost of Empire.* Berkeley: University of California Press.

————. 1930b. *Anza's California Expeditions.* Vol. 4, *Font's Complete Diary of the Second Anza Expedition.* Berkeley: University of California Press.

Bonilla García, Luis. 1959. *La mujer a través de los siglos.* Madrid: Aguilar.

Borah, Woodrow, and Cook, Sherburne F. 1966. "Marriage and Legitimacy in Mexican Culture: Mexico and California." *California Law Review* 54 (May): 946–1008.

Bowman, J. N. 1957. "Prominent Women of Provincial California." *Historical Society of Southern California Quarterly* 39 (June): 149–66.

Brack, Gene M. 1973. "Mexican Opinion, American Racism, and the War of 1846." Pp. 60–66 in *Chicano: The Evolution of a People,* ed. Renato Rosaldo, Robert A. Calvert, and Gustav L. Seligmann. Minneapolis: Winston.

Bradshaw, Benjamin S., and Bean, Frank D. 1972. "Some Aspects of the Fertility of Mexican-Americans." Pp. 140–64 in *Demographic and Social As-*

pects of Population Growth, ed. Charles F. Westoff and Robert Parke, Jr. Commission on Population Growth and the American Future, Research Reports, vol. 1. Washington: U.S. Government Printing Office.

Cabeza de Baca, Fabiola. 1954. *We Fed Them Cactus.* Albuquerque: University of New Mexico Press.

Calderón de la Barca, Madame. 1931. *Life in Mexico.* New York: Dutton.

Calvillo Schmidt, Lorenza. 1973a. "Califas." *El grito: A Journal of Contemporary Mexican American Thought* 7 (September): 63.

————. 1973b. "Como duele." *El grito: A Journal of Contemporary Mexican American Thought* 7 (September): 61.

Carrillo Azpéitia, Rafael. 1975. *Ricardo Flores Magón.* Mexico City: Centro de Estudios Históricos del Movimiento Obrero Mexicano (CEHSMO).

Caso, Alfonso. 1958. *The Aztecs: People of the Sun.* Translated by Lowell Dunham. Norman: University of Oklahoma Press.

Castañeda Shular, Atonia; Ybarra-Frausto, Tomás; and Sommers, Joseph. 1972. *Literatura chicana: texto y contexto.* Englewood Cliffs, N.J.: Prentice-Hall.

Castellano, Guadalupe. 1975. "To a Mandolin." Pp. 145–46 in *Sighs and Songs of Aztlán,* ed. F. E. Albi and Jesus G. Nieto. Bakersfield, Calif.: Universal.

Castillo, Caroline. 1974. "Chavalitas mocosas." *Miquiztli* 2 (Winter): 6–9.

Chaplin, Ralph. 1948. *Wobbly: The Rough-and-Tumble Story of an American Radical.* Chicago: University of Chicago Press.

Chávez, Ezequiel A. 1975. *Sor Juana Inés de la Cruz.* 3d ed. Mexico City: Porrúa.

Clark, Victor S. 1908. *Mexican Labor in the United States.* Department of Commerce and Labor, Bureau of Labor Bulletin no. 78. Washington: U.S. Government Printing Office. (Reprinted in *Mexican Labor in the United States,* pp. 466–522. New York: Arno, 1974.)

Cobos, Georgia M. 1969. "Suffer Little Children." *El grito: A Journal of Contemporary Mexican American Thought* 1 (Summer): 36–38.

Colton, Rev. Walter. 1850. *Three Years in California.* Stanford, Calif.: Stanford University Press.

Cota Cardenas, Margarita. 1977. "Por nosotras." *Hojas poeticas* 1 (mayo): 3.

Cotera, Marta. 1972. "Chicana Caucus." *Magazín* 1 (August): 24–26.

————. 1973. "Mexicano Feminism." *Magazín* 1 (September): 30–32.

————. 1976. *Profile of the Mexican American Woman.* Austin: National Educational Laboratory.

Dakin, Susanna Bryant. 1963. *Rose, or Rose Thorn? Three Women of Spanish California.* Berkeley: Friends of the Bancroft Library.

David, Henry. 1936. *The History of the Haymarket Affair.* New York: Farrar & Rinehart.

De Hoyos, Angela. 1977. "Words Unspoken." *Hojas poeticas* 1 (mayo): 3.

De la Maza, Francisco. 1967. *Sor Juana Inés de la Cruz en su tiempo.* Mexico City: Talleres Gráficos de la Nación.

Del Castillo, Adelaida R. 1974. "Malintzin Tenépal: A Preliminary Look into a New Perspective." *Encuentro femenil* 1 (2): 58–78.

Delgado, Sylvia. 1972. "Epitaph for 'Maria, Maria, Maria la Vandida.'" *Regeneración* 2 (2): 1–3.

Díaz Del Castillo, Bernal. 1963. *The Conquest of New Spain.* Translated by J. M. Cohen. Baltimore: Penguin.

Díaz-Guerrero, Rogelio. 1975. *Psychology of the Mexican: Culture and Personality.* Austin: University of Texas Press.

Dozier, Edward P. 1970. *The Pueblo Indians of North America.* New York: Holt, Rinehart & Winston.

Drumm, Stella. 1926. *Down the Santa Fe Trail and into Mexico: The Diary of Susan Shelby Magoffin, 1846–1847.* New Haven: Yale University Press.

Espinosa-Larsen, Anita. 1972. "Machismo: Another View." *La Luz* 1 (August): 59.

Fergusson, Harvey. 1921. *The Blood of the Conquerors.* New York: Knopf.

———. 1954. *The Conquest of Don Pedro.* New York: Morrow.

Firestone, Shulamith. 1972. *The Dialectic of Sex.* New York: Bantam.

Fisher, Walter M. 1876. *The Californians.* San Francisco: Bancroft.

Flores, Francisca. 1971a. "El mundo femenil mexicana." *Regeneración* 1 (10): Editorial.

———. 1971b. "Conference of Mexican Women in Houston." *Regeneración* 1 (10): 1–4.

Flores Magón, Ricardo. 1910. "A la mujer." *Regeneración* (September 24, 1910). Translated by Prensa Sembradora, March 8 1974.

Foner, Philip S. 1965. *History of the Labor Movement in the United States.* Vol. 2. New York: International Publishers.

———. 1965. *History of the Labor Movement in the United States.* Vol. 4. New York: International Publishing Co.

———, ed. 1969. *The Autobiographies of the Hay Market Martyrs.* New York: Humanities Press.

Forrest, Earle R. 1929. *Missions and Pueblos of the Old Southwest.* Chicago: Rio Grande.

Fuentes, Carlos. 1970. *Todos los gatos son pardos.* Mexico City: Siglo Veintiuno.

Galarza, Ernesto. 1971. *Barrio Boy.* Notre Dame, Ind.: University of Notre Dame Press.

García, Genaro. 1910. *Leona Vicario, heroina insurgente.* 2d ed. Mexico City: Carranza.

Garcia, Mario. 1976. "Obreras y esposas: The Mexican Women Workers of El Paso, 1880–1920." Paper delivered at the Southwest Labor Studies Conference, El Camino College, Los Angeles, Calif., April.

García Naranjo, Nemesio. 1906. "Biografía de Sor Juana Inés de la Cruz." *Anales del Museo Nacional de México* 3 (12): 561–73.

Garrard, Lewis H. 1955. *Wah-To-Yah and the Taos Trail.* Norman: Oklahoma University Press.

Gibson, Charles. 1966. *Spain in America.* New York: Harper & Row.

Gilbert, G. M. 1959. "Sex Differences in Mental Health in a Mexican Village." *International Journal of Social Psychiatry* 3 (Winter):208–13.

Gill, Mario. 1957. "Teresa Urrea, La Santa de Cabora." *Historia mexicana* 6 (abril–junio): 626–44.

Gómez-Quiñones, Juan. 1973. *Sembradores: Ricardo Flores Magón y el Partido Liberal Mexicano.* Rev. ed. Los Angeles: UCLA Chicano Studies Center.

Gonzáles, Jovita. 1972a. "With the Coming of the Barbwire, Came Hunger: Folk-Lore of the Texas-Mexican Vaquero." Pp. 81–83 in *Aztlán: An Anthology of Mexican Literature,* ed. Luis Valdéz and Stan Steiner. New York: Random House.

———. 1972b. "Among My People." Pp. 8–16 in *Mexican American Authors,* ed. Américo Paredes and Raymund Paredes. Boston: Houghton Mifflin.

Gonzales, Sylvia. 1974. "Woman and Woman." P. 65 in *La chicana piensa.* Published by the author.

González, Rosalinda M. 1976. "The Chicana in Southwest Labor History, 1900–1975: A Preliminary Bibliographic Analysis." Program in Comparative Culture, University of California, Irvine.

González Obregón, Luis. 1900. "La Decima Musa." Pp. 258–61 in *México Viejo: Noticias, Tradiciones, Leyendas y Costumbres.* Paris: Bouret.

———. 1936. *Las calles de México.* 4th ed. Mexico City: Botas.

Goodman, Mary Ellen, and Beman, Alma. 1971. "Child's-Eye-Views of Life in an Urban Barrio." Pp. 109–22 in *Chicanos: Social and Psychological Perspectives,* ed. Nathaniel N. Wagner and Marsha J. Haug. Saint Louis: Mosby.

Gordon, Michael. 1972. *The Nuclear Family in Crisis: The Search for an Alternative.* New York: Harper & Row.

Gossett, Thomas F. 1963. *Race: The History of an Idea in America.* Dallas: Southern Methodist University Press.

Granado, Virginia. 1974. "Para mi jefe." *De colores* 2 (Spring): 37.

Grebler, Leo; Moore, Joan W.; and Guzman, Ralph C. 1970. *The Mexican American People.* New York: Free Press.

Green, George N. 1971. "The ILGWU in Texas, 1930–1970." *Journal of Mexican American History* 1 (Spring): 144–69.

Gregg, Josiah. 1954. *Commerce of the Prairies.* Norman: University of Oklahoma Press.

Grupo de Voluntarias del INFONAVIT. 1975. *1916 Primer Congreso Femi-*

nista de Mexico. Mexico City: Instituto del Fondo Nacional de la Vivienda para los Trabajadores.

Gutierrez-Christensen, Rita. 1976. "Eulogy for a Man from Jalostitlan." *Grito del sol* 1 (October–December): 59–68.

Hancock, Velia G. 1971. "LA CHICANA, Chicano Movement and Women's Liberation." *Chicano Studies Newsletter, University of California, Berkeley* (February–March), p. 1.

Hanke, Lewis. 1935. *The First Social Experiments in America*. Cambridge, Mass.: Harvard University Press.

Harte, Bret. 1896*a*. *"Maruja" and Other Stories*. New York: Houghton Mifflin.

———. 1896*b*. *Trent's Trust and Other Stories*. New York: Houghton Mifflin.

Hawkes, Glenn R., and Taylor, Minna. 1975. "Power Structure in Mexican and Mexican-American Farm Labor Families." *Journal of Marriage and the Family* 37 (November): 807–11.

Hayden, Robert G. 1966. "Spanish-Americans of the Southwest: Life Style Patterns and Their Implications." *Welfare in Review* 4 (April): 14–25.

Hellbom, Anna-Britta. 1967. *La participación cultural de las mujeres, indias y mestizas en el México precortesiano y postrevolucionario*. Stockholm, Ethnographical Museum Monograph Series, No. 10.

Heller, Celia S. 1966. *Mexican American Youth: Forgotten Youth at the Crossroads*. New York: Random House.

Hernández, María L. 1945. *Mexico y los cuatro poderes que dirigen al pueblo*. San Antonio: Munguia.

Hernández Tovar, Inés. 1977. "Compañero." *Hojas poeticas* 1 (mayo): 3.

Hererra, Gloria, and Lizcano, Jeanette. 1974. *La mujer chicana*. Crystal City, Tex: Crystal City ISD.

Ho, Ping-ti. 1965. "An Historian's View of the Chinese Family System." Pp. 15–30 in *The Family's Search for Survival*, ed. Seymour M. Farber, Piero Mustacchi, and Roger H. L. Wilson. New York: McGraw-Hill.

Hoyle, M. F. 1927. *Crimes and Career of Tiburcio Vasquez*. Hollister, Calif: Evening Free Lance.

Huang, Lucy Jen. 1976. "The Chinese American Family." Pp. 124–47 in *Ethnic Families in America*, ed. Charles H. Mindel and Robert W. Habenstein. New York: Elsevier.

Huerta, Dolores. 1974. "Dolores Huerta Talks about Republicans, César, Children, and Her Home Town." Pp. 283–94 in *An Awakened Minority: The Mexican-Americans*, ed. Manuel P. Servin. 2d ed. Beverly Hills: Glencoe.

Humphrey, Norman Daymond. 1944. "The Changing Structure of the Detroit Mexican Family: An Index of Acculturation." *American Sociological Review* 9 (December): 622–26.

Hunt, Rockwell D. 1949. "Great Women of California." *Historical Society of Southern California Quarterly* 31 (September): 197–211.

Jackson, Helen Hunt. 1885. *Ramona*. Boston: Roberts.

Jackson, Joseph Henry. 1948. "The Creation of Joaquin Murieta." *Pacific Spectator* 2 (Spring): 176–81.

Jones, Robert C. 1948. "Ethnic Family Patterns: The Mexican Family in the United States." *American Journal of Sociology* 53 (May): 450–52.

Kasuhiro Kobayashi, José María. 1973. "La conquista educativa de los hijos de Asís." *Historia mexicana* 22 (abril–junio): 437–64.

Kendall, George Wilkins. 1844. *Narrative of the Texas Santa Fe Expedition*. New York: Harper.

King, Mae C. 1975. "Oppression and Power: The Unique Status of the Black Woman in the American Political System." *Social Science Quarterly* 56 (June): 116–28.

Lara y Pardo, Luis. 1908. *La prostitución en México*. Mexico City: Bouret.

La Rue, Linda. 1970a. "The Black Movement and Women's Liberation." *Black Scholar* 1 (May): 36–42.

———. 1970b. "Black Liberation and Women's Lib." *Transaction* 8 (November): 59–64.

Las Casas, Fray Bartolome de. 1974. *Los indios de Mexico y Nueva España: antologia*. Edited by Edmundo O'Gorman. 3d ed. Mexico City: Porrua.

Lee, Shu-Ching. 1953. "China's Traditional Family: Its Characteristics and Disintegration." *American Sociological Review* 18 (June): 272–80.

Leon-Portilla, Miguel. 1962. *The Broken Spears: The Aztec Account of the Conquest of Mexico*. Boston: Beacon.

Leslie, Gerald R. 1973. *The Family in Social Context*. 2d ed. New York: Oxford University Press.

Lévi-Strauss, Claude. 1969. *The Elementary Structure of Kinship*. Translated by James Harle Bell, John Richard von Sturmer. Edited by Rodney Needham. Boston: Beacon.

Levy, Marion J., Jr. 1968. *The Family Revolution in Modern China*. New York: Atheneum.

Limón, José E. 1974. "El primer congreso mexicanista de 1911: A Precursor to Contemporary Chicanismo." *Aztlán: Chicano Journal of the Social Sciences and the Arts* 5 (Spring–Fall): 85–117.

Liss, Peggy K. 1975. *Mexico under Spain, 1521–1566*. Chicago: University of Chicago Press.

Lizardi, José Joaquín Fernández de. 1955. *Heroinas mexicanas*. Mexico City: Vargas Rea.

Lockwood Carden, Maren. 1974. *The New Feminist Movement*. New York: Russell Sage.

Long, Haniel. 1936. *Interlinear to Cabeza de Vaca, His Relation of the Journey from Florida to the Pacific, 1528–1536*. Santa Fe: Writers' Editions.

Longauex y Vasquez, Enriqueta. 1970. "The Mexican-American Woman."

Pp. 379–84 in *Sisterhood Is Powerful: An Anthology of Writings from the Woman's Liberation Movement*, ed. Robin Morgan. New York: Vintage.

López, Ronald W.; Madrid-Barela, Arturo; and Flores Macías, Reynaldo. 1976. *Chicanos in Higher Education: Status and Issues*. Chicano Studies Center Publications, Monograph No. 7. University of California, Los Angeles.

Lucero, Judy A. 1973. "A Little Girl's Prayer." *De colores* 1 (Winter): 53. © 1973 by *De colores*.

McMurtrie, Douglas Crawford. 1943. *A Report in April 1848, on the Discovery of Gold and Other Minerals in California, and on the People, Commerce, Agriculture, Customs, Religion, Press, etc. of the New Pacific Territory*. Reproduced from the *New York Herald* (August 19, 1848). Edited by Douglas C. McMurtrie. Evanston, Ill.

McWilliams, Carey. 1968. *North from Mexico*. New York: Greenwood.

MALDEF [Mexican American Legal Defense and Educational Fund]. 1977. "Chicana Rights: A Major MALDEF Issue." *MALDEF Newsletter* 7 (Fall): 1.

May, Ernest R. 1947. "Tiburcio Vásquez." *Historical Society of Southern California Quarterly* 20 (September–December): 122–35.

Meier, Matt S., and Rivera, Feliciano. 1972. *The Chicanos: A History of Mexican Americans*. New York: Hill & Wang.

Mendieta Alatorre, María de los Angeles. 1961. *La mujer en la revolución mexicana*. Mexico City: Instituto Nacional de Estudio Historicos de la Revolución Mexicana.

Menefee, Selden C., and Cassmore, Orin C. 1940. *The Pecan Shellers of San Antonio: The Problem of Underpaid and Unemployed Mexican Labor*. Washington: U.S. Government Printing Office. (Reprinted in *Mexican Labor in the United States*, pp. 1–82. New York: Arno, 1974.)

Mexico, Comité Ejecutivo. 1960. *Cincuenta años de la revolución mexicana en beneficio constitucional de la mujer*. Publicación comemorativa del ideario politico de la mujer. Mexico City: Araña.

Mirandé, Alfredo. 1975. *The Age of Crisis: Deviance, Disorganization, and Societal Problems*. New York: Harper & Row.

———. 1977. "The Chicano Family: A Reanalysis of Conflicting Views." *Journal of Marriage and the Family* 39 (November): 747–56.

Mitchell, Richard G. 1927. "Joaquín Murieta: A Study of Social Conditions in California." M.A. thesis, University of California, Berkeley.

Montiel, Miguel. 1970. "The Social Science Myth of the Mexican American Family." *El grito: A Journey of Contemporary Mexican American Thought* 3 (Summer): 56–63.

Montoya, José. 1969. "La jefita." Pp. 232–33 in *El espejo–The Mirror*. Berkeley: Qinto Sol. © 1969, 1972 by Quinto Sol Publications.

Moore, Joan W. 1970. "Colonialism: The Case of the Mexican Americans." *Social Problems* 17 (Spring): 463–72.

Moore, Joan W., with Pachon, Harry. 1976. *Mexican Americans*. 2d ed. Englewood Cliffs, N.J.: Prentice-Hall.

Moquin, Wayne, with Van Doren, Charles. 1971. *A Documentary History of the Mexican Americans*. New York: Praeger.

Morales, Armando. 1972. *Ando sangrando (I Am Bleeding): A Study of Mexican-American Police Conflict*. La Puente, Calif.: Perspectiva.

Moreno, Daniel. 1958. *Los factores demográficos en la planeación económica*. Mexico City: Cámara Nacional de la Industria de Transformación.

Moreno, Manuel M. 1971. *La organización politica y social de los aztecas*. Mexico City: Instituto Nacional de Antropología e Historia.

Morton, Carlos. 1973. "El jardin." *El grito: A Journal of Contemporary Mexican American Thought* 7 (September): 7–37.

Morton, Ward M. 1962. *Woman Suffrage in Mexico*. Gainesville: University of Florida Press.

Murdock, George P. 1965. *Social Structure*. New York: Free Press.

Murillo, Nathan. 1971. "The Mexican American Family." Pp. 97–108 in *Chicanos: Social and Psychological Perspectives*, ed. Nathaniel N. Wagner and Marsha J. Haug. Saint Louis: Mosby.

Nadeau, Remi. 1974. *The Real Joaquin Murieta: Robin Hood Hero or Gold Rush Gangster?* Corona del Mar, Calif.: Trans-Anglo.

Nava, Yolanda. 1973. "Employment Counseling and the Chicana." *Encuentro femenil* 1 (Spring): 20–26.

Nieto-Gómez, Anna. 1971. "Chicanas Identify." *Regeneración* 1 (10): 9.

———. 1973. "The Chicana—Perspectives for Education." *Encuentro femenil* 1 (Spring): 34–61.

———. 1974. "La femenista." *Encuentro femenil* 1 (2): 34–37.

Nimkoff, Meyer R., and Middleton, Russell. 1960. "Types of Family and Types of Economy." *American Journal of Sociology* 66 (November): 215–25.

Norris, Frank. 1924. *MacTeague*. New York: Doubleday, Page.

Ortega Martínez, Ana Maria. 1945. *Conquista de México*. Mexico City: Vargas Rea.

O'Shaughnessy, Edith. 1916. *A Diplomat's Wife in Mexico*. New York: Harper.

O'Sullivan-Beare, Nancy. 1956. *Las mujeres de los conquistadores*. Madrid: Bibliografía Española.

Otero Peralta, Rosalie. 1975. "Las dos hermanas." *De colores* 2 (3): 66–73.

Paredes, Américo. 1958. *"With His Pistol in His Hand": A Border Ballad and Its Hero*. Austin: University of Texas Press.

Paredes, Américo, and Paredes, Raymund. 1972. *Mexican-American Authors*. Boston: Houghton Mifflin.

Paredes, Raymund Arthur. 1975. "The Image of the Mexican in American Literature." Ph.D. dissertation, University of Texas at Austin.

Parkes, Henry Bamford. 1969. *A History of Mexico*. 3d ed. Boston: Houghton Mifflin.

Parsons [González], Lucy Eldine. 1884. "A Word to Tramps." *Alarm* 1 (October 4): 1.

———. 1895. "Cause of Sex Slavery." *Firebrand* 1 (January 27): 2.

———. 1903. *Life of Albert R. Parsons, with Brief History of the Labor Movement in America*. 2d ed. Chicago: Published by the author.

———. 1935. "The Story of Haymarket." *Labor Defender* 11 (May): 6.

Pattie, James O. 1962. *The Personal Narrative of James O. Pattie*. Chicago: Lakeside.

Paz, Octavio. 1961. *The Labyrinth of Solitude*. Translated by Lysander Kemp. New York: Grove.

Peñalosa, Fernando. 1968. "Mexican Family Roles." *Journal of Marriage and the Family* 30 (November): 680–89.

Pérez, Alex. 1975. "Documentos: los derechos de la mujer." *Historia obrera* 5 (junio): 45–46.

Peterson, Frederick. 1959. *Ancient Mexico: An Introduction to the Pre-Hispanic Cultures*. New York: Capricorn.

Pike, Zebulon Montgomery. 1965. *The Expeditions of Zebulon Montgomery Pike*. Vol. 2, ed. Elliot Coues. Minneapolis: Ross & Haines.

Portillo Trambley, Estela. 1969. "The Day of the Swallows." Pp. 149–93 in *El espejo–The Mirror*. Berkeley: Quinto Sol.

———. 1975. "If It Weren't for the Honeysuckle." Pp. 97–109 in *Rain of Scorpions*. Berkeley: Tonatiuh.

Prescott, William H. 1873. *History of the Conquest of Mexico*. Philadelphia: Lippincott.

Putnam, Frank Bishop. 1963. "Teresa Urrea, the Saint of Cabora." *Southern California Quarterly* 45 (September): 245–64.

Ramos, Samuel. 1962. *Profile of Man and Culture in Mexico*. Translated by Peter G. Earle. Austin: University of Texas Press.

Rascón, María Antonieta. 1975. "La mujer y la lucha social." Pp. 139–74 in *Imagen y realidad de la mujer*, ed. Elena Urrutia. Mexico City: SepSetentas.

Rendón, Armando B. 1972. *Chicano Manifesto*. New York: Macmillan.

Ricard, Robert. 1966. *The Spiritual Conquest of Mexico*. Translated by Lesley Byrd Simpson. Berkeley: University of California Press.

Ridge, John Rollin [Yellow Bird]. 1955. *Life and Adventures of Joaquín Murieta, the Celebrated California Bandit*. Norman: University of Oklahoma Press.

Rivera, Tomas. 1971. *. . . and the earth did not part*. Berkeley: Quinto Sol.

Robinson, Cecil. 1963. *With the Ears of Strangers: The Mexican in American Literature*. Tucson: University of Arizona Press.

Rodriguez, Gustavo A. 1935. *Doña Marina*. Mexico City: Secretaría de Relaciones Exteriores.

Rodríguez, Richard, and Rodríguez, Gloria C. 1972. "Teresa Urrea: Her Life as It Affected the Mexican–U.S. Frontier." *El grito: A Journal of Contemporary Mexican American Thought* 5 (Summer): 48–68.

Rodríguez Cabo, Mathilde. 1937. *La mujer y la revolución.* Conferencia Dictada por la Dra. Mathilde Rodríguez Cabo en el Frente Socialista de Abogados. Mexico City.

Romano, Octavio Ignacio-V. 1973*a*. "The Anthropolgy and Sociology of the Mexican-Americans: The Distortion of Mexican-American History." Pp. 43–56 in *Voices: Readings from El grito.*" Berkeley: Quinto Sol.

————. 1973*b*. "Social Science, Objectivity, and the Chicanos." Pp. 30–42 in *Voices: Readings from "El grito."* Berkeley: Quinto Sol.

Romano-U., Octavio I. 1969. "A Rosary for Doña Marina." Pp. 75–93 in *El espejo–The Mirror.* Berkeley: Quinto Sol.

Rosaldo, Michelle Zimbalist, and Lamphere, Louise. 1974. *Woman, Culture, and Society.* Stanford, Calif.: Stanford University Press.

Ross, Stanley R. Ross, ed. 1972. *Ha muerto la revolución mexicana? balance y epilogo.* Mexico City: SepSetentas.

Rubel, Arthur J. 1966. *Across the Tracks: Mexican Americans in a Texas City.* Austin: University of Texas Press.

Rudoff, Alvin. 1971. "The Incarcerated Mexican-American Delinquent." *Journal of Criminal Law, Criminology and Police Science* 62 (June): 224–38.

Saénz Royo, Artemisa [Xochitl]. 1954. *Político-social-cultural del movimiento femenino en México, 1914–1950.* Mexico City: Leon Sanchez.

Sahagún, Fray Bernardino de. 1946. *Historia general de las cosas de Nueva España.* Vols. 1–3. Mexico City: Nueva España.

————. 1961. *Florentine Codex: General History of the Things of New Spain.* Bk. 10, *The People.* No. 14, pt. 11. Translated by Charles E. Dibble and Arthur J. O. Anderson. Santa Fe: School of American Research and the University of Utah.

Samora, Julian, and Lamanna, Richard A. 1967. *Mexican-Americans in a Midwest Metropolis: A Study of East Chicago.* Mexican-American Study Project, Division of Research, Graduate School of Business Administration, Advanced Report No. 8. University of California, Los Angeles.

Sánchez, Corinne. 1973. "Higher Education y la chicana?" *Encuentro femenil* 1 (Spring): 27–33.

Sánchez, George I. 1967. *Forgotten People: A Study of New Mexicans.* Albuquerque: Calvin Horn.

Sánchez, Nellie van de Grift. 1929. *Spanish Arcadia.* Los Angeles: Powell.

Sanz, M. A. 1907. *La mujer mexicana en el santuario del hogar.* Mexico City: Lacuad.

Schneider, David M., and Gough, Kathleen. 1961. *Matrilineal Kinship.* Berkeley: University of California Press.

Secrest, William B. 1967a. *Juanita: The Only Woman Lynched in the Gold Rush Days*. Fresno, Calif.: Saga-West.

———. 1967b. *Joaquin: Bloody Bandit of the Mother Lode*. Fresno, Calif: Saga-West.

Sidel, Ruth. 1973. *Women and Child Care in China*. Baltimore: Penguin.

Siller, Pedro. 1975. "Testimonios: Juana B. Gutíerrez de Mendoza." *Historia obrera* 5 (junio): 4.

Silva Herzog, Jesús. 1960. *Breve historia de la revolución mexicana: los antecedentes y la etapa maderista*. Vol. 1. Mexico City: Fondo de Cultura Económica.

Sosa Riddell, Adaljiza. 1974. "Chicanas and El movimiento." *Aztlán: Chicano Journal of the Social Sciences and the Arts* 5 (Spring–Fall): 155–65.

———. 1973. "My name was changed. . . ." *El grito: A Journal of Contemporary Mexican American Thought* 7 (September): 76.

Sotomayor, Marta. 1972. "Mexican-American Interaction with Social Systems." *Social Casework* 52 (May): 316–22.

Soustelle, Jacques. 1970. *Daily Life of the Aztecs*. Translated by Patrick O'Brian. Stanford, Calif.: Stanford University Press.

Spiro, Melford E. 1958. *Children of the Kibbutz*. Cambridge, Mass.: Harvard University Press.

———. 1968. "Is the Family Universal? The Israeli Case." Pp. 68–79 in *The Family*, ed. Norman W. Bell and Ezra F. Vogel. Rev. ed. New York: Free Press.

Steinbeck, John. 1935. *Tortilla Flat*. New York: Grosset & Dunlap.

Swadesh, Frances Leon. 1974. *Los prímeros pobladores*. Notre Dame, Ind.: University of Notre Dame Press.

Talmon, Yonina. 1961. "Aging in Israel, a Planned Society." *American Journal of Sociology* 67 (November): 284–95.

———. 1965. "The Family in a Revolutionary Movement—the Case of the Kibbutz in Israel." Pp. 259–86 in *Comparative Family Systems*, ed. Meyer F. Nimkoff. Boston: Houghton Mifflin.

Tapia, Betsy. 1975a. "After." *De colores* 2 (3): 49.

———. 1975b. Untitled poem. *De colores* 2 (3): 48.

Taylor, Paul S. 1930. *Mexican Labor in the United States*. Vol. 1. Berkeley: University of California Press.

Temple-Trujillo, Rita E. 1974. "Conceptions of the Chicano Family." *Smith College Studies in Social Casework* 45 (November): 1–20.

Tirado, Miguel David. 1970. "Mexican American Community Political Organization." *Aztlán: Chicano Journal of the Social Sciences and the Arts* 1 (Spring): 53–78.

Truman, Ben C. 1874. *Life, Adventures and Capture of Tiburcio Vasquez, the Great California Bandit and Murderer*. Los Angeles: Los Angeles Star Office.

Turner, Frederick C. 1971. "Los efectos de la participación femenina en la revolución de 1910." Pp. 132–42 in *Chicanos: Social and Psychological Perspectives,* ed. Nathaniel N. Wagner and Marsha J. Haug. St. Louis: Mosby.

Twitchell, Ralph Emerson. 1925. *Old Santa Fe: The Story of New Mexico's Ancient Capital.* Chicago: Rio Grande.

U.S. Bureau of the Census. 1971. "*Fertility Variations by Ethnic Origins.*" Current Population Reports, Series P-20, no. 226 (November). Washington: U.S. Government Printing Office.

———. 1976. "*Educational Attainment in the United States: March 1975.*" Current Population Reports, Series P-20, no. 295 (June). Washington: U.S. Government Printing Office.

———. 1977. "*Persons of Spanish Origin in the United States: March 1976.*" Current Population Reports, Series P-20, no. 310 (July). Washington: U.S. Government Printing Office.

U.S. Commission on Civil Rights. 1971. *The Unfinished Education: Outcomes for Minorities in the Five Southwestern States. Report II: Mexican American Educational Series.* Washington: U.S. Government Printing Office.

———. 1973. *Teachers and Students: Differences in Teacher Interaction with Mexican American and Anglo Students. Report V: Mexican American Education Study.* Washington: U.S. Government Printing Office.

———. 1974. *Toward Quality Education for Mexican Americans. Report VII: Mexican American Education Study.* Washington: U.S. Government Printing Office.

U.S. Department of Labor. 1976. *Women of Spanish Origin in the United States.* Employment Standards Administration, Women's Bureau. Washington: U.S. Government Printing Office.

———. 1977. *Employment and Training Report of the President.* Washington: U.S. Government Printing Office.

Vaillant, George C. 1966. *Aztecs of Mexico.* Baltimore: Penguin.

Valdés-Fallis, Guadalupe. 1975. "Recuerdo." *De colores* 2 (3): 60–65.

Valdez, Luis. 1972. Introduction to *Aztlán: An Anthology of Mexican American Literature,* ed. Luis Valdez and Stan Steiner. New York: Random House.

Vasquez, Richard. 1971. *Chicano.* New York: Doubleday.

Velarde, C. J. 1926. *Under the Mexican Flag.* Los Angeles: Southland.

Vidal, Mirta. 1971. *Women: New Voice of La Raza.* New York: Pathfinder.

Villagrá, Gaspar Pérez de. 1933. *A History of New Mexico.* Translated by Gílberto Espínosa. Chicago: Rio Grande.

Villarreal, José Antonio. 1970. *Pocho.* New York: Doubleday.

Villaseñor, Edmund. 1973. *Macho!* New York: Bantam.

Walker, Kenneth P. 1965. "The Pecan Shellers of San Antonio and Mechanization." *Southwestern Historical Quarterly* 69 (July): 44–58.

Webb, Walter Prescott. 1931. *The Great Plains*. Waltham, Mass.: Blaisdell.

Wislizenus, Dr. Aldolphus. 1969. *Memoir of a Tour to Northern Mexico*. New Mexico: Rio Grande.

Wood, Sylvia. 1976. "La polvadera." *Grito del sol* 1 (July–September): 92–95.

Ybarra, Leonarda. 1977. "Conjugal Role Relationships in the Chicano Family." Ph.D. dissertation, University of California, Berkeley.

Zamora, Bernice. 1976. "Pueblo, 1950." P. 13 in *Restless Serpents*. Menlo Park, Calif.: Diseños Literarios. © 1976 by Diseños Literarios.

Zamora, Emilio Jr. 1976. "Sara Estela Ramírez: A Note on Research in Progress." *Hembra* 1 (Spring): 4–6.

Zamora, Mónica. 1974. "A dónde se fue mi cultura." *De colores* 1 (Spring): 48.

Zendejas, Adelina. 1962. *La mujer en la intervención francesa*. Mexico City: Sociedad Mexicana de Geografía y Estadística.

Zorita, Alonso de. 1963. *Life and Labor in Ancient Mexico: The Brief and Summary Relations of the Lords of New Spain*. Translated by Benjamin Keen. New Brunswick, N.J.: Rutgers University Press.

Index

Abascal, Modesta, 222
Acuña y Rossetti, Elisa, 205–6, 222
Aguiar y Siexas, Francisco de, 48
Aguirre, Lauro, 83
Alegría, Juana Armanda, 29, 211
Allen, Ruth, 228
Allende, Ignacio, 50–51
Alvarado, Pedro de, 6
Alvarado, Salvador, 217
American literature, 143–58; psychological depths probed in, 152; romantic tradition in, 147–53; Social Darwinist tradition in, 147, 153; and travel accounts of Chicanas, 143–47
American Southwest, postcolonial: ambivalent Anglo attitude toward Chicanas in, 75–78; changing feminine roles in, 78; and the Chicano Social Bandits, 71–74, 78–79; examples of Chicanas in, 76–95; exploitation of Chicano labor in, 68–69; Indian rebellions in, 81–83; and religion, 81. *See also* Colonial period, American Southwest; Colonial period, Mexico
Anaya, Rudolfo, 158, 163–64, 169–70
"Anima." *See* Jiménez y Muro, Dolores
Annexation. *See* Mexico, United States annexation of
Anza, Juan Bautista de, 56, 57
Aramoni, Aniceto, 213
Arballo y Gutiérrez, María Feliciana, 60–61
Arias, Ron, 158, 170–71
Arizona. *See* Colonial period, American Southwest
Atherton, Gertrude, 149–51, 152, 155, 156
Aztec family: childrearing in, 103; codices as key to women's roles in, 99; education of women in, 17, 99, 103, 104–5; emphasis on familism in, 99; femi-

Glossary of Spanish Terms

adelantado	title formerly given to the governor of a province
agabachado (-a)	"Anglocized," Americanized
agorero	diviner
a toda madre	"a real live mother," fantastic, "out of sight"
Aztlán	mythical land of the north from which the Aztecs are said to have originated, used today by Chicanos to refer to the American Southwest
baile	dance
barrio	neighborhood
bracero	contract laborer brought to the United States for a temporary period
bruja	witch
caballero	young horseman, gentleman
cacique	Indian chief
californio (-a)	Californian
cantina	saloon, bar
capirotada	Mexican bread pudding
carnal	brother
carnalismo	brotherhood
carrancista	follower of Carranza
casta	mixing of Indian and Spanish blood
colonia	neighborhood
comadre	name by which parents address their child's god-mother
comandante	commander
compadre	name by which parents address their child's godfather
conquistadores	conquerors, Cortés's men
consejo	bit of advice
criollo (-a)	person born in Mexico of Spanish parents
curandero (-a)	healer
diseño	sketch or draft of a map
empleado	employee
español (-a)	Spaniard

familia	family
fandango	dance
gabacha	Anglo-American female
gachupines	Spaniards
gringo (-a)	Anglo-American
hacendero	owner of a *hacienda*
hacienda	large estate and lands
hembra	female
hembrismo	womanhood
hermana	sister
heroina	heroine
huelgista	striker
huertista	follower of Huerta
huipil	smock
indio (-a)	Indian
insurgentes	insurgents, rebels
jarabe tapatió	regional dance from Jalisco, Mexico
jefita	mother, (lit.) little boss
junta	assembly of people
llano	plain, plains
machismo	manliness, masculinity
macho	male, masculine
maderista	supporter of Madero
malinchismo	concept in Mexican and Chicano culture which equates selling out, in whatever form, with Malinche's selling out to Cortés
mariachi	Mexican folk band, originally from the state of Jalisco
mescal	intoxicating drink made from a cactus plant
mestizaje	mixing of Indian and Spanish blood
metate	curved stone used as a pestle
mexica	tribe of Indians
mexicano (-a)	Mexican
mexicano norteño	person from northern Mexico
mujer	woman
monte	card game
pachuco	term used in the 1940s to refer to Chicanos who wore zoot suits; see *vato*
partera	midwife
patria	country
patrón	boss
peninsulares	Spaniards born in Spain
peon	modern-day serf
pobres, los	the poor
pocho	"Anglocized" or Americanized Mexican